YOUR CAREER

IN CHANGING TIMES

MOODY PUBLISHERS
CHICAGO

All Scripture quotations, unless otherwise indicated, are taken from the *New American Standard
Bible*®, Copyright © 1960, 1962, 1963, 1968, 1971, 1972, 1973, 1975, 1977 by The Lockman
Foundation. Used by permission. (www.Lockman.org)

The use of selected references from the Bible in this publication does not necessarily imply publisher endorsement of the version in its entirety.

Editor: Adeline Griffith
Cover Design: The Puckett Group
Interior Design: Ragont Design

ISBN-10: 0-8024-2713-8
ISBN-13: 978-0-8024-2713-7

We hope you enjoy this book from Moody Publishers. Our goal is to provide high-quality,
thought-provoking books and products that connect truth to your real needs and challenges. For
more information on other books and products written and produced from a biblical perspective,
go to www.moodypublishers.com or write to:

Moody Publishers
820 N. LaSalle Boulevard
Chicago, IL 60610

5 7 9 10 8 6

Printed in the United States of America

Contents

Preface

*D*uring the years I was counseling families on their finances, I frequently observed people in career fields that didn't match their talents and abilities. Consequently, they didn't seem to have any joy in their work. I'm confident they also were not as proficient as they could have been at something more suited to their natural abilities. Even more important, from a spiritual standpoint, their disdain for their occupation undermined their witness in the workplace.

Studies show that the majority of people are unhappy in their work. Work stress has become a serious problem, and many are burning out from trying to work in areas where they aren't naturally talented. This applies to Christians as much as to anyone else.

As I look toward the future of our economy, I see that finding good employment will be a major challenge of the nineties. I believe this book will help to equip you to meet that challenge.

Larry Burkett

*D*uring my time on the faculty of the University of Georgia, I was amazed at the high percentage of young people who had no plan for their future, other than just to get a degree and go look for a job. At the core of the problem was an almost total absence of any criteria for career decision making, other than money. Much of my time was spent helping students identify their strengths and weaknesses and choose an appropriate college major.

When Larry offered me the opportunity to come to Christian Financial Concepts, it was probably the easiest career decision anyone ever could have made. I knew the career guidance problem, I knew God had equipped me to work in this particular area, and I was excited about the opportunity to help people be better managers of their God-given talents.

Clearly the world of work is changing rapidly, and career decisions will be more difficult and will have to be made more frequently. For many, the job security once expected has vanished. No one can guarantee employment, but by following the principles in this book, you can know your talents, interests, and, most importantly, develop a Christ-honoring perspective about work.

Lee Ellis

Acknowledgments

*S*hortly after we began the Life Pathways outreach in 1990, it became obvious that people needed more information on how to make career decisions from a biblical perspective. About that same time, Greg Thornton and Bill Thrasher from Moody Press began to talk to us about the need for a book covering the principles we were using in our program. They had vision for this book, they were persistent, and their encouragement has been especially meaningful.

Adeline Griffith, our editor, deserves special recognition for her diligence and professional contribution to this project. Her efficiency is remarkable and enables incredibly fast turnarounds on edits and re-edits. Adeline is a great asset to the CFC team and we really appreciate her.

The Life Pathways' staff has done a remarkable job in developing and carrying out the assessment program. Their dedication to the mission of helping others has been crucial to our success.

The entire Christian Financial Concepts' staff plays a direct role in supporting the activities of Life Pathways. Every department supports Career Pathways in some way, and it really has been a team effort.

We especially appreciate the many clients and *Money Matters* newsletter readers who have allowed us to reprint their letters and testimonies. As you will see, their stories are an important element of this book.

We also owe special thanks to our wives Judy Burkett and Mary Ellis and our families who have supported us so faithfully during our own career journeys.

Finally, we say thank you to all those who have participated in the Life Pathways assessment. Without you, this book would not have been possible.

It is our prayer that this book will help us all to better understand that Jesus Christ is the true Shepherd who stands ready to guide us on a career pathway that will bring honor and glory to Him.

SECTION ONE
Understanding Changes in the Workplace

CHAPTER ONE
The Workplace Is Changing

*T*he twentieth century has been an era of unbelievable changes. We literally have gone from the horse and buggy days to outer space in less than 100 years. At the turn of the twentieth century, 90 percent of Americans worked in agriculture—usually on small farms. Now less than 5 percent earn a living growing our food.

We have seen the evolution of mass production technology, such as the automobile assembly lines, shifted from people to machines and the office work force capability expanded a thousandfold by computers.

New technologies have accelerated changes in transportation, manufacturing, communications, and nearly every other area of our lives. But all changes bring with them some pluses and some minuses. Certainly our technology revolution is no exception.

For instance, at the turn of this century a high school dropout could expect to get a good job. Why? Because the technology of the time required little formal education. By mid-century, a high school diploma was a minimum requirement for most production jobs; and by the beginning of the next century, at least some post-high-school education will be needed for virtually any job.

Technology brings increased productivity, but it also necessitates increased skills and complexity. Unprepared workers will be relegated to the status of menial labor.

Through the end of this century and further, these changes will have a dramatic impact on future jobs. One of our main goals in writing this book is to inform you of these changes so you can prepare now for the future. In many ways we're playing a "new ball game" and many of the old rules don't apply anymore.

Let's take a look at the way careers were developed under the old system—the one most of us who entered the work force during the last 50 years understand.

The Old System, 1946–1990

During the period following World War II, it was normal for someone to get and hold a job with the same company for a lifetime. Many people came to view their lives and their jobs as totally interrelated.

Most young people graduating from high school or college expected that a good job would be waiting, because the actual starting point in the work force usually depended on education and experience. Even the routine job, such as an assembly line worker, paid a very livable wage. After all, America ruled the (economic) world, and "Made in the USA" really meant something.

Whether someone worked in a textile mill, a steel mill, a coal mine, or a corporate giant such as Sears, General Motors, or IBM, having a job for life was a reasonable expectation for dedicated and diligent workers.

In the past, there was a fixed pattern to how companies were structured and operated. Most were organized with layers of executives, management, supervisors, and workers. Workers who showed initiative, hired at any level, had a chance for "upward mobility." Career planning often was as simple as getting a job and working upward in the organization.

Americans of earlier decades were accustomed to some structural changes in industry, but they were generally gradual, and we had a growing economy that could accommodate the people displaced by automation and technology.

For instance, in 1940 about 23 percent of the work force earned a living through farming. By 1990 this had declined to about 2.3 percent, yet our economy was able to absorb this segment of the work force without much problem.[1]

Generally the decades of the fifties, sixties, and seventies were prosperous times, with enormous potential economic growth. To be sure, there were slow periods (recessions), but even the workers who were laid off during these slow periods knew there would be abundant jobs when the economy "perked up." After all, the U. S. economy had capital, technology, a good public educational system, low energy cost, and good access to cheap raw materials.

Perhaps best of all, American industry had developed a tremendous production capability during World War II that hadn't suffered the devastation experienced by other world powers. Consequently, we had a tremendous head start when the war ended. The world was poised for a period of unparalleled prosperity as the rebuilding began, and the U. S. would lead the "pack."

Because of our position, our wealth, and our leadership role, we became overconfident, sloppy, wasteful, and arrogant. There is an old saying: "prosperity is hard to handle," and this certainly was the case with post-World War II America.

ECONOMIC SLUGGISHNESS BEGINS TO SET IN

In time, both businesses and employees began to "expect" good times. Customers, profits, and paychecks were taken for granted, while the unique international conditions that had allowed easy profits were rapidly changing.

Our leadership position was eroded through blatant arrogance toward our customers. Our attitude was, "If you don't like it, lump it!" Thus we opened the door for our eventual competitors to step through. At the same time, government services, as well as regulatory agencies, were growing rapidly and beginning to consume a larger portion of business profits and personal incomes.

The seeds of government welfare and control that were planted during the depression years began to sprout and grow. Government at every level, but especially in Washington D.C., swelled and bloated, while assuming more and more of a "provider" role. The social reformers thought the government could solve all of society's ills if enough money was thrown at the problems. To do this required lots of money—more than the politicians were willing to tax their constituents to pay.

In order to fund the shortfall created by these social experiments, our government borrowed and borrowed and borrowed. The politicians borrowed from the taxpayers, their children, their grandchildren, and their great grandchildren. They even borrowed from our competitors—in return giving them free access to our markets. But the borrowing wasn't limited just to the government.

By the mid-seventies, the whole country was hooked on credit: consumers, businesses, governments—even college students. The artificial growth of the eighties was the result of debt-spending more than anything else.

As the economy slowed down in the late eighties, properties deflated in value and business collateral began to decline, which curtailed further borrowing. By this time, consumers had exhausted sources of collateral for more loans, and consumer spending slowed dramatically.

Coincidental with our economic shift to debt-spending during the seventies and eighties, the economies of Europe and Asia were just hitting their full stride. Even though American industry being untouched by World War II was an asset in the forties, fifties, and early sixties, it now became a liability.

Europe and Asia had rebuilt their factories using newer, more efficient technologies. Worst of all, American labor and management were in a malaise: living on past accomplishments and falling steadily behind the rest of the world.

In the Far East and Asia, relatively inexpensive labor, lean management structures, new technologies, and support from national governments enabled many overseas companies to become very competitive and profitable. While protecting their own markets, Japan, Taiwan, Hong Kong, and Korea began systematically to corner ours. As they did, American manufacturing jobs began to decline.

During this same time period, new technologies in communications and computers played a major role in reshaping the economic world. In the sixties and seventies, corporate giants such as IBM could overwhelm their competition by owning the entire operation—from making their own computers to writing their own software. But as competition increased and *downsizing* made emerging technologies more productive, those very same factors that made IBM and

GM profitable in the fifties and sixties became their biggest stumbling blocks.

The term *downsizing* was coined to describe the restructuring process that most companies are undergoing as they seek to cut back some of the extra layers of management that accrued during the earlier decades.

Production technology shifted from total integration to decentralization. For example, while Ford, GM, and Chrysler attempted to maintain in-house capabilities for everything from engines to electronics, a competitor like Honda set up independent suppliers for everything from wheels to radios. The sub-systems were built to Honda's specifications, and the cost savings were significant.

> *The need is for flexible,*
> *well-educated employees*
> *who can respond*
> *quickly to changing*
> *consumer demands.*

In the U.S. all attempts to decentralize and develop a flexible team concept in the manufacturing plants were resisted by the unions. With decentralization comes greater productivity but loss of jobs as well. It was not until it became clear that survival was the issue that the real changes began to take place.

The onset of relatively inexpensive, high-tech equipment has enabled small companies to spring up quickly and respond with new products. Corporate giants, who stayed too long with the old system, now struggle for their very survival. Employees and employers have discovered that volume, not price, determines profits. Technology and competition have created the need to be leaner and more cost conscious. In turn, these efforts to become competitive (profitable) have brought on the need to downsize.

Just as many levels of middle management are being eliminated, so too are jobs that allowed the extreme specialization of the
integrated companies. No company that wants to remain competitive
in the nineties can afford the luxury of an employee who only does
one task or a plant that only turns out one type of product.

The need is for flexible, well-educated employees who can respond quickly to changing consumer demands. The last words of a
dying company are: "We never did it that way before. I can't. . . ." In
the nineties, the business world is coming to grips with problems
generated by changes in technology, economics, overregulation, and
overindulgence.

The purpose in reviewing these facts is not to criticize but to put
into perspective some of the events that brought about the changes
in the U. S. economy and work force. In the future, workers must be
willing to adapt—or be unemployed.

ECONOMIC CHANGES

Many more changes will shape the workplace of the future. In a
feature article of the *Chicago Tribune*, William Neikirk gave several
insights into what is happening to our economy. He notes that millions of workers have lost their jobs as part of the current corporate
restructuring.

Neikirk says, "They [the workers] have been swept up in a new
industrial revolution that many business analysts believe is a long
way from complete. Some think that downsizing will continue during
the nineties as American corporations reinvent themselves to survive
in a new, even more competitive century."[2]

Any thinking person should have concerns about the employment future for all American workers. The downsizing of the early
nineties is not just the result of an economic slump. Rather, it is a
restructuring that will fundamentally change the way we think about
jobs and careers. As many are already beginning to realize, the majority of those who have been laid off never will return to their old
jobs because they are gone forever!

Structural unemployment is a term used to describe what is actually happening in our economy. You almost can think of the next
few years as a metamorphosis—much like the life cycle the sluggish
caterpillar goes through to become a graceful butterfly.

Many of our corporate giants are going through painful contortions as they try to find a new shape that will give them the flexibility to keep up with the changes in the marketplace today. Unfortunately, most of the pain will be felt by those who lose their jobs in the process. American industry no longer sets the rules—and must either adjust or fail.

ACCEPT CHANGE AND PREPARE FOR THE FUTURE

If there is one absolute for the future, it is change; and this change likely will come at an ever-accelerating rate. Think what life was like just 100 years ago, then 50 years ago, or even 25 years ago. The rate of change that has occurred is breathtaking. We have gone from horses and buggies to stealth fighters in this century. Change is not uncommon—it is inevitable.

> *Much of the structural unemployment we see today is a direct result of businesses, governments, and especially individuals not being able to anticipate and prepare for these changes.*

I grew up in the fifties, so I still can remember what life was like before television. In those days, people usually traveled by bus or train. Propeller airplanes that traveled 150 miles an hour were considered fast, and commercial air travel was a somewhat hazardous adventure. Most people didn't travel long distances regularly, and families usually had one fairly unreliable car. Life certainly has changed a lot since then.

When I entered the Air Force in 1959, the basic electronics course consisted of the vacuum tube theory, although a few days were devoted to the still-unproven technology of transistors. Most of the transistors that were in production were used primarily in analog circuits (as opposed to digital), and were more unreliable than glass radio tubes.

Fixing your television in the early sixties consisted of pulling every tube in the set, taking them down to the local TV repair shop, where for a dollar or so the owner would test them for you.

After the Air Force, I went to work at Cape Canaveral in Florida. In the early sixties the primary computer system at the space center (then known as the ballistic missile testing range) was an IBM analog computer that required its own building, cooling system, and a host of technicians just to change vacuum tubes every day. Today, a hand-held calculator has more computing ability than that entire system.

By the mid-sixties all the computers were solid state (transistor-ized) digital systems. The on-board computer that steered Apollo XI to the moon's surface was a technological marvel of that time. The package weighed only 80 pounds and had more than 50,000 words of memory. Compare that to a portable computer today that weighs 5 pounds and has 12 *million* words of memory!

All of the computing power available at the space center during the moon landing in 1969 would not come close to matching the power of one IBM PC today.

The revolution that took place in automobiles at the turn of the twentieth century, and in flying machines a decade later, in rockets two decades later, in commercial aircraft during the seventies, and in computers during the seventies, still continues today. It is not the change that is abnormal; it's the pace of the change. If you reflect on the last 30 years, it's clear that the changes are accelerating.

Lee Iacocca, past chairman of the Chrysler Corporation, coined an expression that bears repeating: "In our society today you have to lead, follow, or get out of the way." That is absolutely true. And although change can be a little unnerving, we must adapt to the change in our world and profit from it. If we don't, others will.

In his book entitled *Margin*, Richard A. Swenson documents the changes taking place in every area of our lives. Through a series of graphs, he illustrates that since about 1940 industrial processes have

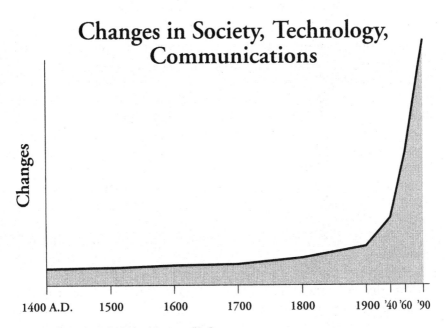

Changes in Society, Technology, Communications

Changes

1400 A.D.   1500   1600   1700   1800   1900 '40 '60 '90

Adapted from *Margin* by Richard Swenson, NavPress.

changed at a rate that is unparalleled in history. In studying the 29 graphs of various changes, in the appendix of Swenson's book, one thing stands out very clearly: All the changes are compounding.

Depicted above is a representative view of Swenson's graphs, which directly follow the rate of change in technology. For instance, on the graph shown, you can see that, starting about 1940, the volume of technological innovations began to change.[3]

As time progresses, the changes accelerate. Our "progress" has been a two-edged sword. It has brought us a better life through improved health care and modern conveniences that relieve burdensome toil; yet it has brought us problems and stresses never known before—particularly in the area of vocation.

Much of the structural unemployment we see today is a direct result of businesses, governments, and especially individuals not being able to anticipate and prepare for these changes.

PREPARE NOW FOR THE CHANGING WORKPLACE

So far I have sounded a rather pessimistic trumpet regarding the future of our economy and the workplace. In reality, there is much to be optimistic about for the future of both employers and employees, if you are willing and able to adapt.

The United States has many strengths that will help us adapt to the future. First of all, we still have a fundamentally capitalistic system—the most responsive and versatile economic system in existence. When companies don't make a profit, they either regroup and develop a strategy for becoming profitable or they go under. In our current "economic revolution," some will go under, but most will take a hard look at what they are doing and adjust as necessary in order to make a profit.

Perhaps the greatest deterrents to our long-term financial growth are twofold: one, too much government interference in the free enterprise system and, two, the lack of good vocational training in America. We might add an additional factor: the lack of quality education for our young people. Our schools may be "politically correct" today, but they don't teach students basic living skills anymore.

In the short run, the restructuring of corporate America will be painful for many, but it is a necessary process in order to compete and survive in a global economy. A lot can be learned from companies that restructured early on and now are beginning to reassert themselves in world competition. General Electric and Chrysler have been featured in *Fortune* magazine as examples of companies that have adapted and are now positioned to compete in a world economy.[4]

On the other extreme, *Fortune* singled out IBM, General Motors, and Sears as companies whose management structures failed to keep up with the changes taking place and are paying the price.[5]

Before writing off these old blue-chip companies, however, let's remember that capitalism rewards those who respond to the market. It is likely that these companies also will survive the painful metamorphosis and emerge as successful companies in the twenty-first century.

You may be asking, "How does all that affect me? I just want a job where I can earn a decent living and have my weekends off." The point I want to reemphasize is that all of the corporate and economic changes ultimately come to bear on the employees. The bottom line is: *You need to understand the rules of the new economic game and prepare accordingly.* Those who fail to do so risk experiencing the same fate as the corporate dinosaurs mentioned earlier.

THE WORKPLACE OF THE FUTURE

The needs of companies are changing, and that's transforming the way they look at employees. Let's examine some of the changes that will directly affect the American worker.

As mentioned earlier, as companies restructure, layers of management are removed. Replacing these layers will be work units, teams, modules, and even small businesses that develop around core functions. *Empowerment* is a new buzzword that describes this decentralization of decision making. Rather than dictate and control everything from the top down, work teams will be allowed and encouraged to make many decisions that affect product excellence.

If you want to be a part of a winning team, you must choose your vocation based on your God-given talents and skills.

Likewise, work teams will be responsible for resolving most of their own problems rather than sending them up the corporate chain for management decisions.

It has been proved that employees who previously have been discouraged by exclusion from the decision process generally will respond positively when allowed to participate in product development and production decisions. After all, the notion is not new; virtually everyone wants to feel like he or she has some input into their jobs.

This feeling of involvement and control is what causes many Americans to quit good jobs and start their own companies. Large companies that can capture and cultivate that entrepreneurial spirit will prosper. It's literally like having hundreds of people running their own companies—but with good management help and adequate capital.

With a well-educated and trained work force, empowerment is bound to raise productivity because it taps the natural creative potential of God's most excellent creation: humankind. Companies will have less overhead because this lowering of responsibility will enable a streamlining of management and elimination of costly overspecialization.

Another by-product of empowerment will be a faster decision cycle and a quicker response to the customer. Remember, in order to compete in global markets, businesses must be more responsive to changing market demands.

As I said earlier, when the U.S. dominated world markets, businesses could ignore many aspects of quality and price because consumers had few alternatives. But the early nineties have seen a dramatic shift toward a merger of price, quality, and service. Companies (and employees) who ignore this movement will find themselves out of work.

As more of our overseas competitors come of age, often with newer production facilities and a hungry work force, they will surely force U. S. companies to hone their skills even sharper. If you want to be a part of a winning team, you must choose your vocation based on your God-given talents and skills. The old, tired theme of going to work at a boring job and hiding out until retirement is a thing of the past.

The word excellence is being used almost like a religious symbol to motivate management and employees to improve products and services, and the key to doing this is fitting the right people to the right job.

As Christians we should be excited about the new emphasis on excellence since this is what God's Word calls us to do anyway. As the apostle Paul said: "*Whatever you do, do your work heartily, as for the Lord rather than for men*" (Colossians 3:23).

CHAPTER TWO
Adapting to Changes in the Workplace

FUTURE SKILLS FOR THE FUTURE WORKPLACE

Technical Expertise. Let's face it. We live in a technical world, and almost everyone who expects to be employed is going to need some technical skills. That's true whether we're talking about a sophisticated industrial plant or a one-person insurance agency. Just as the pony express gave way to the telegraph and the telegraph to the telephone, so the card file and note pad will give way to pocket-sized personal computers.

This may sound scary to many who aren't *Popular Science* magazine readers, but it shouldn't be. Actually we are already accustomed to a daily life focused on using high technology equipment: VCRs, CD players, checkout scanners in stores, programmable thermostats, copy machines, digital instrumentation in our cars, cellular phones, home computers, and many of the medical processes we have come to take for granted. These all rely on high-tech equipment, and using them has given us a good base of knowledge for understanding the concepts and applications needed by the modern work force.

You can expect that new technologies will come at an ever-increasing rate as companies compete to supply new products that will make our lives easier and improve productivity in the workplace. Mass production and unbelievable competition in the semi-conductor industry has made hi-tech affordable for almost anyone in business today.

Although the maze of the computer world may look complicated to older workers, in actuality it is not. In fact, as the power and speed of computers have increased, their operation has become more simplified. New sophisticated operating systems, such as Microsoft's *Windows*, have brought the use of computers down to the "user friendly" level. Eventually these systems will be voice responsive and no more complicated to use than a telephone.

The key to the future for most of us is to understand how to use the computer, not how it operates. But first you'll need to become computer literate—know the language of the computer world.

If you don't have a good foundation of technical knowledge, begin by subscribing to a basic computer magazine, such as *Personal Computing*. Then you should continue the learning process by taking a course in computer basics at a community college. Just by learning some of the basic concepts, you'll eliminate the fear of not being able to function in a high-tech workplace.

Remember, it is not necessary to understand how to build or repair computers in order to understand how they work. Few pilots can repair a jet aircraft; nor do they need to. Pilots need to understand the basics of mechanics in order to make the aircraft perform properly, but that does *not* include disassembly and repair. Virtually everyone today needs a basic understanding of computers because, for better or worse, they're the wave of the future.

Even in our career testing, computers are used for several functions, including scoring, processing data, statistical analysis, and printing reports. One of our staff members, with only minimum technical knowledge of computers, set up all our scoring and data programs. Using "user friendly" programs, she is able to fully utilize a complex machine designed by engineers and programmed by mathematicians.

As H. Ross Perot once commented, when asked how he could grasp the technical complexities of his computer-based EDS Company, "I only want to know what the computers do. I don't care how they do it."

OTHER SKILLS

In summarizing a survey of over 100 business executives, Frank Grazian, executive editor of *Communication Briefings,* says "Employees can't depend on manuals or rule books to find answers to tomorrow's problems. They must adopt a mind-set that lets them process and apply information—and never stop."[1]

If you really want a career in our future work force, turn off the TV and break out the books.

Workers in the twenty-first century will need to develop the skills that enable them to be critical thinkers.

1. *Learn to be creative.*

Most people need to read more and watch television a lot less. If you watch television at all, develop a taste for documentaries, not sitcoms.

2. *Cultivate leadership skills so you don't need to be told what to do all the time.*

Develop this area by volunteering to lead a committee and by reading biographies and good books on leadership.

3. Learn to envision the future and develop new ideas.

Study the lives of great people, such as Edison, Bell, and Ford (and, more recently, Bill Gates). These people had both vision and tenacity. They often failed—but never quit.

4. Become a team player but not a mindless follower.

In the book on management, *Control Your Destiny Or Someone Else Will*, Jack Welch, CEO of General Electric, explains why it's important for everyone to get involved in developing new ideas. He strives for an environment at GE that encourages every worker, regardless of position, to contribute to new product development. Having such a pool of creative thinkers is an essential resource in today's highly competitive marketplace.

Describing GE's new corporate attitude, Welch says: "I wish we'd understood all along how much leverage you can get from the flow of ideas among all the business units. Now that we've got that leverage, I wonder how we ever lived without it. The enormous advantage we have today is that we can run GE as a laboratory for ideas."[2]

Although GE is a technological company, it's clear that all levels of employees are invited to participate in the idea process. You can anticipate this trend to expand as global competition intensifies.

Our future work force needs to be able to solve problems without direct management intervention. This ability is as much a mind-set as it is education, training, or experience. Formal schooling and training are important, but free thinking and a team mentality are essential. If you really want a career in our future work force, turn off the TV and break out the books.

5. Develop communications skills.

We have discussed "empowerment" already—allowing workers to be more involved in decisions regarding products and services. But if you are going to exercise this new authority, you must communicate well.

Stop for a moment and consider the impact of modern communications. Through fax machines, mobile telephones, and computer modems, we are able to request information, negotiate, make offers, change instructions, and literally conduct business directly from our offices. But high speed communications won't be very effective if customers have to wait for answers to be processed through several layers of management.

So the future trend in business will be to allow individuals to make decisions within their areas of authority (within prescribed limits). For instance, I recently read an article describing how the Holiday Inn hotel chain allows service repair employees the discretion to spend up to $2,000 to correct customer problems without management approval. Obviously controls must be applied to curb abuses but, as a result of this policy, customer complaints have dropped substantially and worker satisfaction has increased.[3]

In our society, clients, customers, and suppliers are growing more and more impatient for quick responses to their needs. We live in the "quick-fix" age. Giving employees both responsibility and authority is the growing trend. Communications is the key to career growth.

Having the technology to transmit quick responses is of little benefit if you can't communicate succinctly and clearly. The ability to communicate with customers in a pleasant and intelligent manner is absolutely critical to the success of every business. Consequently, it is also critical to future employment.

As a result of too much government regulation, which is forcing companies to move out of the U.S., our economy is rapidly becoming a service economy. Instead of working in factories, more and more people will be employed in selling and planning and other areas requiring good communications skills. Failure to adapt will likely result in fewer opportunities.

6. Develop human relations skills.

International competition is forcing everyone to look more closely at the service side of business. As the price and quality gap between products narrows, what usually determines repeat sales is *service.* If you don't believe that, just think about your own buying habits. Will you buy a product costing more than a few dollars from a store where the employees are rude, information is scarce, and there is a no-return, no-exchange policy? Hardly so.

Businesses are waking up to the fact that customers are concerned about price and quality, but they're also concerned about how they are treated before, during, and after the sale.

As Christians, we have a great advantage in this area because we're inclined to be nice to people because we *care* about them—

not because we "need to." Once you adopt an attitude of service to others, people will sense it.

I have personally hired more than one young person out of a retail store I frequented, simply because they were so polite and cooperative. I knew we could train them to do the job we needed, but their attitude was a matter of choice—theirs.

I often stop by one of the many fast food places in our town to get a cup of coffee on the way to work. Since many of these eateries are the testing grounds for first-time workers, I'm always alert for a prospective employee. Unfortunately many of the young people are careless and disrespectful and, without even realizing why, most of them will have a hard time getting and keeping good jobs.

In the workplace of the future there won't be any place for those who simply want a job as a place in which to hide.

But one young lady working the drive-thru window at the local Hardees seemed especially bright and pleasant. She went the extra mile to help me by always including the implements to stir the coffee and asking the logical questions about cream and sugar and so on.

One day I decided to test her commitment to service. When I stopped at the window, I asked her if she would mix the cream and sugar in my coffee and spread some jelly on the biscuit I ordered. (I have done this with many of the teens working the drive-thru windows, and you wouldn't *believe* their reactions.) This young woman paused for a second to consider what I requested, then said "Yes, sir," and promptly completed my order.

I did two things as a result: I tipped her $10 and called a friend who manages a local bank and asked him if he needed a good teller. He did. She now works there during her college breaks.

Just bear in mind what Proverbs 22:29 says: *"Do you see a man skilled in his work? He will stand before kings; he will not stand before obscure men."*

The skills needed in the age of communications are technical expertise, creativity, leadership, vision for the future, team playing, communications, human relations, and courtesy.

Remember: Turn that television off and get involved with *real* life.

KEEPING A JOB AND LIKING IT

In the workplace of the future there won't be any place for those who simply want a job as a place in which to hide. Companies are going to operate as lean as possible; that means very little slack.

As tax dollars get harder and harder to come by, even governments will be forced to cut out the excess. The traditional attitude that a job with a big company or with the government is security for a lifetime will disappear just as surely as the attitude has that you can make a bad product and still stay in business.

In my opinion, this is a very good trend. What a waste it is to have people stuck in positions where they are miserable and, consequently, they make almost everyone around them miserable too. The key to fulfillment (not to mention profitability) is placing the right people in the right positions.

I have felt for many years that dismissing someone is not the cruelest thing a manager can do to an employee. The cruelest thing is to allow someone to remain in a position where he or she is unable to function properly.

In our "politically correct" society we seem to think that everyone must be maintained and protected. In my judgment, to be released from a fruitless job is not punishment; it is a reward. When you know what you can do and do it, there always will be a place for you.

In good times, when there is more than enough business to go around and plenty of profits, maintaining marginal employees is possible, even though it is foolish. But in a highly competitive environment where economic survival is the issue, such policies change; there is no alternative. Often what happens is that companies wait until the economy dictates change and the politicians, who themselves are in economic peril, are less sympathetic to "political correctness," and these misplaced employees are released. Unfortunately, it is often late in their working careers, and the opportunities are very limited.

Don't let this happen to you, regardless of your race, handicap, or any other factor. Find out what your God-given abilities are and settle for nothing less than a job that allows you to fully utilize them.

Obviously the first job you hold may not fit that requirement, just as your first home doesn't fit all of your long-term housing needs. But don't allow yourself to get trapped in a job that you know is a dead end. Peace and contentment are far more important in the long term than any amount of money.

Without a doubt, our current politically correct attitudes about job security will change as the economy changes. It's going to be difficult to survive economically in the next century with all the competition that countries like China will bring to bear. In times of survival, people and government do what they have to to survive. The best employees will always have a place. *All* others are subject to early withdrawal.

TECHNOLOGY IS NEITHER GOOD NOR BAD

The point has already been made that workers in the twenty-first century will have to adjust to new technologies and changes. Unless you plan to find a cave somewhere and hide, you'll need to learn to utilize this new technology. And even if you decide to hide in the mountains, you're liable to find yourself confronted by some ecologist with a portable computer, checking to see if you're polluting a forest or stream.

It isn't unusual for people to resist changes, especially as they grow older. But when carried to an extreme, this resistance can make them unemployable. You certainly don't want to be in this position over the next decade because the usual alternative of retirement will be greatly reduced.

Simply put, the system of retirement as we now know it will be absolutely impossible in the next century. There will not be enough young taxpayers to support retirement for the vast majority of people. You and I will need to work well into our 70s in order to maintain any reasonable standard of living. Inflexibility will condemn the intractable to the welfare roles.

Our office is a small microcosm of the American workplace, and it has been only a few years since we introduced electronic word processors into our daily routine. When I first made the decision to replace the old typewriters with word processors, it was met with a great deal of opposition. One woman even quit rather than learn to use a computer.

In spite of my assurances that computers would be more productive in the long run, many of our best typists continued to use their typewriters—while the computers sat on their desks. After all, they surmised, they were doing quite well on their typewriters and they didn't need to change—thank you very much!

But I was certain that the office of the future (which is now) would be heavily dependent on computerized systems, so I finally took their typewriters and locked them in a closet. Within a couple weeks, all of the typists were using the word processors and loving them. The ability to call up routine information—addresses, standard paragraphs, and the like—reduced their work loads significantly. Eventually a good typist using a word processor was able to turn out the work of three equivalent typists using the old system.

Those who are willing to adjust and learn will find their places in the new job market. Those who refuse to learn will be bypassed.

Today practically every office in the country uses computerized word processors. When linked to a central data base, these machines can improve productivity by a factor of 10, compared to the old system. The ability to do instant rewrites, edits, additions, and sharing of information is now commonplace.

We are currently changing our office to an E-mail system. E-mail is a term used to describe the electronic transfer of information within an office. Instead of people writing notes or letters to each other, they simply leave a message in the other person's electronic message box.

Obviously there is some resistance to E-mail from those who like the handwritten system they are used to. But technology brings with it changes, and total electronic communications is the trend of the future, so our office will change.

It is easy to envision a time when handwritten letters will be the exception, rather than the rule. Instead of writing a letter, buying a stamp, and mailing it across the country, you will simply sit down at your work station, draft the letter, and transmit it to the recipient's computer mail box.

Many businesses and individuals already do this, using fax machines. But eventually the fax will give way to the totally electronic transfer system. With existing technology it is already possible to scan any written document into a computer and transmit it anywhere in the world where the recipient computer then reconstructs the document and prints it out. In many areas, contracts drafted and signed this way are as binding as those written and signed face to face. Witnesses at each end attest to the signatures.

In the very near future technology will enable a household to pay all their bills, access library books, and even attend classes—all electronically. Hopefully we will learn to use these advances without compromising our freedoms or privacy; that's really up to us. But the certainty is that huge changes are coming. Those who are willing to adjust and learn will find their places in the new job market. Those who refuse to learn will be bypassed.

Many things of the past are to be preserved and treasured, including our spiritual heritage; technology does not threaten that. We need to keep the best of the past and adopt the best of the future—as many of our parents did.

SECTION TWO
Making Career Decisions

CHAPTER THREE
Your Vocation and Your Income

*W*hen I attended Rollins College in the early sixties, the U.S. space program was in full swing. The college, in central Florida, was obviously affected by the influx of scientists to the area and, consequently, offered a broad variety of engineering and math courses.

Virtually all the good jobs in the central Florida area were in the space industry and, as a result, most of the students were steered in that direction. There was only one problem: I wasn't particularly good at math, and I didn't really want to be an engineer.

However, since I was already working at Cape Canaveral in a scientific experiments laboratory, I took several courses in math and science. To my surprise I found that by applying myself to the courses I did pretty well. But with each additional course the work load got progressively more difficult. My friends at work seemed to study a lot less than I did, but they got better grades.

I learned to work my way through algebra, trigonometry, and even differential equations—all the while dreading the next series of classes. I knew that I would far rather study law, history, or something unrelated to engineering. But since there were very few career opportunities for history majors, I stuck with the science classes.

Since the company I worked for paid for the classes as long as I maintained at least a "B" average, I did what was necessary and even maintained a low "A" average.

I didn't know enough then about vocational aptitudes to realize that I would have made a poor engineer if I had continued on the same track. Actually I was already working as a quality control engineer, and since I had a good memory and was able to learn quickly, I was able to get by on the job. Where other people could use their education to help solve some of the engineering problems we had, I drifted toward ways to solve some of the people problems we had.

Eventually I inherited the job of scheduling people, keeping the activities reports current, and briefing the NASA officials to whom we were responsible. Without realizing it, I was "doin' what comes naturally," as the old song goes.

It was not by luck or chance that, once I began doing those things I enjoyed, I began to get some recognition. In a department made up primarily of engineers and scientists who wanted to be able to do their "thing" unencumbered by paperwork and meetings, I was appointed their official representative. When the space program expanded and a new department was formed, I was asked to assume responsibility over it.

Suddenly I was no longer doing any engineering; instead I was supervising and coordinating an engineering and programming staff, and I loved it. Instead of constantly looking for ways to avoid more work, I was excited to go to work. The challenge of coordinating our operations and setting schedules was much closer to my temperament than solving electrical glitches in a guidance package.

At college I stopped taking engineering courses and began taking business courses. Perhaps the discipline I had developed in the science and math courses had taught me how to study, but I found the business courses were exciting. Instead of struggling to maintain an A or B average, my grades became a solid A. I breezed through the business classes and began to see a direction for the rest of my life.

My experience is not too different from that of millions of other college students of my generation who studied the wrong subjects because that's where the jobs were. The advantage I had was that I worked my way through college and, therefore, had the opportunity to find the right path before I had invested four or five years in an education I would never use.

The reason I ended up in an engineering job at the space center actually took root in high school. My father was an electrician, and because of his contacts with an electrical union I could get summer jobs as an apprentice electrician. Since I am fairly mechanical by nature, I was able to do a reasonably good job, in an era when teenagers weren't all that reliable. Once I began to get some raises, I was locked into working in the construction trade, even though I didn't particularly enjoy it.

In order to progress (in income), I was required to attend weekly classes on electrical theory. When I entered the Air Force after high school, the experience and training I had received in the electrical field automatically qualified me for training in electronics. Mine was a classic case of being trapped, due to circumstances, into a career field where I had no real interest.

The vast majority of people who make career decisions early in life are motivated primarily by their income expectations.

A friend, who is now a practicing physician, related a similar story about how he was funneled into an engineering career because his father owned a commercial construction company, where he worked throughout high school. He graduated from engineering school with honors, and yet he had no interest in the field.

It was only after spending three miserable years as a structural engineer that he finally decided to apply for medical school—a career he had always dreamed about. He now practices family medicine and thoroughly enjoys going to work every day. He sacrificed a very lucrative career running the family business to accomplish his goals, but the long-term rewards of doing what God equipped him to do best were well worth it.

HOW CAREER CHOICES AFFECT INCOME

Anyone who thinks that career decisions are not related to income expectations is very naive. Perhaps there are a few dedicated individuals who know exactly what they want to do for the rest of their lives at age 17 or 18, but they are decidedly in the minority. The vast majority of people who make career decisions early in life are motivated primarily by their income expectations.

The mere fact that someone is motivated by income expectations is not necessarily wrong. After all, earning a living is a fact of life. What *is* wrong is making career decisions based *primarily* on future income considerations.

A doctor who chooses the medical field because of its income potential generally will make a poor physician. He or she might actually be a reasonably good doctor, just as I was a competent engineer (so I have been told). But I could never have excelled in the engineering field because it was not what God had equipped me to do best in life.

If I had been able to invent a highly profitable product that would have generated millions of dollars for me, I would have taken my money and walked away from the engineering field without a look back. If, as is more likely, I had never come up with that terrific product I more likely would have stayed on and been miserable until I quit, was fired, or retired—like most Americans today.

With the colossal changes taking place in the health care industry today, we will see many doctors taking the money they have made and retiring to fish, golf, or travel. These are the ones who were drawn into a career field by the financial rewards—not aptitude, abilities, and desire. Other doctors will stay, in spite of the extra burden of government regulations, because it is their chosen and preferred career field. These are the men and women who practice their trade because they love it, not because it pays well.

All too often, the advice given by college career counselors to students seeking career guidance is based on future economic trends and available jobs. This is understandable. Guidance counselors would like to help students get jobs after they finish their college education. And, likewise, students would like to find employers waiting with open arms to hire them at exorbitant salaries.

But at some point, we must help people to adopt a longer-term perspective about their futures. The only way to find true success and fulfillment (not to speak of financial success) is to determine what you will do the best and then go do it!

One of my childhood friends was an avid golf enthusiast. We both lived near an exclusive country club in Winter Park, Florida and, while growing up, we often caddied on the weekends. I did it strictly because of the money. The pay per hour was great, especially if a local duffer had a good game.

I quickly realized that if I knew a little about golf and could advise a golfer on how to play the course better, he often would give a better tip. So I studied the game and the course and listened as the local golf pro gave tips to his clients. As a result I was able to make some good money, although I didn't care much about golfing.

But my friend took up golf seriously. He played in all the "pee-wee" tournaments and, eventually, went on to the national golfing circuit. Because he focused his efforts in an area in which he had both an aptitude and desire, he has been able to make a good living from what was only a hobby for me. He is now a golf pro at a local country club.

The key to my friend's success is the same as for most truly satisfied workers: He matched his interests and abilities. Obviously being a golf pro won't make anyone a multi-millionaire, but peace and contentment are far more important than money in the long run.

RECOGNIZING YOUR APTITUDE

I have a close friend who says he knew at the age of eight that he wanted to be a physician. I wish that had been the case with me, but it wasn't. I really didn't know what I wanted to do until I was in my thirties. However, as I stated earlier, at least I knew some things I didn't want to do. I didn't want to crawl under houses to pull electrical wires; I didn't want to bag groceries; I didn't want to deliver newspapers; I didn't want to be an engineer. And there were several other career alternatives I wanted no part of.

However, as I look back over my varied work experience, I realize that what I do now (write and teach) was a desire that simply had not been fulfilled. I took a creative writing course in college that was absolutely one of the most boring classes I ever endured. The instructor was a frustrated writer who could not get published, so she took it out on her students. She tested us on the 12 rules of creative thinking, the 10 methods of evaluating good literature, the best way to outline a macro study in ergonomics, and so on.

How do you weigh income against satisfaction?

Obviously these would be absolutely useless for any really creative writer. But in spite of her best efforts to discourage me (by repeatedly redlining my poor punctuation) and my obvious failure to correctly outline before I started writing (which I still don't do), I found that I thoroughly enjoyed creative writing.

It would take nearly 10 more years before I would actually write my first book. And even then I had to pay the publisher to print the first copies. But here I am 20 books and 2 million copies later doing what I truly love to do: write. I had the aptitude and desire to write throughout my entire working career, but I lacked the opportunity and message until I was 32 years old. I trust that your ultimate career decision will be hastened as a result of Lee Ellis' efforts in this excellent book on career decisions.

VOCATION VERSUS INCOME

Assume that you're facing some critical decisions about your vocation, and chief among them is how much you will make. How do you weigh income against satisfaction?

It would be easy in a book like this to fall back on platitudes like "Do what makes you the happiest," but that's not always wise. I have a friend who would like more than anything else to play professional golf for a living. He is a better-than-average golfer and plays every chance he gets. He is employed by a company he dislikes, at a job where he is seldom challenged, so he would appear to be an ideal candidate for a career change.

However, two important elements are missing: He is not a good enough golfer to earn a living at it, and his golf fixation is a consequence of being stuck in a job that is neither challenging nor rewarding.

As with many people in similar situations, he lives for weekends, vacations and, ultimately, retirement. Certainly he is a candidate for a vocational change, but not into professional golf. He might operate a golf shop or even teach golf at a small country club, but for him the risks are too high and the pay cut too steep to make the change; so he will stay where he is. In his case, he has allowed his income expectations to overrule whatever God's vocational plan is for his life.

A young woman I'll call Sherry came to see me several years ago when she was a freshman in college. She wanted to study English literature but her father, who was an accountant, wanted her to study something practical: accounting. As he correctly pointed out, she could always get a job in the accounting field, but finding jobs in English literature would be very difficult. Unless she was fortunate enough to land one of the few teaching jobs available, she might never find employment in her field of study. And even if she did, it would require at least a masters degree and, probably, a doctorate. Her parents could not afford to send her to graduate school, and they certainly could not invest the better part of $100,000 to help her get a job that might pay $25,000 a year.

Sherry's personality was such that she would have made a good accountant, if that had been her goal. The same temperament (a supporter perfectionist) would also serve her well as a teacher, so the choice really came down to one of desire and practicality.

Sherry was absolutely committed to the study of English literature—even to the point of working her way through college and going part-time if necessary. After several sessions with both Sherry and her parents, I recommended a compromise.

Since her parents had committed to helping her in undergraduate school, I suggested that they continue their commitment with the clear understanding that all financial aid would end when she graduated. If she could fund the rest of her education herself, that would be her choice. If not, then she would have to take whatever job was available to her.

Obviously her father wasn't too happy. He could see his daughter spending four years in college, then working in a fast-food restaurant after graduation. But at some point all parents must allow their children to make their own choices, and this was one that Sherry had prayed about, and she was willing to accept the consequences —good or bad.

My counsel to Sherry, outside of the meetings with her parents, was to look for any opportunities that came her way in the area of English literature during the four years she would be in college. If she waited until after graduation to seek a career she probably *would* end up flipping hamburgers.

If either Sherry or her parents had asked me back then what I thought the chances were of finding something in her field, I would have replied "slim to none." I had known more than one English literature major who went on to graduate school to study something more oriented to the business world because there were no jobs available. Fortunately neither Sherry nor her parents asked.

In her second year of college, Sherry noticed a New York newspaper ad for English-speaking teachers to teach in Japan. She responded to the ad but was told she would have to be fluent in Japanese to be considered since the job would be in a Japanese school. Since she did not speak a single word of Japanese, she obviously was not qualified.

Success in any field is 90 percent perspiration and 10 percent inspiration.

But what this incident did was plant an idea in her mind. She realized there were probably career opportunities in English literature in other countries if she spoke their language. Since she had taken courses in French and German in high school, she knew that she could learn a second language if motivated. She chose Japanese since it was obvious that the Japanese were anxious to learn as much as possible about America and the English language.

Her college offered no courses in Japanese but she talked her advisor into allowing her to take classes by correspondence that would be applied toward her college degree. She enrolled in a class through an accredited institution in Tokyo.

During the summer of her junior year she applied for and received a grant to study in Japan through a program offered by a major Japanese company. By the end of her senior year she was rapidly becoming proficient in the Japanese language and the relationship with the Japanese company landed her a teaching job upon graduation—at a salary of $40,000 a year!

Sherry spent nearly six years in Japan teaching at two major universities, as well as consulting with several Japanese companies. The company that had provided the initial grant was so impressed by her commitment and abilities that she was given a full grant-in-aid to complete her doctorate.

Sherry returned to the United States to start her own consulting firm, teaching American executives on Japanese culture while also teaching at a California university. She proved that if you know what you are best equipped to do and prepare accordingly, you can do well in any field. Success in any field is 90 percent perspiration and 10 percent inspiration.

God has equipped each of us to do one thing better than anyone else in the world. Find out what that is for you, and you can't help but succeed.

CHAPTER FOUR

Career Decisions: Peace or Prosperity?

*I*f you looked objectively at how career decisions were made at or about the turn of this century, you'd find that, in many instances, they were actually more logical than they are now. Over 90 percent of all private entrepreneurs were not high school graduates, and only a minuscule percentage were college graduates.

The necessity of earning a living forced most young men into the workplace at a young age. By trial and error they made their way through several career fields until they found the one that best suited their talents and temperament.

Later these men, who had amassed fortunes doing what they loved best, passed their wealth along to their offspring. This second generation had careers thrust upon them, and the seeds of discontentment are obvious in most of their lives.

In some cases the children did exceedingly well because their temperaments fit the jobs available. But in other cases the offspring degenerated into what are commonly called "spoiled brats," who accomplished virtually nothing and, in fact, lived miserable lives.

The children of successful men and women are stark testimonies to the principle that each of us must find what God has equipped us to do best—not what our parents or grandparents did. In my opinion, modern education is a major detriment to accomplishing that goal.

Based upon nothing other than the most superficial data, the 18-year-olds of today are expected to decide what their lifelong vocations will be *prior* to going to college. Consequently, many are studying for careers they will never master—and the vast majority will not even enjoy.

All of this is to say that anything that can be done to avoid making career mistakes should be done.

It is my personal conviction that no college professors should be allowed to teach until and unless they have 10 years of work experience in their field of concentration. Once they had worked in the "real" world for 10 years or so, they would recognize what is necessary for their students to succeed.

It is also my conviction that the vast majority of college students would be better served if they had to work at least two years *before* entering college. To be sure, it would take them two years longer to finish, but it would save most of them 20 years of grief because of making the wrong career choices.

All of this is to say that *anything that can be done to avoid making career mistakes should be done.*

Several times over the last 20 years I have taken small surveys of how many people are still working in the career fields they studied for in college, and the results are almost always the same: About 10 percent are actually working in their field of study.

Some of this can be explained by the abundance of choices that have been available in our economy, and others are probably the result of the lack of jobs in a particular field. In great part, however, we are seeing the reflection of our society as a whole: Most people just don't know what they are best equipped to do. As I said earlier, too often career decisions are based on projected income—not satisfaction.

THE COST OF PROSPERITY

Randy was a very successful attorney in Washington, D.C. He had studied history at the University of Virginia and had attended law school at Georgetown University. He had an excellent aptitude for the field of law and was blessed with a keen mind, as well as a superior memory, which are great assets in the field of trial law.

After graduating from law school he was courted by several major firms in the Washington, D.C. area and had offers ranging from $40,000 to $50,000 per year. Randy's father tried to encourage him to return to his hometown and practice general law. He was concerned about the liberal bias Randy had acquired in college, and he was particularly concerned over Randy's obsession with material success.

Randy had talked about joining his father's practice before going to college, but when he saw that general practice attorneys were held in low esteem by his professors, his attitude changed.

"Get a political background," one of his law professors told him, "and you can write your own ticket." That's exactly what Randy did. He joined the staff of a U.S. senator as a legal aide. His sights were set on the really big money that could be made by practicing law where the government money flows.

As with most senatorial aides, Randy worked for pretty low wages for the first five years of his career, all the while developing contacts within some of the most prestigious law firms in Washington. He often met with other senators' staffs, worked directly with government officials on special committees, and quickly was recognized as a rising star. Consequently, Randy was given access to some of the most powerful politicians in America.

For those who have never traveled the Washington scene, it may be difficult to imagine the power and prestige that emanates from our capital. With billions (and now trillions) of dollars flowing into the economy from Washington, nearly every major corporation in the world is vying for anyone with contacts within our government; and Randy had them.

At 30 years of age he left the senator's staff and accepted a position with one of the major law firms specializing in government contracts. His starting annual salary was $200,000 plus bonuses. Within two years he was earning more than half a million dollars a year. By that time he had married his childhood sweetheart, had two fine children, a beautiful home in Virginia, and the whole world before him.

The only thing Randy really didn't have was peace in his life. He felt he had "paid his dues" and the system owed him something. His goal in life was to become rich—very rich—and he worked extremely hard at it.

His career required him to work 100 hours a week or more, and he had to travel extensively to meet with clients. He was able to travel in the best style, fly first class, and stay in five-star hotels, but inside he knew his talents were being wasted. There are many forms of prostitution; Randy became a success prostitute.

The more money he made, the less important it became. He began to look objectively at some of the clients he represented and realized that he was helping them to cheat the U.S. government out of tax dollars provided by people who earned a fraction of what he made. He wasn't helping to advance mankind; he was helping greedy people to make more money, and he was syphoning off some of it for himself.

He went back to his boyhood home in Virginia less and less because too often his father would ask him penetrating questions, such as: "Are you happy? Do you spend enough time with your family?" and "What will your work be worth in eternity?" In reality, Randy didn't want to think about those things. He had career goals.

Randy had come from a Christian home where his parents regularly attended church. He had seen his own father make career choices to his financial detriment. Once when he had been offered a position with a national firm, he turned the job down saying he couldn't dedicate the time it would take to do the job well.

As Randy was advancing in the field of political law, his father repeatedly asked him about his own family and spiritual goals. His response was that he was doing what he had been trained to do, to which his father usually would reply, "But how about what God wants you to do?"

Randy brushed aside the questions and concentrated on becoming a wealthy Washington attorney. There was much about his career he didn't enjoy, but he assumed that when he had made enough money he could always retire and practice law with his father—if he wanted to. So he continued to spend the time necessary to gain influence, make money, and develop the attitudes of the very people he disliked most.

Randy's wife Kaye often asked him to stop working so much and spend more time with his family. His normal response was to get angry and tell her he was doing all of this for his family and when he had "made it" he would take some time off; maybe he would even quit and get out of Washington.

Two events were to occur in the mid-seventies that would alter forevermore Randy's ideas of success.

One rainy morning Kaye was driving to a meeting with their children when a drunk driver slammed into the side of her car, instantly killing her and the two children.

Randy was totally devastated by the tragic death of his family. In one brief moment, everything he knew had been changed forever. After the funeral he returned to their beautiful home under the most oppressive guilt trip Satan can lay on anyone. He had more than a million dollars in investments, a $500,000 home, a Mercedes, and no one to share his grief.

The week after his wife and children were killed, his father suffered a heart attack and died. In less than two weeks his whole life was changed completely.

All the hours that had gone into making his wealth now came back to haunt him. He had spent hundreds of hours with greedy clients, many of whom reminded him of slimy eels. These people had seen more of Randy than his own children had. All the little league games he had missed now came to mind. His sacrifices to material success were made at the expense of the important issues of life.

It was during this dark time that a friend of Randy's latched unto him and would not let go. Randy tried to hide in his work, but this friend would call and ask him to meet for breakfast or lunch. Randy would go because he had no other real friends (in a real crisis, few people on the "success treadmill" do).

This friendship was a rather strange one because his friend Charles was an auto mechanic. One of the "toys" Randy had bought was an expensive sports car that he drove sometimes on weekends. But as expensive toys are prone to do, this one took a great deal of maintenance. Another attorney suggested that Randy take the temperamental machine to a small shop where the mechanic was a true genius. Randy did, and he developed a friendship with Charles that had lasted for more than five years.

Charles was about Randy's age, bright, and extremely gifted in the mechanics of complicated automobiles. He and Randy hit it off right away. Randy often chatted with Charles while he was tuning the sports car, and one day he asked Charles why he decided to become a mechanic when, clearly, he could have become a good engineer and earned a great deal more money.

Charles usually shrugged off the question, but as they became friends he shared his story. He was a graduate of Texas A&M and had worked in the aerospace industry until the cutbacks in the late sixties. Unable to find a job in the aerospace business and with a keen interest in high performance automobiles, he started a specialty garage for sports cars in Houston.

Initially he thought the garage would be a stopgap between jobs, but after a couple of very successful years he sold the garage to a local sports car club and moved to the Washington area to take a lucrative job as a service manager for a sports car import company.

Over the next couple of years, Charles gained a reputation for his honesty and expertise among the sports car enthusiasts in the D.C. area, and he eventually started his own garage. That's where he met Randy.

Charles was a committed Christian, as several of the signs around his shop reflected. He had often shared his beliefs with Randy and some of the other clients, although he tried never to be pushy about it if someone objected.

The thing that most impressed Randy about his mechanic/friend was that he was totally unimpressed by the titles and positions of his clientele, many of whom were senators, representatives of Congress, and judges. He was thoroughly professional in his field, but he seemed to keep his priorities in balance.

He would always close his shop at 7 P.M., regardless of how insistent his customers were or what position they held in the Washington hierarchy. He closed at noon on Saturdays so he could spend the rest of the weekend with his family, and no amount of persuasion or money could alter his decision.

Although after the death of his family Randy tried to avoid Charles and drown himself in more work, Charles refused to be dissuaded. Not only would he call Randy, but sometimes he would drop by Randy's home and refuse to leave until he agreed to get together again.

As the months went by, Randy confided in his friend that he lacked the will to live since his family had died.

"It seems like my whole life has been wasted," Randy shared one day. "I've made a lot of money, but I failed at being a husband and father."

"You're probably right," Charles agreed. "Now, what are you going to do about it?"

"I don't know what to do," Randy replied as they sat in the garage, sipping coffee. "It's too late."

"Do you really like what you do?" Charles asked.

"Actually I hate it," Randy replied. "But it's all I know. I feel like I gave up my family to get to where I am."

"If you could do anything you wanted, what would it be?" Charles asked.

"I guess I'd like to set up a practice in my dad's old office and help people," Randy replied, "but I don't know if I could do that; my expenses are so high."

"Sure. I understand," Charles said sympathetically. "I never thought I could afford to be an auto mechanic. Besides, it's a big comedown for a guy with an engineering degree to be a grunt. But you know what, Randy? I wouldn't trade jobs with the president. No, even more than that, I praise God every day that I'm *not* the president, or an aerospace engineer, or anyone who's on a treadmill to nowhere."

To make a long story short, I met Randy because of a case he was working on to help defend a Christian liberty issue. Charles had the privilege of leading Randy to the Lord, and shortly after that Randy set out to get his priorities straight.

He moved back to his hometown in Virginia and set up shop where his father had practiced for 40 years. When the local high school principal had refused a Christian teacher the right to speak at a youth rally, Randy took on the case pro bono and became involved with the issue of religious liberties.

Randy now works nearly full time researching and confronting issues that involve the constitutional rights of all Americans. Since he became a Christian, he has given the majority of his wealth away and lives a fairly modest lifestyle.

> *I doubt that many Americans truly have ever experienced real poverty—at least not in this country.*

He also has remarried—a widow whose husband was killed in a plane accident—and he inherited another family. He makes about 10 percent of what he did in Washington and works about twice as hard.

I can say honestly that I have never met anyone more at peace with himself and God than Randy. He chose the right career but for all the wrong reasons. It took an ex-aerospace-engineer-turned-mechanic to teach him that peace and contentment are worth a lot more than wealth and fame. We could all stand to remember that lesson.

PEACE AND POVERTY

If prosperity doesn't guarantee peace in your vocation, then how about poverty? First I need to qualify the term poverty, because in America the term does not have the same meaning it does in places like Somalia or Bangladesh.

Poverty in America usually means living in public housing, not having a car (or driving an old battered one), eating starchy foods, and wearing worn or hand-me-down clothes. Poverty in Somalia means watching your children die of malnutrition or killing rats for food. I doubt that many Americans truly have ever experienced real poverty—at least not in this country.

Having made the distinction that true poverty is not exactly what we think it is, I would like to discuss the issue of peace through poverty. Americans, especially Christians, think that if one extreme leads to error, then the opposite extreme will correct it. Almost never is this true; balance is the key term.

Deciding on a life of self-imposed poverty, or at least severely reduced income because there are so many people who have made the wrong career choices in the quest for prosperity, does not insure happiness. In fact, it can actually lead to more frustration, because by the time you learn the truth you are too old to correct your errors and too poor to do much else.

There are many people who have consciously chosen a career that will never pay well. In fact, many careers will never pay what most of us consider a livable wage. I certainly would put Mother Teresa in this category. Anyone who chooses to become a priest or a nun for the material success it can bring will be woefully disappointed. Obviously some of those in any career field who rise to the top will live well, but they are the exception (in the case of priests and nuns).

I don't know many priests or nuns personally, but I do know a lot of missionaries who have chosen to give up potentially lucrative careers for what we would consider poverty-level incomes. Those who know their calling is from God and have matched their talents and temperaments to their chosen careers have found peace. In fact, many of them dread returning to the United States because of our materialistic lifestyle.

But any honest missionary will admit that the lack of economic resources is a concern from time to time. Without matching their careers with both temperament and aptitude, the lack of material success would be overwhelming—especially when it comes to educating their children. If the rest of us were doing what we should be doing, we would be helping to meet those needs and thus freeing them to minister better. But that's another issue; the issue here is one of career choices.

Most missionaries have met others who chose the mission field for the wrong reasons and were miserable. The fact that they were living on less income did not set them free from worry, anxiety, and even greed. Choosing the wrong career for the right motives is just as bad as choosing the wrong career for the wrong motives.

In the early part of 1981 I sat talking with a couple about their financial problems. The husband, Josh, had worked several years for the I.R.S. as an investigator, which seemed to fit his temperament perfectly. He had advanced to the highest government service rating in his career field and was making nearly $40,000 a year when he quit his job.

The reason he quit a job he had held for nearly 18 years was as a result of becoming a Christian. As with many new Christians, Josh felt God was calling him into full-time ministry. Perhaps God was, but it seemed clear to me that it was not with a non-profit organization. Josh's salary had dropped from $40,000 to $18,000, but his expenses had not dropped proportionately, and they had accumulated several thousands of dollars of debt as a result.

In addition, Josh's new responsibilities required that he interact with people as a fund-raiser. Basically his job was to encourage supporters to leave the organization a bequest in their estate. The motive was good, and all the people he called on were active supporters of the organization he represented. The problem was, the job was totally wrong for Josh's temperament. He was a rather reclusive and shy person who felt very comfortable doing financial audits and very uncomfortable asking people to give.

In addition to calling on potential donors for the ministry he represented, Josh also was required to raise his own salary through the support of friends and family. The net result of both the job and the personal support-raising had made Josh a nervous wreck. His health was rapidly deteriorating; he dreaded going to work; and his marriage was falling apart.

Josh was a victim of what could be called "other people's expectations." After becoming a Christian, Josh and his wife Shirley started attending seminars and training classes. During one of these seminars, a teacher challenged members of the group to quit their jobs and "do something for the Lord," as he put it. Being a new, impressionable Christian, Josh assumed the challenge was from the Lord and quit his job with the government. Their lives started downhill from that point forward.

Josh joined a national ministry as a fund-raiser and discovered quickly he had no aptitude for the job. From there he transferred to another department as a recruiter, with the same results. He then transferred to his present position as a deferred-giving specialist, with no great degree of success. Since the organization required that all staff raise their own support, Josh had virtually no income; he lacked the basic temperament to ask others to help support him.

In the meantime, the bills continued to pile up and, having no other visible alternative, they used their credit cards to live. By the time Josh and Shirley came to see me, Josh was an emotional basket case.

After talking with Josh and Shirley I determined two things: Josh's basic temperament and personality did not complement what he was doing, and it was unlikely that God had called him out of his previous position.

Obviously no one can ever say for certain what God's will is for another person, but the total lack of peace in Josh's life clearly indicated he had made that decision based on "feelings" rather than conviction.

Those who strive after prosperity without regard for their God-given aptitudes end up being miserable and frustrated.

Josh had been duped into believing that to serve God requires one to be in a "full-time ministry" and that sacrificing worldly goods is an essential step in finding peace. Neither is necessarily true.

The vast majority of people who make a surplus of money do so as a by-product of doing what they enjoy most. Most would continue in their chosen field regardless of the economic rewards. On the other hand, those who are good at their vocation and don't make a great deal of money would stay with their jobs because of the personal satisfaction they receive. Often other non-financial benefits, such as community acceptance, outweigh the financial.

Perhaps the classic example of this in Christianity is seen in the pastorate. A hundred years ago practically no pastors would have been counted among the materially prosperous of their society. They basically earned a small stipend, plus a place to live. Often their congregation was rural and couldn't tithe money, so they would share a portion of their produce with the pastor and his family. Ministers usually ate pretty well, but they didn't have a lot of money.

From reading the books and letters written by pastors of previous generations, it's obvious they didn't feel their calling was sacrificial. Perhaps they didn't have all of the material things others had, but they were satisfied. The one thing pastors did have as a group was community respect.

I rather think that most pastors today would willingly trade some of their additional income for the respect achieved by their peers of previous centuries. These men didn't choose their vocation because it came with poverty. They chose their vocation and accepted the income that came with it. The same principle is applicable today.

Those who strive after prosperity without regard for their God-given aptitudes end up being miserable and frustrated. Those who give up all worldly ambition while choosing the wrong career fields ultimately end up being just as miserable. It's not poverty or prosperity that makes the difference; it's doing what God has equipped us to do best.

By the way, in Josh's case I recommended that he reapply with the I.R.S., which he did. He now serves God by being an honest, ethical tax auditor. Yes, they do exist.

CHAPTER FIVE

Career Stories: The Good, the Bad and the Ugly

*W*orking at a ministry that provides assistance in the areas of personal financial management and career planning provides us a unique opportunity to share in the lives of others.

At Christian Financial Concepts and Life Pathways, we receive many letters with exciting testimonies of how God has blessed people who are using the talents He gave them. Of course we also receive many letters that share the stress and discouragement many are feeling as they struggle with various issues in their work.

As Larry and I discussed the purpose and concept of this book, we decided to illustrate how people make both good and bad career choices. Throughout this book, we have used many illustrations of situations and people we know personally.

To broaden our coverage of career issues, we asked a number of our Life Pathways clients for permission to use their stories. You also may have seen the announcement in the April 1993 *Money*

Matters newsletter asking for volunteers to send in their career stories.

CAREER STORIES NEEDED

Larry Burkett, founder and president of CFC, and Lee Ellis, director of CFC's Career Pathways program, are about to begin a book on career planning. They will use actual case studies (anonymously) to illustrate the good, bad, and ugly of career decisions.

Please consider sharing your story, your mistakes, and your triumphs for use in this book. Just mail a note to Career Pathways asking for details or send your story to: P.O. Box 1476, Gainesville, GA 30503.

MARCH 15,1993

We received so many that we were not able to use them all but, as you will see from the selections in this chapter, we got a pretty good cross section of all three categories (good, bad, ugly).

Since many of the letters were several pages long, editing was necessary. However, the selections used are given in their unedited wording. As promised, the names and locations have withheld to protect the privacy of the individual contributors.

To all those who shared their stories with us, we say a heartfelt thanks. We know many will be blessed through your testimonies.

#1

I started college already set on a career in electrical engineering. I had chosen this because it had been my consuming hobby through all of high school. I was unsaved as were my parents. They had saved sacrificially for years to be able to put me into a quality private school.

I was saved near the end of my junior year. I knew that this gave Christ claims on my life, but was a little slow in surrendering in some areas. My mom in particular was worried that I would want to become a preacher and they would have wasted the money that had been used to train me as an EE.

After salvation, my first "surrender" was being willing to be anything as long as it was an electrical engineer. As you might suspect, God was not impressed with this. Next, I surrendered for anything as long as it wasn't being a missionary. Thirdly, I surrendered to anything but foreign missions.

By this time, I was in graduate school and at a point where I was being held up on several fronts. God was still dealing with me about that last holdout. When I finally surrendered it too, there was an immediate and decisive string of circumstances that finally set me off on a straight line toward a career of teaching electronic engineering.

This has been a very satisfying career for me. At the age of 52, I've never even gone through "mid-life crisis"! But I now believe I never would have had this career contentment if I had not surrendered that last reservation. God (as it turns out) did not want me in full-time missions, but He did want me full-time committed to His will for my life.   —P.H.

#2

Let me begin by saying that I ended up discovering I was in the right career already. I just needed to have an attitude adjustment and correct a few things I was doing.

My jobs have never, until now, been the result of some well thought out career search. I was a little curious about the work I am in now, but I was most attracted to the money potential and the potential growth I saw in the financial services industry in the years ahead. I have now been with the same firm for 9 years in which I provide financial planning advice and sell insurance and investment products to my individual clients.

About 18 months ago I was really grasping for what I wanted to do career wise with my life. Being in a position where I was having to sell insurance and investments to make a living was giving me a lot of problems with feeling like I was being manipulative. I also hated the rejection that comes with any form of selling. We were struggling financially through major income swings. Finally I decided enough was enough and that I was going to get to the bottom of what I should be doing with the abilities which God had given me.

I learned the following from this self examination process: The talents and motivated skills I possessed were perfect for the field I was already in. Therefore, I must be doing something to sabotage my enjoyment in the field. I also learned that all of us are inherently self-consumed. I saw clearly for the first time how little I focused on serving the needs of other people rather than always being concerned about what was in it for me.

I learned that . . . I should do everything with excellence, as unto the Lord, and not as unto men, but that I should let God be concerned about the end result. I learned that my motives in working must be to serve people with honest concern for them and absolute integrity. . . . Also, I made a firm commitment to do only what was best for the client no matter what the consequences. . . . This was the attitude adjustment I had to make and once I did, God began blessing me as never before.   —R.H.

#3

Through the example of hardworking parents I grew up knowing that hard work is a good part of life—things are not simply handed to you.

By the time I was in fifth grade I realized that math and working with numbers was the greatest love of my studies. By the time I was a pre-teen I had already begun to earn my own money delivering newspapers and baby-sitting. When I was a junior in high school I signed up for a special program at school which helped teens find a part-time job and then gave them half a day off school every day to work the job and still keep up their studies. I look back now and see how God began right then to mold me for the work He would need me to do in His kingdom later.

My first "real" job was in a dry cleaners. The owner had a reputation for helping troubled teens which at that time I was. During the time I was there he gave me the special opportunity to learn some of the office work—most importantly, how to efficiently handle money and keep records. For several years after that I worked a variety of jobs. . . . Then I got saved! Eventually I became a department manager in a K-Mart.

It was at that time that I discovered I not only loved to work with numbers and money but could also manage both people and business dealings. About a year later, I enrolled in a junior business college to earn an Associate in Accounting. I loved every minute of it because it was one of my natural talents.

After several years and changes in my life, God's plan for my life came to pass by my becoming the Office Administrator /Bookkeeper in a 400 member church which also has a day care. Here God has used me not only as the accountant, secretary, receptionist but also as the day-care assistant director and bookkeeper when needed.

I praise God for all that He has done for me. By following after my God-given talents I am fulfilling the role God created me to fulfill for Him. I praise Him for every good and perfect gift which is from Him alone.   —M.S.

#4

The general criteria that guided me in my career choice was the salary I would be earning. . . . I was still seeking a job that would provide me security. . . .

I do not feel that going to college was an error, but I do feel that I could have been more prepared in choosing my course of studies. I feel that the major mistake I made was listening to what other people thought I needed to do without seeking what the Lord had for me. Also the Lord spoke to me in such a clear way through the events of the oil industry going down. He showed me that he was in control and that he made me to be unlike anyone else. He made me for a specific reason and that he had a specific task for me to do.

During that year I made a commitment to do what the Lord wanted me to do. Once I made that decision to let him have the reigns of my life, my career began to go on the upward swing. I wanted the Lord to lead me wherever he wanted me to go. The Lord took me from a position in the oil field of making a lot of money into a youth pastor position paying $250 a month. He opened this position in 1986 after the oil field bust. Through this the Lord taught me to trust Him because benefits and money were not everything. I soon found out that working with youth was more rewarding than just focusing on the money. . . .

I feel the career assessment was helpful in helping me to realize that my talents and personality are perfect for the positions I am involved in at this time. The personality profile was as if I was reading about myself. . . . I am still looking forward in changing careers in the future and it has helped me to focus more on what areas are in proportion to my personality, enjoyment, and most of all what direction Christ will have me go.   —M.O.

You may have noticed a trend in these first four letters: the emptiness in trying to serve ourselves and how God blesses us when we commit our efforts to serving Him. By our natures, this is a difficult concept to accept. In fact, to be able to turn loose of our own ideas of success and trust Him for direction is the essence of faith in Christ.

#5

If I were to share anything I've learned with my career decision making experience, I would say seek the Lord with all your heart, mind, spirit—find what you desire, learn what your skills, talents and personality match up with—and take one step at a time, praying every bit of the way. . . .

If my faith were not being strengthened and being able to see that I am in God's hands and special to Him, I'd never be able to do what I'm doing. Counseling and my church family have helped in my healing and in seeing God's goodness.

I guess the most important principle God has taught me during my career journey is that God cares for me, He has His best in mind for me for His glory and He will keep me as well as guide me. I never have to fear as long as He's in charge and I keep a humble heart before Him, seeking him in all things and being quick to thank Him for all things.   —T.F.

#6

. . . . The Lord showed me that He had never forgotten my dreams, nor turned His face from me. Instead, when I followed His ways, according to His ways, He was then able to immensely bless. I worked very long hours, but my work no longer meant that much to me. I could not put my trust and security in it, because it had failed me miserably already. . . .

By now, I was thoroughly convinced that our Lord is not only faithful to hear our prayers and our hearts' desires, but He will eventually work things out for His glory, in His own time.

The Lord had other plans, too. From 1989 until 1991, the Lord laid it upon my heart to help several Southeast Asian high school youth and some of their friends and siblings to earn money through a number of landscape planting projects. . . . it gave me the treasured and eternal reward of being a role model in their influential life phase, plus opportunities for witness and discipleship to them and their families. . . . I was blessed from these teenagers more than I could have given to them.

Now it is 1993, and California is once again mired in a deep, prolonged recession. I find comfort in that I am not the only one in my profession who is suffering financial hardship, as stories abound about job layoffs and insecurities of those who still have relatively stable jobs. I ask myself what is it that the Lord wants to teach me now, and what to do with the increase in time that comes with a slow workload. . . . perhaps time to rest in Him more, and reflect on His abundant blessings.   —D.L.

#7

I was employed in the corporate audit department of a multi-divisional corporation with facilities in assorted geographical areas. I was one person in a four person audit team. This was my first audit assignment to spend several weeks operational auditing in a TV station. Before I went to the TV station, my new boss instructed me to give special attention to a named person and his work. They hoped to use my audit report as a basis to fire the employee.

I tried to conduct an objective audit. My report declared that the named person's boss was causing lots of problems instead of the person they thought was to blame. My boss stated that since I was not able to follow instructions I no longer had employment with them.   —H.S.

#8

My career path is still somewhat of a mystery to me. I feel as though God has held my hand and led me the whole way. I do not know for what reason I have been so blessed or why I have been surrounded by such wonderful and talented people who have been far more responsible for my successes than I and I hope some day that I will find a way to fulfill my obligation to repay the blessings that have been bestowed upon me.   —D.C.

#9

[In] almost every job I ever had before opening my own business I witnessed dishonesty, corruption, greed, and blatant criminal behavior, on the part of employers, managers, and co-workers. And now that I have my own business, I find myself competing with the same, and quite often losing to it. The only way I can handle this is to focus that Christ is my purpose, and not money or wealth.

I believe that unless an individual clearly knows himself or herself and is self confident, understands his or her dislikes, and has healthy family relationships or has a healthy understanding of their relationship with their family, that person will have difficulty with career and finances.

One's integrity is far more important than wealth, success, or fame.   —R.H.

Quite often our adversities are not the results of anything we have or have not done; it's because sin exists in the world. A positive attitude founded on faith in a Sovereign God is the secret to facing these difficulties. The psalmist Asaph wrestled with the unjustness of a sinful world, confessing "My feet came close to stumbling; my steps had almost slipped. For I was envious of the arrogant, as I saw the prosperity of the wicked" (Psalm 73:2-3). After sharing how he struggled, he continues in verses 23 and 24: "Nevertheless, I am continually with Thee: Thou has taken hold of my right hand. With Thy counsel Thou wilt guide me, and afterward receive me to glory." Remember, God always honors those who honor Him.

#10

[The errors/mistakes I made in my career decisions are] not seeking career counseling early or earlier in life [and] not knowing what I was best suited/equipped to do or not to do.

[The impact in my work of using my best talents has been] greater contentment, peace, and [doing] a better job for my employer.

[The most important principle God has taught me during my career journey is to] seek Him out daily for guidance, pray over your work. Work on your bosses priorities rather than your own. Take criticisms as on-the-job training. Take notes on these things and look for character traits God wants you to work on. Be punctual. (This is hard for me and I'm still learning on it.) Be customer oriented. I've seen businesses lose out just because of a slothful or negligent employee. And I've seen others flourish due to hustle!

I graduated from high school in 1969, went to a college that fall and graduated in December 1973 with a Bachelor of Science Degree in math. I studied about two years toward a Master's Degree. I borrowed $2000 the final year to go after it. I burned out on college, books, professors, and inspiration and quit short only six hours of my degree. I went to work as an odd job and handyman earning about $3 an hour. For almost three years I struggled to pay back the $2000 plus interest by the sweat of my brow. I was so happy and relieved when I finally got it paid off.

That lesson alone was the final six hours of my Master's Degree (a Master's in common sense and prudent financial management)! Shortly after that I interviewed with the telephone company and landed a good job with them in another city. There I met my Savior (through a fellow employee), my wife, and an abundant life. Now, fourteen years later, I'm saved, happily married, we're the parents of adopted twin boys, and we are debt free!   —B.S.

#11

[The most important principle God has taught me during my career journey is] do not ask for an easy shift!! But say, "Lord, I thank You for being with me at work today, thank You for giving me wisdom and insights, thank You for being with me whatever the day may bring. I know with Your help everything will work out OK."

This took me a long time to figure out; not to ask for things to be easy, but thanking the Lord for being with me and helping me through any and every situation.

Once I worked in a small hospital with another Christian nurse. We would start each shift out, asking for "an easy shift". Our scheduled twelve-hour shifts would turn into the worst of worst's sixteen-hour shifts, with many superlative horror stories. We changed our attitude and prayers and it sure helped. I figured out that "easy" is not a word or an attribute that the Lord is interested in!   —D.M.

#12

[The mistake I think I made in my career decision is] not taking a long-term view of where a job would lead. Looking primarily at the money side of the job.

[Many clients indicate they have problems due to a conflict with their values and those of the company or their boss. The problems I experienced in this area are] I have often been faced with illegal and/ or unethical requests or orders. I've let the employer know that I refuse to be involved in anything illegal. Sometimes they try to convince me that no one will know [or that] I'm worrying about nothing. As for the ethical problems, we just don't see eye-to-eye.

[The most important principle God has taught me during my career journey is] that you can't put a square peg in a round hole. The world system seems to think you can educate and train into almost anyone the skills, abilities and interests needed to do a job. Sure, techniques can be taught and people can be manipulated and even shown how to manipulate others. But in the long run, it takes a toll on people in terms of burnout and emotional and spiritual problems, etc.   —W.R.

#13

[The way my commitment to Christ affected my career decisions is] if I had it to do over again, I would do what I feel led to do—regardless of the marketability of the job—and be willing to move to where the job was.

[The most important principle God has taught me during my career journey is] the best way to work in a bad job situation is to realize everyday we work for God—like God is our boss—it cheers me and I do my best.

[The problems I had when I tried to do a job which required talents I didn't have were] extreme stress and job dissatisfaction.

—D.D.

#14

My senior year in college (1971–1972) was not a good year for engineering graduates. I had a few interviews, including one with Baltimore County, Maryland, and one interview trip to Illinois for an oil company. By April I had got no job offers. My co-op employer finally gave me an offer after I asked them. . . . an engineer who was helping me with an independent study for my last seven credits in college offered me a position with his employer. . . . I was ready to say yes immediately (as I was getting "desperate"), when he said that I should not rush my decision and to think about it. The *next* day I went to a Baltimore County spring festival where many County agencies had booths describing their activities. I vividly remember. . . . discussing with my girlfriend whether I should be so bold as to ask the man [at a booth for the Bureau for Sanitation] whether they had any job openings for an engineer. After much hesitation, I did ask. He said as a matter-of-fact yes and to come to their office on Monday. On Monday I met with the Bureau Chief. . . . I went to see the Deputy Director, who was an engineer and the Chief's supervisor. On June 5, 1972, (in less than a month!), I was working for the County.

I began a job for which civil engineering was a good background, but for which I had no formal education, though I had interest in recycling and in the environment. . . . I am still in the same Bureau and the same "position," still enjoying the variety of work and degree of responsibility given to me by my two different Bureau Chiefs. Though in the same "position", as the engineer for the Bureau, I have been reclassified over the years from an entry level engineer to the highest engineering grade below an Assistant Bureau Chief.   —S.L.

When choosing a career field, so many use either no criteria or wrong criteria to make their decisions. Keep in mind: You have been given a unique pattern of strengths and desires for a specific reason. By taking a long-term view toward your career, you'll be motivated to overcome whatever barriers there are in order to learn your bent and understand how it can be applied in the workplace.

#15

I decided to study engineering partly out of interest and also as a challenge. All my peers said it was the toughest curriculum, so I accepted it as a challenge. The error I made in my decision is that I never had my entire heart into studying engineering. Whenever I had thoughts of "getting out" and changing majors, I said, "This is something I started, and I'm going to finish it."

I've since learned commitment runs much deeper. . . . when one commits himself to a job he truly chooses and wants to be in. I'm still adjusting!

My commitment to Christ certainly affected my career decision in that I refused to work for a dishonest company. I could not present a case to my customer based on a lie devised by my employer. I firmly believe my employer to be honest, fair and up front with their business policies and decisions, otherwise I would have to leave.

The problem in doing a job with mismatched talents is a lack of zeal and enthusiasm in the job. I also find a drain on myself when I'm in a job I don't really like. I feel stress not only on the job but also at home.

I look back and would suggest that the time to really think about our career and talents is very early in high school. I can promise the majority of today's work force is mismatched in their careers. . . . How much different would high school and college [have] been had I had the insight of my career path and how my studies would apply.

—E.B.

#16

Living with the consequences of a wrong career decision has been a personal devastation to me. The effect of this one decision upon my life has effected ruin far beyond what I could have ever imagined. It has touched every area of my life: marriage, parenting, spiritual, leisure, etc. Prior to graduating from college I believed that my career would be a challenge and something to look forward to everyday. Instead, this last fifteen years in my chosen field has been a source of intense boredom and mental anguish. I spend an entire workday watching the clock and feeling frustrated. By the end of even a not-too-busy day, I am emotionally drained. I can't wait until it's time to go home, and at the thought of having to return, I become internally distressed.

I completed the tough five-year curriculum in four years by attending school during the summers. I graduated with a 3.4 GPA only to discover in my first few months of internship that I had made a terrible mistake in my choice of a career. It was too late, I could not un-do what had been done. I realized I was stuck in a career that was a good one, but it was totally wrong for me. And I have been in this predicament for the past fifteen years. Although now I only work part-time, it is still a struggle.

How I wish that I could have had the privilege and opportunity of using the services of a ministry like Career Pathways when I needed to make the right career choices. The pain of a decision made so many years ago still runs very deep, but I have learned lessons that I could not have learned otherwise and I believe that when the time is right, God will relieve me from my distress and still provide financially.

—R.L.

#17

My question to young people is "What's the rush?" They rush to get to college, through college, to get married, to get an MBA, to start a career and have a mid-life crisis at 40. Not all industries allow you to make as much money without a degree as advertising does, but a college degree is no longer a guarantee of anything. Nor is a job any guarantee, as my layoffs attest. Might as well follow your heart and do what you enjoy all day.

Of course, God does not deal with everyone the way he deals with me. While the steps of a righteous woman are ordered by the Lord, He was ordering mine long before I acknowledged Him. The only plan he shows me is his *goal* of conforming me to Christ's image. Between here and there is tremendous creative freedom. —L.R.

Boredom, mental anguish, clock watching, and stress can be good indicators that you are in a job mis-match. Some people get into this situation out of ignorance; they just don't know their talents. Others know their talents but ignore them in order to pursue wrong priorities (pride, money, power). Our first calling is to Jesus Christ and His way and to use our talents to serve Him. Next, we are called to be skilled in our work and, through love and excellence, to be a light to the world and a blessing to others.

When Abraham offered up Isaac as a sacrifice, it was symbolic of offering up everything of importance: life, future, security, and heritage. God's response to his obedience was "Indeed I will greatly bless you . . . and in your seed all the nations of the earth shall be blessed, because you have obeyed My voice" (Genesis 22:17–18).

#18

I went to college at night after putting in nine hours at the office, maintaining a house, and being a wife and mother. That lasted two years until I realized I was neglecting my husband and daughter. During this time, I was also trying to change my personality to fit the expectations of my managers. Unfortunately, they encouraged this type of "development." I judged my own self-worth by career success. I was driven toward career goals and had no spiritual goals. I was not praying that God's will be done. I wanted my own will to be done. I allowed rejections to affect my outlook on life. I got to the point where I felt worthless.

Finally, I cried out to God! He has helped Me to accept and love myself the way I am, and to focus on and utilize my strengths. I'm educating myself with God's Word and learning His values. Now I understand my value based on His love for me, not how far up the ladder I get. The more I learn of Him, the stronger my relationship grows with Him. I'm putting God's Kingdom first, and now my career goals are working out nicely. My relationships with others have blossomed as I try to see people as Jesus sees them. . . .

I have not given up my goal for obtaining a degree. If it's God's will, He'll help me find a way. My priorities are straight now and He gives me peace and contentment. I'll be patient and allow God's plan for my life.   —T.D.

#19

I believe this was the place God was taking me. This was His classroom and this was the final exam. I did not want to fail and have to take the course over again. It was tough getting to this point. All of my efforts to keep my job, including good performance, networking, contacts, and extra training were washed away with one decision by one company president. However, unlike the time when I changed from construction to training, I was not particularly anxious. I constantly shared with my co-workers that when the time comes and the need arises, my God will provide for my needs. During this time my wife Carol and I had been praying and really getting the message from scripture that when it seems God has lost control, He hasn't!

The time came on a Monday morning at 10:00 when I received my notice that I would be targeted for the layoff. Twenty-two years of commendable and excellent performance evaluations ended. But then, God showed His power! At 2:00 that same day a Christian friend, not knowing my needs, called and asked if I would work as a management consultant in Puerto Rico. . . .

What an education God has given me. Not only was He in control of my future and career on that fateful Monday, but He had been in control for many years. . . .

To sum up in one sentence the most important principle God has taught (is teaching), it would have to be: "Be anxious for nothing, but with prayer and thanksgiving let your request be made known to God, and have the peace that passes understanding."   —B.T.

#20

I asked the Lord . . . "Why did you put me in such detail-oriented work when I am a big-picture person?" The response was quick: "Because I want to add detail to your life." Oh. And for the last 14 years, he has certainly done that! This work has been good provision for my family, and for that I am eternally grateful. . . .

I believe career counseling is a very valuable service indeed. I wish I had had some! On the other hand, I can see that the highest good may not require my functioning in the area of my own greatest gift and personal interest. Perhaps there are other factors to consider, such as being faithful with what the Lord puts in your hand to do, whether you love it or not. The last fourteen years might have been easier, and doubtless more fun, if I had been fulfilling my heart's desire. . . . What *has* become totally clear is that my heart's desire is to love our Lord with all my being and serve Him wherever and however He wants me to. . . . Day by day, I seek Him yet again for the ability to work in the field in which He has placed me. And truly, He has given me much more than I could ever ask or think.   —C.R.

#21

After all the prayer that went into my job change and all the effort, my wife pointed out that I didn't really seem any happier in my new job than I had been in my old job. About the same time, I noticed the January "Career Track" feature in your newsletter. I realized that even though I had said they weren't important to me, I had let materialism, pride and lack of trust control my job change decision. When I had identified my values during my job search, I didn't list income, title, or security as important. However, when I honestly evaluated my motives, I was determined to show my old corporation how great I was and that I could land a big job with high pay (and wouldn't they feel sorry they lost me!).

After much more prayer, I have again made a career move. I have accepted a job which pays less and will hopefully be a blessing to others.   —D.K.

MAKING GOOD, BAD, AND UGLY CAREER DECISIONS

A. How to Make GOOD Career Decisions
   1. Surrender your life to Jesus Christ and make serving Him your life purpose.
   2. Learn about your natural strengths, talents, interests, needs, and personality. Develop a written profile of who you are—your pattern.
   3. Investigate various career fields by reading, interviewing people, visiting work sites, and so on.
   4. Look for occupations that seem to require your particular group of strengths and talents. Identify these and investigate them closely.
   5. Choose an initial direction and prepare yourself through education and training.
   6. Refine your career as you go along. After you're in the job, you'll see areas where you can grow and develop. Prepare and move along when the doors open.

B. How to Make BAD and UGLY Career Decisions
   1. Choose the first/easiest job you can get.
   2. Choose a job based on the amount of money it pays.
   3. Choose a job because it sounds like a good title.
   4. Choose a job because your friends are working there.
   5. Choose a job because your parents do that job.
   6. Choose a job to fulfill your parents' unfulfilled dreams.
   7. Choose a job just because you have the ability to do it.

CHAPTER SIX

Good Career Decisions Are Based on Truth

*I*n the previous chapter you read about some of the problems that cause bad career decisions. Based on our experience, we can say that almost all career problems come from the same spiritual problem that affects every other area of our lives: We are attracted to short-term, worldly choices because we don't really trust that God's love, grace, and power are sufficient for our needs.

That may sound like a radical statement, so let me elaborate through the story of a friend and then examine some truths of career planning. It's so easy to think "If I could reach my goals, I really would be satisfied." But is that actually true? My friend's story illustrates a truth we all need to learn.

Gary has been blessed with many talents—especially those that seem to help people "succeed" in our society. He's a natural leader, has strong communications skills, and has excellent judgment. He cares about people, and his standard of ethics is extremely high. All his life he's been a very moral person.

Early in his career Gary got into marketing and then management. These areas suited his interests and talents perfectly. He loved his work and was good at it. So good, in fact, that he had 13 promotions in 12 years. Each promotion brought an increase in income, recognition, status, and perks. Money and rewards came easily, so Gary and his family lived well; they also saved and invested.

By the time he was 36 Gary was the head of his company's German division. It was a top-notch company, one of the world's largest, with a good mission. He was highly regarded for his talents and, basically, he had everything he'd ever wanted.

Gary and his family were not regular church attenders; to his knowledge there was not an English-speaking church nearby. They didn't read the Bible either, but they thought of themselves as Christians.

One day Gary took a good look at himself and his family, to see what they really had. It shook him to the core when he saw that his work was his idol, and the materialistic lifestyle they lived was hollow. He observed his children, saw their attitude about "things" and, at first, it made him angry. Then he realized they were just emulating what he and his wife were living.

Gary says, "It was obviously the Holy Spirit that moved me that day because, though I had been blind to the truth, I saw clearly that all I lived for was of no real value. I got on my knees and asked Christ to come into my life and let me live for Him." Two days later Gary's wife Nancy also accepted Christ. The change in their lives was so dramatic that one of their children also was saved two months later.

Gary knew he had to make a clean break with his idol. He knew he had to resign from his company. When he turned in his letter of resignation, his European president shook his head in disbelief. Gary describes that meeting this way. "My boss knew how much I loved my work and the company and to him it was incomprehensible that I would resign. I tried to explain, but he couldn't understand. At the end he did say, 'I think you may have found what I'm still looking for.'"

Most people in Gary's company thought he'd just had a nervous breakdown, and they tried to get him to go to the Mayo Clinic for psychiatric evaluation and help. Instead, he and his family returned to the states, where he attended Bible college.

Over the next three years, Gary exhausted their savings because he was unable to find a good job. Getting a job had never been a concern to him; he'd always lived on a fast track. But now no one would hire him because he was overqualified. Gary had to do manual labor at minimum wage just to feed his family. His faith was truly tested, but God was always faithful.

Eventually, Gary was hired to a marketing position with a Christian company. As before, he loves his work and his company; he's doing well and has been promoted to a management position. But this time there's something different in his life. Serving Jesus is his first priority and that has given him the peace he was missing before.

Gary's story clearly points out the misrepresentation that has been sold so successfully to most of our society. What is needed is the truth.

What Is Truth?

I challenge you to consider all the assumptions upon which people base their career decisions—power, position, wealth, fame, excitement, even talents—and see if you can find any criteria that will provide peace and fulfillment.

Those conditions can't satisfy because they are not founded in the fundamental truth that governs human nature. In these days it does sound radical but, the truth is, we were created to serve in the kingdom of our God and Creator. Our service must come through His power and be done His way.

A History of Following Our Own Truth

Unfortunately, most people in our society, even Christians, seem to be just as hardheaded as the Jews of the Old Testament. You may recall they had very short memories of God's faithfulness and blessings. Even though He demonstrated His commitment through many miracles, they seemed to forget and turn away.

God told them over and over again, "I care about you. If you will trust me and follow my ways, I will bless you and be your God. Honor me and I will deliver you, I will redeem you from your sins and your burdens, and I will give you a new heart." All He asked was that they be willing to rely totally on Him.

"Obey My voice, and I will be your God, and you will be My people; and you will walk in all the way which I command you, that it may be well with you" (Jeremiah 7:23).

But, like Eve, they fell for the lie, thinking that they could be like God and determine what truth was for themselves. Repeatedly the Jews turned their backs on God to go their own way, only to suffer the consequences of their separation.

Again and again, God delivered them from trouble, only to see them rebel against Him and choose to go their own way. The story of their rebellion, suffering, and God's faithfulness and mercy is the basic theme of the Old Testament.

With the problems of God's people so well documented, you'd think we would learn from their mistakes. But we don't. This inherited legacy of wanting to define our own truth and do things our own way has never been more prevalent than in our current society.

God is still saying, *"Come to Me, all who are weary and heavy-laden, and I will give you rest. Take My yoke upon you, and learn from Me, for I am gentle and humble in heart; and you shall find rest for your souls. For My yoke is easy, and My load is light"* (Matthew 11:28–30). But we turn away from His blessings and look to what appears to be a more attractive pathway.

So often we are like teenagers who turn their backs on the wisdom of loving parents, while assuring themselves that they know a better way, or like drug users or alcoholics who claim that what they are doing is not affecting their lives because they can handle it. The desire to do their own thing completely obscures their view of the most obvious truth and denies them the fulfillment they seek.

Isn't it amazing how an outsider can see how bad choices are wrecking the lives of rebellious teens or alcoholics or drug users, but those who are caught up in these bad choices usually don't see the truth? I think this must be how God sees our desires to invent our own truths about what will bring fulfillment and peace in our work.

When I'm counseling someone who is facing a decision or when I'm faced with choices in my own life, I like to use visual concepts to help simplify and clarify what is really happening. The following illustration verifies what I know to be truth.

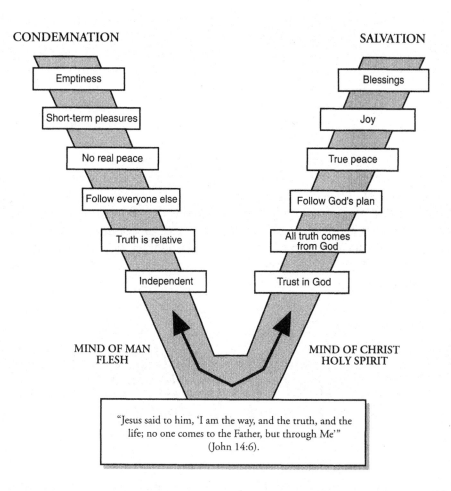

CONDEMNATION

SALVATION

Emptiness

Blessings

Short-term pleasures

Joy

No real peace

True peace

Follow everyone else

Follow God's plan

Truth is relative

All truth comes from God

Independent

Trust in God

MIND OF MAN
FLESH

MIND OF CHRIST
HOLY SPIRIT

"Jesus said to him, 'I am the way, and the truth, and the life; no one comes to the Father, but through Me'" (John 14:6).

TO DEPEND ON HIM IS TO KNOW THE TRUTH

If you think about it, we all face choices every day and we must have a basis for making them. We need wisdom to be able to see things for what they really are. We need the ability to understand truth while avoiding the deceptions and half truths that attempt to pull us away from our dependence on God.

What is the truth that God wants us to understand regarding our work and our lives? If we want to know truth, we must look to the Author of Truth and observe His character and principles.

"If you abide in My word, then you are truly disciples of Mine; and you shall know the truth, and the truth shall make you free" (John 8:31–32).

The primary truth that affects all our decisions is that God has committed to be our God and He desires our commitment to Him. He knows a relationship with Him will benefit us more than any pleasures of this world, any get-rich-quick plan, or any short-term expediency.

Our goal should not be to get results but to work the process.

God is always reaffirming his covenant promises to those who will commit to being His people. The covenant he made with Abraham, the Last Supper, and the shedding of Jesus' blood on the cross symbolize His sacred covenant of commitment to us.

HIS TRUTH PROVIDES A FIRM FOUNDATION AND PERMANENT REWARDS

God is going to be around throughout eternity and is interested in things that have lasting value. Scripture uses terms like wood, hay, chaff, and grass to describe the temporary things and those that are not built on a strong foundation. On the other hand, Jesus uses the analogy of refined gold to illustrate something that will not rust or rot, and he uses rock to describe foundations that will last.

By using these concepts, Jesus has communicated what is really important: Temporary pleasures will never provide fulfillment here, let alone bring rewards in the hereafter. Our relationship with Him will be the only thing that counts.

"For no man can lay a foundation other than the one which is laid, which is Jesus Christ. Now if any man builds upon the foundation with gold, silver, precious stones, wood, hay, straw, each man's work will become evident; for the day will show it, because it is to be revealed with fire; and the fire itself will test the quality of each man's work. If any man's work which he has built upon it remains, he shall receive a reward. If any man's work is burned up, he shall suffer loss; but he himself shall be saved, yet so as through fire" (1 Corinthians 3:11–15).

We are affected by sin and rebellion, so we are drawn to the temptations of the world in which we live; these result in short-term pleasures. After all, straw, wood, and hay are much easier to obtain than gold, silver, and precious stones. But think how much better off we'd be if we would heed the following: *"Trust in the Lord with all your heart, and do not lean on your own understanding. In all your ways acknowledge Him, and He will make your paths straight"* (Proverbs 3:5–6).

WORK THE PROCESS BUT LEAVE THE RESULTS TO HIM

A second, and related, truth that affects career decisions and success is that our goal should not be to get results but to work the process. I know this may be contrary to everything you've been taught, but I assure you it is true. Think about it this way: If you assume responsibility for the results, this indicates that you don't need God.

You definitely should have a goal and a general plan, but you must leave the door open to the Lord so that He can direct your path. *"The mind of a man plans his way, but the Lord directs his steps."* (Proverbs 16:9).

I first began to see this principle operating while still in the Air Force. As a commander, I would meet with all new personnel to welcome them.

These were bright and ambitious young men and women and, when it came their time to ask questions, they would frequently ask "What do I need to do to get promoted?" I saw that many of them were much too focused on achieving results that would benefit them, as opposed to being the best servant possible. It wasn't that they weren't good people; they were very dedicated to their work, but they felt there was something they must do to expedite their promotion.

My response to them was that their promotion was my responsibility; in fact, it was one of my major responsibilities. The best thing they could do to assist me in getting them promoted was to be the best servant-leaders they could possibly be. If they truly cared about our mission and applied themselves to accomplishing it better every day, then they had done all they could do and all that I could expect them to do.

Back then I didn't recognize that this was a biblical principle, but as I got into career counseling, I observed a pattern: People choose results they think they have to achieve in order to be fulfilled, or happy, or satisfied with their work. Often the results have nothing to do with their talents or even their true interests; it might just be something a friend has done and they feel they have to do it to be successful. Unfortunately, those results don't guarantee success.

Another reason to avoid focusing on results is motive. When *we* pick the results, we usually can count on a tarnished motive. Somehow our own selfishness or ego will come into play when we start picking outcomes.

In time I began to see how much of our lives has been misled by one fundamental error—that we are responsible for the results. Once you start to understand the principle of process over results, you will notice it being used throughout the Bible.

Was Abraham blessed because he achieved great results or because he faithfully followed the process and left the results to God? What about Joseph? Was he selected to be the governor of Egypt because of his great results or because he was faithful to the process and got thrown into jail.

Consider Moses. He certainly had a good opportunity to be the successor to Pharaoh; and wouldn't that have been a successful outcome—at least by the standards of many? But the following verses sum up Moses' choice quite well.

"By faith Moses, when he had grown up, refused to be called the son of Pharaoh's daughter; choosing rather to endure ill-treat-

ment with the people of God, than to enjoy the passing pleasures of sin" (Hebrews 11:24–25).

Without regard to what the outcome would be, by faith, Moses chose to follow the process of faithfully doing what God called him to do .

Paul is one of my favorite examples of someone who was a process person. How would you judge his results? He was beaten, persecuted, and spent much of his adult life in jail. I'm sure that was not the kind of results Paul would have picked for himself. But we should be thankful that Paul was a man of process. Because he was, God could use him for the results He had in mind: namely, to bring the gospel to the Gentile world.

There is another truth related to the process-results concept. His results are always better for us than what we would have planned.

Looking back, I can see how a concern for process guided me during my five-and-a-half years as a prisoner of war in Vietnam. I had no control over the outcome of the war. The only thing I could control was my choice to faithfully keep my commitments and serve my country (process). I trusted God and our government to take care of my life, the war, and my repatriation (results).

I know this may be a new idea, so I'll use a diagram to illustrate the concept.

This concept is especially helpful for career or any type of decision-making situation. As you can see, usually this is not an overnight event; rather, it is in itself a process of walking in faith.

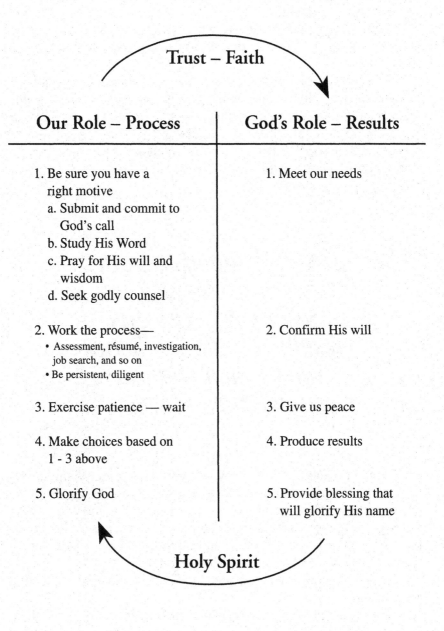

Trust – Faith

Our Role – Process	God's Role – Results
1. Be sure you have a right motive a. Submit and commit to God's call b. Study His Word c. Pray for His will and wisdom d. Seek godly counsel	1. Meet our needs
2. Work the process— • Assessment, résumé, investigation, job search, and so on • Be persistent, diligent	2. Confirm His will
3. Exercise patience — wait	3. Give us peace
4. Make choices based on 1 - 3 above	4. Produce results
5. Glorify God	5. Provide blessing that will glorify His name

Holy Spirit

Too often we work things backward. We decide on the results we want and then pray that God will bless us and make them happen. When we do this we deny Him full control, and we deny ourselves His full blessings. There is another truth related to the process-results concept. His results are always better for us than what we would have planned. Turning the results over to God is a critical, but necessary, step if we are going to know His will and live by truth. It also guarantees us the best possible outcome.

BEING IS MORE IMPORTANT THAN DOING

Do you ever stop to think about the fact that our society tries to assign who we are by what we do? This is a deception, because our true nature is spiritual not physical. We are children of God and, in eternity, it isn't going to matter what we "do for a living."

In his challenging book *Everything You've Heard Is Wrong*, Tony Campolo addresses this subject.

> A common pitfall on the way to establishing identity is to allow ourselves to be defined by whatever job we happen to fall into when we finish school. Our being becomes our doing. Who we are is established by what we do. It's all so easy and natural that we hardly notice it's happening. Without even realizing it, we can "slip-slide away" into letting the identities provided by our work become the "ultimate" basis for defining who we are.
>
> Of course the problem with letting our jobs provide our identities is that sooner or later we all lose our jobs. Whether it comes sooner through layoffs or later through retirement, it will happen. And then, for those whose identities have been wrapped up primarily in their work, there is a horrendous crisis. Who of us has not encountered those persons who are devoid of any identity or meaning to their lives because all that they were was synonymous with their job? So many, particularly men, die very shortly after retirement simply because they cannot figure out any good reason for living.[1]

In the long run it is your "being" that will count—the obvious evidence of Jesus Christ in your life. Does He abide in you?

Naturally, we will be "doing" and we will produce results, as a by-product of being faithful to the process of serving. The real issue is about control or who will be Lord of our lives. Do we think we can control our lives and, through our own doing, generate outcomes

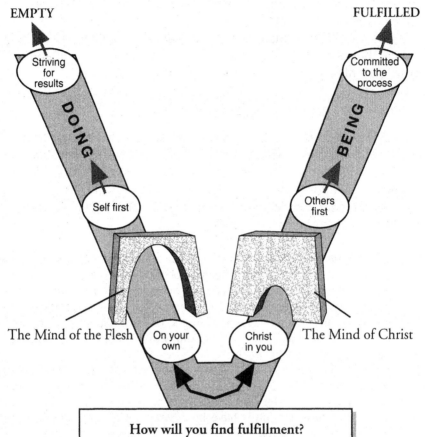

EMPTY   FULFILLED

Striving for results

DOING

Self first

Others first

BEING

Committed to the process

The Mind of the Flesh   On your own   Christ in you   The Mind of Christ

How will you find fulfillment?

"But a natural man does not accept the things of the
Spirit of God; for they are foolishness to him, and he
cannot understand them, because they are spiritually
appraised" (1 Corinthians 2:14).

that will be better than the blessings that come from faithfully using our talents for the Lord?

"I am the vine, you are the branches; he who abides in Me, and I in him, he bears much fruit; for apart from Me you can do nothing" (John 15:5). What will be the source of your fruit and how will you find fulfillment?

YOU CAN'T WALK TWO PATHS

I counsel many Christians who have not yet realized what it means to live truly for the Lord. Their minds are so accustomed to thinking that life is divided into secular and sacred spheres, they haven't realized that they can and should trust Him in all areas of their lives.

We must commit to one path and follow it in every choice we make. James referred to this concept when he said, *"For let not that man expect that he will receive anything from the Lord, being a double-minded man, unstable in all his ways"* (James 1:7–8). Also, the Lord said, *"I would that you were cold or hot. So because you are lukewarm . . . I will spit you out of My mouth"* (Revelation 3:15–16).

You cannot serve God on Sunday and yourself on Monday through Saturday. You cannot serve God and mammon. As Doug Sherman and Bill Hendricks point out so well in their book *Your Walk Matters to God*, it's all one package—God does care about every part of our lives.[2]

It is this very issue that makes the work priorities and values part of our assessment so difficult and yet so essential to sound career decisions. You will have many occasions to look down two paths as you choose your career. One is based on faith, the other flesh. They are mutually exclusive and you must choose one. Which will it be?

YOUR PURPOSE GUIDES YOUR LIFE

What is your purpose? Have you thought about it? I don't believe you can make a good career decision until you have decided on your life purpose. In other words, what purpose will all your work serve?

Tony Campolo calls this the basic question of life: "Those who do not ask and answer the ultimate questions about life may be making record time so far as career advancement is concerned. But if they do not know where they are going in life, their record-making advancements will prove to be absurd and ludicrous in the end."[3] Have you developed your answers to these "ultimate" questions?

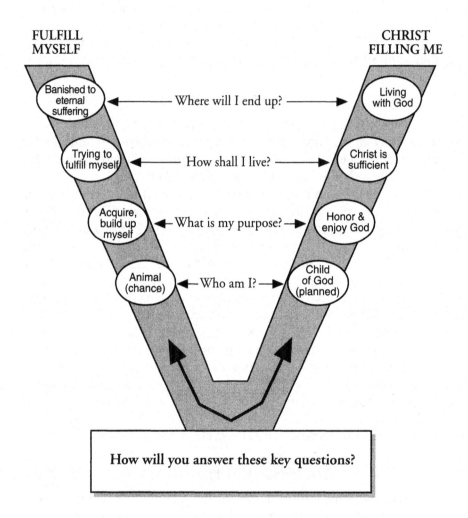

FULFILL
MYSELF

CHRIST
FILLING ME

Banished to eternal suffering ← Where will I end up? → Living with God

Trying to fulfill myself ← How shall I live? → Christ is sufficient

Acquire, build up myself ← What is my purpose? → Honor & enjoy God

Animal (chance) ← Who am I? → Child of God (planned)

How will you answer these key questions?

Even though most people haven't defined their purpose, they naturally want their lives to count for something. If you don't believe that, just look at the way people donate money to get their name placed on a plaque somewhere. Most of us would like to have our names in some "hall of fame" or have something named in our honor because it would indicate that we had made a difference in this world.

It's probably our inborn desire to live forever that ties in to our need to do something that will be eternal. Unfortunately, most of what we do in our work will not have much lasting value. More often than not, the visible products of our work are merely for the present time.

In Jeremiah, the Lord gives a clear warning against trusting in our work when He says *"Cursed is the man who trusts in mankind and makes flesh his strength, and whose heart turns away from the Lord"* (Jeremiah 17:5).

The activities of our work are, in a way, the media or the stage for the growth and development of character and for revealing Christ to others. The results (the doing) of our work will rust, rot, or be burned up, but the good news is that the way we live our lives at work (the being) can have great meaning and will have an eternal impact on others.

As you consider your work and career choices, remember your purpose in life. If you haven't written out a purpose statement yet, we urge you to spend some time contemplating this most important of life's questions.

As we said at the beginning of the chapter, not having a good fix on truth is the fundamental cause of most of our problems in life—especially bad career decisions. I can give you the best career counseling in the world, but if you make a choice that isn't consistent with God's truth concerning your relationship to Him, then I can assure you that fulfillment will be lacking in your life.

I challenge you to turn the outcome (results) of your life over to the Lordship of Christ as the first step of your career plan. He's the only One you can trust totally to manage your career.

CHAPTER SEVEN

Factors That Affect Career Decisions

*I*n the last few years the problems associated with work have received a lot of attention in the press. We've read various studies showing that 40 to 80 percent of the work force is unhappy at work.

Because of the nature of our work at Life Pathways, we hear about these problems every day, not just through numbers and statistics but from real people who are struggling with work issues.

It shouldn't be a surprise that so many people have a difficult time achieving contentment in their work; there are many factors that affect a person's outlook toward work.

In later chapters you'll find many practical aids to finding your career niche, but first it's important to cover some of the basic issues that affect work satisfaction. After considering these factors, some of you may decide you don't need a career change at all. (Factors 1 and 2 were covered in Chapter 6.)

1. We can never find true fulfillment through work alone.

Our primary need is for a spiritual relationship with God, and this can't be filled by the process or the results of work.

2. Your work should enable you to fulfill your overriding life purpose.

Another characteristic we have inherited from our Heavenly Father is the desire to do something that has meaning. Without ever thinking about it, we naturally want our lives to count for something important and eternal.

Most of our waking hours are spent at work, so it seems logical that our work serves as a focal point for carrying out our purpose. You were designed by God for a special mission—to honor Him and to be a blessing to others.

3. Work can fill many of our needs.

Survival. Work produces a return, which is used for food, clothing, shelter, and other necessities of life. In our current society it is also expected to produce a surplus with which we can purchase many of our wants and desires—or what has come to be known as "the good life."

> *We naturally need to be productive and fruitful, to accomplish, to do, to fulfill, and to complete tasks.*

As you consider your situation, ask yourself: "Considering the totality of history, are my material expectations realistic, or are they a product of a 'Great American Dream' that has lost touch with reality?"

Creativity. In addition to our survival needs, work also provides us an opportunity to express the characteristics we inherit because we're made in the image of God.

We normally think of creativity being related to artistic people, but we all have a need to improve, construct, design, resolve, organize, arrange, order, originate, make, conceive, cause, author, or produce things or ideas.

To be satisfying, work should offer an outlet for this drive. Granted, we will administer our creativity in different ways, but if the need isn't met, we'll feel like something is missing at work. Indirectly, that's what is bringing about the demise of the industrial revolution and the restructuring of management in this country.

The management philosophy of treating employees like machines was doomed to failure because it suppressed one of our key human attributes and, correspondingly, denied industry one of it's most valuable resources: the creative ideas and energy of its employees. Thankfully, the new management concepts solicit the creativity of people.

Achievement. Closely linked to creativity is the need to achieve. We naturally need to be productive and fruitful, to accomplish, to do, to fulfill, and to complete tasks. When we were a more agricultural and craft-guild-oriented society, it was much easier for people to see their achievements because the finished product could be seen and touched.

Much of the job dissatisfaction we see today is due to the complex nature of the work done in an information-oriented, high-tech society. It's increasingly more difficult to see how our labor is contributing to a meaningful product.

The drive to achieve may take a different twist in various personalities. Some will want to see concrete results; others may need to know only that they have resolved a problem; while still others may need to know they have helped someone personally in order to fulfill the need to achieve. Achievement can take many forms but, ultimately, we all need to see results from our efforts.

Feedback, recognition, and reinforcement. Regardless of their level of humility, people need feedback regarding their work. Individual personalities will vary in how much feedback is required. Some will decline public recognition, but just the fact that they achieved results and were identified as being deserving of recognition is important reinforcement.

On the other extreme, others need frequent, personal reinforcement and will tend to migrate unconsciously toward the center of attention just to get their recognition needs met.

Although our needs for recognition may vary from low to high, the bottom line is that we all need to know that we're doing okay. Being recognized for being competent and knowing that we're making a meaningful contribution is an important factor of career satisfaction—and this includes homemakers.

Order. Our Creator is a God of order, and since we are created in His image we have a need for order. Depending on our personalities and background, some of us will need more than others, but our work needs to have a degree of organization and stability to it.

When we go to work, most of us need regular hours, and we want to know generally what is expected of us. We want accountability, and we want to know the boundaries in which we are expected to operate. In other words, we want to know the rules, the restrictions, and the lines of authority. Just as children need order and structure in the family as a form of security, we need order in our work.

Authority. At the Creation, it was God's design for us to exercise authority over the earth and our work. Authority is really a prerequisite if we are to achieve creatively, because creativity and achievement imply control over decisions—not robot-like activity.

---

*A lack of authority
to make even simple
decisions is one of the
biggest complaints in
the American work force.*

It is true that the amount of authority each of us has varies with our specific circumstances, maturity, and expertise. It's comparable to the relationship of parents to children. As young people grow older, they are given more and more freedom in their decisions. In giving them authority, parents also give them the opportunity to make mistakes. Sometimes they will err, but they must have this freedom, or they never will be what God intends for them to be. The same is true of a person at work.

We find that a lack of authority to make even simple decisions is one of the biggest complaints in the American work force. People don't like to be treated like children; yet, too often supervisors are afraid they will look bad if one of their employees makes a mistake. It takes a lot of faith and courage to delegate responsibility to workers and then give them the authority to do their jobs.

If current trends continue, the changes taking place in the workplace will benefit everyone by giving more authority to workers. As the American work force is restructured, two or three layers of management will disappear and the lower levels will have a greater opportunity to make decisions and resolve problems at work.

Variety. After surveying thousands of clients with our work priorities evaluation, it's clear that variety is something everyone needs at work. Like some of the other needs above, this will vary quite a bit, depending on the personality of the individual, but it is definitely a human need and without it we run the risk of burnout.

Variety is coming back to the workplace, due to the restructuring of companies and the resultant broadening of worker duties. Both management and unions are having to rethink their ideas on specialization. For their own good, workers need to move away from the idea that has been ingrained in them in the modern workplace of "that's not my job, I only do (this or that)."

The new workplace will require workers to expand their skills and be adept at a variety of functions, but this will be a blessing rather than a curse. As workers take on a variety of tasks during their day, their job satisfaction will increase. It will be a natural stress reliever because variety is an important part of our nature and all creation.

Fellowship. John Donne's famous verse is so true: "No man is an island, entire of himself; every man is a piece of the continent, a part of the main."

We all have a need to belong. At work we share our burdens, build relationships, find counsel, and help others grow. Through relationships with fellow workers we nurture and are nurtured. With the mobility of our society, many live a long distance from their extended families, and relationships at work become the primary support system.

4. We can gain the maximum fulfillment from our work by using the interests and talents we have been given.

Pursue your interests. All the research bears out what common sense would tell us: People do better at what they enjoy than at what they dislike. The simplest and most fundamental career counseling is "do what you enjoy most." This is excellent advice.

The biggest problem we see in talent identification is that people are preoccupied with comparing themselves to someone else.

As Larry has pointed out, most of us don't have the talents to succeed at all our interests (we can't all be movie stars or pro-athletes), but within our range of interests there are usually one or two vocational areas in which we can excel.

Exploit your talents. Our talents encompass natural abilities, learned skills, and personality strengths. After assessing over 7,000 people, we have yet to find a single person with no talents; statistically, everyone is talented.

The biggest problem we see in talent identification is that people are preoccupied with comparing themselves to someone else, (usually it's someone who has a lot of talent in an area they don't). It's often a case of "The grass is always greener on the other side."

Without becoming fixated on themselves, people should take an objective look and find out what they do well. A survey of more than 250,000 successful people concluded that the highest levels of achievement come when people work at activities that use their strengths.[1]

Section III of this book will lead you through a self-assessment to help you identify your interests and talents.

5. Career decisions are an individual responsibility.

One of the biggest challenges our clients face is understanding how their talents can be used at work. We point out their interests and their talents and then offer some typical career fields and occupations that will match their particular situation. But one thing we've learned is that many people have a hard time actually making the match and would rather have someone else do that for them.

Finding a good career match is difficult because it requires mental effort to research various occupations, jobs, and organizations and then compare them to your pattern of interests and talents. This is the same kind of mental toil required to solve word problems in math and write research papers in history. It requires pushing out into new intellectual frontiers, and that's not the kind of thing most of us enjoy.

Even though there is a lot of help available, such as counselors, friends, books, assessments, and professional placement agencies, ultimately you'll have to put it all together and make your own career decision.

After a person identifies a good career match, it still requires courage and effort to actually get a job. Following a strategy that has proved effective for others should take away some of the unknowns and calm fears enough to enable the most timid to get the job done.

6. We must use discernment to refine our career decisions.

Refine your match. At Life Pathways, we see many people who are in the right general career field but just need some refining to get a better match with their talents.

Within a given career field there will be many variations in the duties involved, so it's helpful to distinguish between career fields, occupations, and specific positions. For instance, you may be well suited to the marketing career field, with talents especially suited for sales. But within sales, there are many specific positions: you could be in wholesale sales or retail sales; you could be in traveling sales, cold-call sales, or inside sales. And your fit could be good or bad, depending on your exact blend of talents.

Organizational mis-match and personality. Find an organization that matches you. You could have an ideal match between the career field, occupation, and position, but if it were with the wrong company you'd still be miserable in your work.

When all is said and done here on this earth, relationships will have eternal value, but material things will be left behind.

The most common problem is a conflict between your values and those of the company. The issues could relate to honesty, philosophy, or even the products of the company. As our society moves further and further away from its Judeo-Christian heritage, Christians are encountering more and more divergence between their standards and those of their employers.

Depending on your talents, you also could have an organizational mis-match if there's no opportunity for you to achieve higher responsibility as your skills develop. It could be that the organization is too small, or it could be political or operational factors that limit you.

7. Our values affect work decisions.

Family. The issue of "family values" has been highlighted in recent years. And it's about time! Our society is unraveling, in large part due to the demise of the family. Deciding how much priority to give work when it conflicts with family makes for a tough decision. It usually helps to look at issues from an eternal perspective, and that's especially true in the case of how much priority to give to family.

Men tend to get consumed with their work. For those who enjoy their work, it can be addictive—crowding out family and, often, key life priorities. We've talked to some degree about those problems already, but what about the question of whether women who are mothers should work?

The priority of family can be especially critical for mothers. With all the discussion about choosing a career and with a social climate driven by materialism, it may seem natural for mothers to believe they have to work outside the home to be fulfilled. But, fulfillment comes from carrying out God's purpose (remember, "process" takes faith).

Men and women both should share the responsibilities for rearing the children, but it seems that women have been gifted much better than men to be the nurturers of the home and family. The focal point for love and quality instruction to children in the home is the mother. Of course, to do her job she needs the sacrificial love and support of her husband.

I have married children who are facing the decision of whether mom should work "so we can afford decent housing" or stay home with the young child. This is a tough decision, and my advice to them is to go back to Larry's budget workbook and evaluate their absolute needs, versus their wants and desires.

Every situation is different and every family must evaluate its own situation. Just remember, when all is said and done on this earth, relationships will have eternal value; but material things will be left behind and, eventually, burned like a field of grass.

Speaking for myself and many of the "successful" people I've known, I wish I had placed a higher priority on my family when my children were younger.

Geography. This factor is usually one of the most obvious, but when it comes up it can pose some tough issues in our choices. What do you do if you live in a farming village in southern Iowa and your talents and interests are in marine biology? You could have a conflict, especially if you and your spouse both grew up there and think it's important to rear your children in a rural setting near family and friends.

Deciding whether or not to make a move for occupational reasons is usually a difficult task. As in any other situation, you must weigh all the factors and prayerfully seek guidance and godly counsel. As a rule, it helps to evaluate your options in light of how well they allow you to meet your most important priorities and values.

Ministry. As mentioned earlier, there can be no separation into secular and sacred worlds. Everything we do is for the Lord and, ultimately, represents Him for better or worse. Yet some will be called into paid ministry positions, while others will conduct their ministries from the platform of a job the world views as secular.

Christians must consider how their work will affect their own spiritual walk, as well as the potential their jobs offer for witness. As the apostle Paul said, *"All things are lawful . . . but not all things are profitable"* (1 Corinthians 6:12).

This must be a personal evaluation, because where one person could see a real mission field in an organization another could see a mine field. Just remember it is important to consider how your ministry will be affected by work in a particular environment.

8. Some non-work-related issues affect work.

Dysfunction and sin. How you feel about this area will vary greatly, depending on whose books you've read. All individuals are affected to some degree by sin and the sins of their families. Typically, problems are a result of physical abuse, sexual abuse, shame, guilt, anger, neglect, or similar childhood problems.

Emotional baggage brought from our childhood can undermine the ability to be our best or to be content in our work.

Our clients often share insights into these very private issues, and this has enabled us to see that these dysfunctional problems are more the rule than the exception. This shouldn't be a surprise, though, considering the Old Testament documentation of how the sins of parents impacted their children and grandchildren.

In severe cases, dysfunction is sufficient to make it impossible for people to perform jobs to their full potential.

Typical of this situation is a lady whose drive to do everything perfectly made her set standards for herself and others that were totally unrealistic. So she was driven to be perfect to validate her worth. As a child she had never been able to measure up to her mother's standards and, therefore, earn her love. (Her mother had always criticized her for everything she'd ever done.)

Now, as an adult, she didn't want to run the risk of making a mistake, for fear of losing approval at work. Of course, her problem came to light when her work piled up as she strived to do everything to an unrealistic level of perfection.

Another example is the person who can't handle authority. One man brought to his work a deep hatred for authority figures because of the terrible abuse he had experienced during his childhood from his alcoholic father. Without realizing it, this man transferred his anger at his father to his bosses. Whenever they questioned him or challenged him, he blew up.

Emotional baggage brought from our childhood can undermine the ability to be our best or to be content in our work. Even more important, it can destroy our witness to fellow workers. Recognizing that the conflict may be within ourselves and not related to our work is the first step toward solving these types of problems.

Character and maturity problems. These issues definitely relate to spiritual problems and often are tied to the dysfunctional problems discussed above. Problems of integrity and reliability can sabotage the work success and satisfaction of the most talented person.

It should go without saying that people who can't get to work on time, or those who really do not care about the quality of their work, will have career problems. The Bible has the answer for every problem associated with this area. If we truly want to be ambassadors for Christ, we will want to be above reproach in every aspect of our life and work.

Young workers or "young" Christians should seek out role models or mentors to serve as examples of good character and to help us grow. At the same time, we should remember that there are probably others looking to us for behavior clues.

Relationship problems. A number of personal problems, such as marriage conflict, dealing with rebellious children, and concern over aging parents, can generate stresses that affect our joy in life and enthusiasm for work. Sometimes the issues are so intense we are unable to see the source of our pain. Under these circumstances it can be easy to conclude: "If I just had a different job, things would be better."

Good counsel can often help a person identify the source of problems, as well as strategies for resolving them. It's usually a big help just to have someone to talk to about the situation and, preferably, someone who is not involved and able to see the issues in a more objective light.

Financial problems. It is common for those who are having financial problems to consider changing occupations or jobs in order to make more money. Unless the change is based on a good match of talents and a sound evaluation of all the other career decision-making factors, however, such changes may be like jumping from the frying pan into the fire.

Indebtedness is usually a symptom, not a cause. The cause is almost always a spiritual problem. It could be greed, covetousness, slothfulness, or a related issue, but more money will not solve this type of problem. The answer lies in adopting an attitude of stewardship (God owns it all and I am to be a good manager) and then applying discipline in all areas of spending.

If you have financial problems, get involved in financial counseling and get on a budget. See Chapter 21 for further information on budgeting.

All any of us can do, and all God expects of us, is to be faithful with whatever we have been given, whether great or small.

Mental illness and psychological factors. Unfortunately some people are not capable of carrying out "normal" work responsibilities due to mental problems, such as schizophrenia, manic-depression, and other brain disorders. Often this can go undiagnosed for many years.

Patty Duke comes to mind as a typical example of someone who had a great acting career going, only to see her world fall apart. As Patty matured, she developed a chemical imbalance in the brain that caused severe manic depression. Her story, documented in *A Brilliant Darkness* (by Patty Duke and Gloria Hochman, Bantam, 1992), gives some excellent insights into mental illness.

Anyone who has experienced such problems or who has had a family member go through the pain of mental illness can understand the accompanying fear and sense of helplessness. If you or someone in your family is dealing with such a problem, your faith will be tested. In these situations it is through faith in His sovereignty and unconditional love that we are able to accept the situation and work it out to His glory.

Faith, hope, and love, along with a lot of patience and support of others can make a tough situation bearable. Good medical care, knowledge, and counsel will be important to make the best of the situation.

Physical disability factors. Since the Americans with Disabilities Act (ADA) passed, many of the unnecessary restrictions on the physically disabled are disappearing and work opportunities are increasing. Probably a good way to look at these situations is to recognize that we all have both strengths and limitations.

For those who are disabled, the best advice is to do what everyone else must do: (1) Accept the fact that there are some things you can't do well; (2) identify those things you enjoy most and do best; (3) develop to the maximum your skills in those areas; (4) keep a positive attitude; and (5) do everything possible to help others succeed.

All any of us can do, and all God expects of us, is to be faithful with whatever we have been given, whether great or small. Remember: We are responsible for how we live—not the results.

We would do well to recall the words of the blind poet, John Milton, in his poem *On His Blindness.* "They also serve who only stand and wait." Of course Milton did much more than wait. His writings have influenced almost every English speaking student for over 400 years.

God is sovereign, He loves us with a supernatural love, and our lives have meaning and purpose regardless of any disability. Our challenge is to figure out how God wants to use us to advance His kingdom.

Learning disabilities. We frequently hear from learning-disabled people who want to know if we can help them find an appropriate occupational field through our assessment program. Our normal response is that we are not sure, but we are willing to try. Almost everyone has some strengths that can be used in employment; it's usually just a matter of identifying the strengths and then doing some creative research to identify occupational matches.

It does seem harder for those with learning disabilities to get the opportunity to prove themselves. The most common problems we see relate to communication skills, especially writing and comprehending written material. In an information age, these disabilities seem to automatically preclude many jobs and that's unfortunate.

One of our clients had great difficulty getting a job because he could hardly fill out an application. Yet our experience with him showed that he was very bright, had excellent judgment, and had a gift for supervision. All he needed was an opportunity. Somewhere along the way we were given an opportunity; the physically and mentally disadvantaged deserve no less.

9. Some people cannot work.

What about those who are unquestionably not capable of holding a job? What role do they play? One of my nephews has Down's syndrome and never will be able to work, in the normal sense of the word. His limitations have had a significant impact on my brother's family—and our extended family, to a lesser extent.

But there has never been any doubt that his life has a purpose. His childlike faith, humility, and love remind us of Jesus' words *"Unless you are converted and become like children, you shall not enter the kingdom of heaven. Whoever then humbles himself as this child, he is the greatest in the kingdom of heaven"* (Matthew 18:3–4).

It seems that those who cannot work have a special role in life: to help the rest of us understand the nature of Christ and His kingdom. What greater purpose could anyone have?

10. We cannot expect a perfect work situation.

Too often we see clients who are waiting for the perfect work situation. They are setting themselves up for disappointment because it isn't a perfect world, and there will never be a perfect job or work environment. Just as every gardener struggles with weeds, so every aspect of our lives encounters snags that keep things from running smoothly. Work is no exception.

Sin affects everything. Our career choices and performance at work will be affected by pride, rebelliousness, greed, and selfishness. Likewise, we will be affected by those same attributes in others. We have to accept that the consequences of sin will always bring rocky roads and detours to our career paths. We will never be able to meet all the needs we've listed above through our work. At best, our work can fill some approximation of these needs, but it never will be a perfect situation.

When we encounter difficulties, we must remember that our greatest calling is not to success, or doing, or even results, but to being: being the earthly representative of our Lord Jesus Christ.

We bring some of our problems on ourselves, and some are due to circumstances beyond our control. Whatever the source, trials and difficulties usually provide our greatest opportunities for Christian growth. For that reason, if no other, we should be encouraged to *"Consider it all joy, my brethren, when you encounter various trials, knowing that the testing of your faith produces endurance"* (James 1:2–3).

CHAPTER EIGHT

How Parents Influence Career Decisions

*M*ost of us are familiar with the verse *"Train up a child in the way he should go, even when he is old he will not depart from it"* (Proverbs 22:6), but few realize the implication: that we should dedicate and train our children according to the bent of their talents. The promise is, if you'll do this they won't depart from God's design for them.

This interpretation recognizes that each child is unique and has been given special talents for service in God's kingdom. As parents, we are to groom them in biblical principles and in the use of their gifts.

You may not have thought about it, but parents have the greatest influence on career decisions of anyone in society; and this is as it should be, because parents have been given a special trust to serve as stewards or managers of their children. Unfortunately, some parents view their role as *owners* rather than stewards, and this causes many problems.

Parents must ask themselves: Do I view myself as an owner or a steward? If you see yourself as an owner, you likely will feel responsible for what your children will do as adults and apply pressure to mold them into your desired career.

On the other hand, as a steward you are concerned only about helping them develop their talents through sound guidance and encouragement. With this kind of help, they can become what God has equipped them to be.

As parents, it's hard to detect an attitude of ownership because the differences between ownership and stewardship are very subtle. Your first clue will be that you find yourself trying to control their occupational choices.

Many parents struggle with being a good steward, especially if their child's bent is different from theirs or different from what they would like it to be.

> *Too much pressure from parents can be harmful because it can put a guilt trip on the individual, which can have very adverse effects.*

I found it quite threatening for my first child to have a career assessment, because I was afraid I might not like the results. What if they didn't recommend what I wanted him to do? As you'll read later, God used that situation to teach me about trusting Him with my children.

When I studied career counseling during my masters program, there was no emphasis placed on the good and bad influence that parents have on the vocational choices of their children. But, a few years later when I went on staff at the University of Georgia, I was amazed to learn how much parents influenced their children's career choices.

The first insight I had on this was when we did a survey of the Air Force students to see how many of them were from military families. The percentage was astonishingly high. Later, as I began to meet with these students and discuss their motivation for pursuing a commission in the Air Force, the influence of their parents was even more obvious.

I learned that young people will look first to what they know best. If they have grown up in a military family and enjoyed it, it is automatically a strong choice. Likewise, if they come from a business family, they will look first at a business-school-related occupation.

Although you may feel that today's youth are overly affected by movies, television, and peers (and they probably are), I can assure you that parents still have the greatest influence. Even the career choices of very rebellious children will be heavily influenced by their parents.

I'd like to share some of the bad and good ways parents affect their children, beginning with some of the problems that are most prevalent. I'm not trying to give anyone a guilt trip for mistakes made. As a father of four, I must confess to many mistakes, but I know God is faithful to forgive and to help us grow in this area.

HOW TO AVOID THE COMMON MISTAKES PARENTS MAKE

Don't pressure them to become pastors or missionaries.

It's normal for Christian parents to want their children to be involved in the Lord's work; we all should be. But it can be harmful if children are pressured into being pastors or missionaries just to fulfill their parents' dreams.

As Doug Sherman and Bill Hendricks point out so well in their book *Your Work Matters to God*, we are all called to minister, but we are not all called into the paid, professional ministry. I know one of my mother's dreams was that I would be a preacher, but I don't believe God called me to preach. He did call me to serve, and I have been teaching the Bible and speaking in churches for the last 20 years.

Too much pressure from parents can be harmful because it can put a guilt trip on the individual, which can have very adverse effects. Let me explain.

I had just finished teaching at a CFC conference and, as usual, a few people came up afterward with personal questions. One man waited until after everyone had left and asked if he could walk back to my room with me. He said he needed to talk to me about his career situation. I could see he was quite troubled, so I agreed to talk to him.

As we walked along, he described how he'd been a successful engineer in one of the cutting-edge fields of electronic communications. He had come from a very religious home; his father was a pastor, and his parents had always prayed for him to be a pastor also. As his parents grew older and their health began to fail, their dream had begun to weigh heavily on the son. He felt guilty that he hadn't chosen the career his parents wanted for him.

The biggest problem that most parents face comes from a legitimate desire to see their children become successful.

Reluctantly, he quit engineering and went to the seminary. It was a hardship on his family, and the ensuing years were even harder. Being a pastor was difficult for him, and he confided that he really hadn't been very successful at it. Eventually, he suffered a nervous breakdown, due to the stress of trying to be a good pastor, not succeeding, and still trying to reconcile the issue of his parent's desires. When I met him, his denomination had moved him to an administrative job to give him time to recover and reconsider his future.

My counsel was to consider the general intent of his parents rather than the specific way they expressed it. Their goal was that he would be a godly man who would serve the Lord and help others come to know Him. In their denomination and in their era, people typically thought that you had to be a pastor to fulfill those roles. I pointed out that everything we do should be "as unto the Lord" and that he could be a great servant as an engineer.

From our conversation, I believe he was able to see that God needs ambassadors who will go into the workplace as engineers— just the same as he needs pastors who will teach and prepare such ambassadors. After all, most of the unsaved will never go into a church, but they will go to work.

If you've been suffering from guilt because you haven't been a pastor, it could be legitimate. But more than likely it's false guilt. I hope the contents of this book will help you sort that out. On the other hand, if you are a parent, encourage your children to take delight in the Lord and seek to serve Him, using the talents He has given them in the occupations He has made the desires of their hearts.

"Delight yourself in the Lord; and He will give you the desires of your heart" (Psalm 37:4).

Don't pressure them to live out your dreams of success.

The biggest problem that most parents face comes from a legitimate desire to see their children become successful. This is a natural and desirable dream to have. We want them to do well and to be financially independent.

However, when a parent pushes or manipulates a child toward a career field because it has high income potential or it will satisfy the pride or ego of the parent, the young person is set up for disaster. Let me give you some examples.

A young man I'll call Michael came into my office one day to ask about the ROTC program. Michael couldn't look me in the eye; he even stared at the floor while we talked. His questions about the Air Force were somewhat bizarre and, in general, he seemed very depressed.

After Michael left, I called an academic advisor and asked him to check with some of Michael's professors to see if he was acting depressed or strange in their classes. It turned out that he was, so the advisor contacted Michael's parents, who lived in a neighboring state.

A few days later Michael's father showed up in my office; he'd come to find out what I knew about his son's situation. I told him Michael had apparently been thinking about trying to go into the Air Force and had come by to find out more about military life. I also explained my concern over Michael's behavior and recommended an evaluation by a mental health professional. The father's reply knocked me over.

He said, "I don't know what his problem is. He just needs to buckle down and get to work on his grades. Since he was five years old his mother and I have planned that he would be a lawyer."

Now I admit I didn't know all of Michael's problems, but one of them was very clear that day. The boy was caught between wanting to please his domineering parents or rejecting the career they had picked out for him and choosing one for himself.

The pressure was evidently too much for Michael to handle. There is no question in my mind he was about to snap and was crying out for help the day he came into the office.

Two years later I saw the movie *Dead Poets' Society*, and it was all too real. In the story line a father rejected his son because he wanted to be an actor rather than the successful lawyer the father had always wanted him to be. Ultimately, the boy committed suicide because he couldn't deal with the lack of acceptance by his father.

In most situations the pressure is not as direct and the mistakes aren't as costly or obvious. But our experience shows that the problems caused by pressure from parents are very widespread.

Don't pressure them for the sake of money.

I was shocked at the number of parents who would push their children into the ROTC program just for scholarship money, even when their sons or daughters had no interest in the military. Some would do this even though they could afford the tuition.

Generally it didn't work out and only brought stress and a sense of failure to the student. If the young people were truly interested in being in the military, scholarships were great opportunities. But if they weren't, it was much like prostitution—a sacrifice of something special God has given in exchange for a short-term financial benefit.

It never ceases to amaze me how much our society puts its trust in money. We have had many Career Pathways' clients who say they weren't allowed to pursue the career of their dreams because their parents felt it wouldn't earn enough money.

Several have related how their parents didn't feel they should invest in a degree, such as teaching or recreation management, because it wouldn't bring a good return. This attitude represents one of the great lies most of us buy into at one time or another: that a person who earns a high income has succeeded.

Implied in that lie is another lie: that more money will bring more happiness. Of course the ultimate lie at the bottom of this whole problem is that God is not sufficient for our happiness.

If you don't think the problem is widespread, consider these figures. A survey of 23,000 students, grades 8–11, showed that the most popular occupations were lawyer and physician, in that order. Engineer was number 12; corporate manager was 19; and banker was 35.

The single most important thing parents can do to help their children find suitable careers is to make sure their own definition of success is based on biblical truth.

Now I ask you: Do you think that young people want to be lawyers because they like to read thick books and write papers and deal with criminals or divorce cases? Of course not. Most of them want to be lawyers and doctors because those are the people who live in the nicest houses in town, drive the snazziest cars, and take vacations in Europe or ski trips to Aspen.

Let's face it. It's the money they're after. They've bought the lie just like our generation did. Incidentally, ours is the same generation of parents who say they hate their jobs and are stressed out by their work.

Based on the Life Pathways' Questionnaire and Work Priorities Evaluation (values survey) we use in the assessment, we can't see much difference in the values of society and those of kids from Christian homes. In fact, most young people are very honest about it and tell us their main career goal is to make a lot of money.

The single most important thing parents can do to help their children find suitable careers is to make sure their own definition of success is based on biblical truth. Proverbs sums it all up very well: *"It is the blessing of the Lord that makes rich, and He adds no sorrow to it"* (Proverbs 10:22).

Don't pressure them because of your pride.

As I said, I've had my problems but they haven't been related to money—just pride. About ten years ago, when my oldest son was in high school, we put him through a career assessment program very similar to the one offered by Life Pathways. The results came back saying he was very artistic and should be an artist, musician, or writer.

I'll be quite honest. I don't like that one bit! You see at the time my values about life and work were totally centered around Christianity and the military. I didn't know any Christian artist, and even if I had, I was sure they wouldn't be anything like what I wanted my children to be.

In my values system at that time, you got up early, worked hard, dressed neatly, wore short hair, and lived a fast-paced schedule, so for my son to be an artist seemed to be a rejection of everything I stood for. Besides, as a long-time prisoner of war, I still had some animosity toward the extreme artsy-type people; they were the most visible leaders of the anti-war movement.

As I said, I didn't like it, but I knew enough about testing and people to know they were right. Over the next few years God allowed the pain and suffering necessary to deal with my pride and judgmental attitude. Eventually, I began to understand how God had made us all different for a purpose.

My son has graduated from college with a degree in art and a minor in music. He has a regular job to support his family, but his love is music and he practices every day. He also composes Christian songs and is especially talented at putting Scripture to music.

My youngest son is very artistic also and, although he looks a lot like me, he's really a chip off the same artistic block as his brother. In recent years God has been showing me the power of art, drama, and music to communicate the gospel. My prayer is that the church will rediscover the arts and use them to reach the lost.

How I thank the Lord for giving me sons who have different talents and for using my sons to teach me the new attitudes and principles I needed to be a better Christian, father, and career counselor.

I'm thankful to God for opening my eyes before it was too late to give my sons my blessing. I can now encourage them to use the talents He gave them and be what He created them to be.

Rather than thinking our children are chips off the old block, we need to recognize they are works of art created by the Master Potter.

The problems caused by the pride and ego of parents are widespread and have a devastating effect on their children. A typical example is Eddie, who had an incredible gift of mechanical aptitude. Even as a young boy he could fix things most adults couldn't. He learned to repair automobiles and, by his late teens, he could rebuild an engine.

Unfortunately for Eddie, it was not acceptable to his parents for their son to be a manual worker. They were well educated and had always been employed in "professional" jobs. Instead of encouraging Eddie's bent for automotive mechanics, they constantly nagged him to complete college.

Eddie is in his late twenties now, and he's never completed college, despite several attempts. The problem is not one of intelligence (Eddie is brilliant) but of motivation.

Eddie's parents are not totally destroyed; he does have a white collar job, as a clerk in a department store, but Eddie is miserable. What a waste of talents and potential. With his gifts, Eddie probably could have been one of the best mechanics in the country.

In contrast, let me tell you about Tyler, a high school classmate who also was gifted in mechanical ability. Tyler was reared on a small farm, and his parents worked at the local apparel plant. In high school Tyler spent his spare time working on tractors, cars, and motorcycles.

By the time he was in his thirties, Tyler was one of the premier engine builders in the country for NASCAR race drivers. His engines were in the winner's circle at Daytona, Charlotte, and all the big tracks.

Tyler has made a good living at his work and, more importantly, he loves what he does. He was fortunate that his parents were proud of his gifts and encouraged him rather than letting their pride keep him from following his bent.

Rather than thinking our children are chips off the old block, we need to recognize they are works of art created by the Master Potter. Each is different and designed for both a practical and eternal purpose. As stewards our tasks are to recognize their design and then help them develop their potential.

BEING A POSITIVE INFLUENCE

Encouragement is a critical element in training children because it motivates them and gives parents credibility for further influence.

Once you have accepted the fact that your children are not you, it's much easier to encourage them in the direction of their bent. Still, giving encouragement is not a natural thing for everyone to do— especially to their children.

True encouragement implies confidence in the individual and the direction the individual is going. If you are resisting the person or the direction, your encouragement will tend to be for purposes of redirection, and that often results in manipulation.

Young people may be immature and unskilled in many ways, but they are quite accomplished at recognizing our attempts to manipulate them. And when they detect it, usually they resist, either directly or passively. I bring this out because I know how hardheaded parents are; and I personally know it's not easy to change from an attitude of ownership to stewardship.

If you have a problem encouraging your child in the way of his or her natural gifts, pray about it and ask God to help you accept your child in the same way He has accepted you.

Look for their bent and encourage it.

Not everyone needs an assessment to know what they should do with their lives. Marty, one of Christian Financial Concepts' more involved lay counselors, earns a living in construction and remodeling. Last year CFC contracted with him to convert some warehouse space into office space to accommodate the growth in our organization.

When work began, I noticed that Marty was doing a lot of manual labor and, out of curiosity, I asked if he normally kept a crew to work for him. He said no, he really liked to do most of the work himself because he enjoys working with his hands. In our conversation, Marty made it clear that he is one of those people who really loves his work, so naturally I asked him how he got into it. The following is Marty's story.

"It really happened one summer when I was about 12 years old. After school was out I went to Vacation Bible School for a week, swam every day for a week, and then I was bored. I told my parents I needed something to do. My dad bought some lumber, gave me some of his tools to use, and told me to go to it. I started building bird houses, picnic tables, and all sorts of practical things, and I found I loved it. You know, it's like God just built into me an ability and desire to do things with my hands. I like to see the results of my work, and I really wouldn't want to do anything else."

Evidently Marty's parents recognized his bent and were willing to take some risks to encourage it. You see Marty's family background is more blue blood than blue collar.

In *Discovering Your Child's Design*, Ralph Mattson and Thom Black give some good pointers on how to recognize your child's bent. They point out that we all tend to follow patterns (they call them motifs) of behavior and these can be seen recurring even in young children. They describe how we are drawn to certain types of activities and processes.[1]

By closely observing your children, you can see the ways in which they have been formed. The same processes they like to use as youths will play a key role in their career successes as adults. Although Marty's family didn't know anything about the motif theory, they used it very well.

If you and your children aren't sure of their bent, give them an assessment.

William and Betty were the proud parents of two fine high school youngsters. Tommy was a senior and Jenny was a junior. Both had good grades and planned to go to college, but they didn't know what they wanted to do. When I first met William, I was concerned that he might be pressing Tommy and Jenny too hard to be what he and Betty thought they should be, but I decided not to say anything.

Tommy graduated from high school and went to a tough engineering school. There still seemed to be some tension between Tommy and his dad because Tommy had not really settled on a career direction. He thought he wanted to major in science or engineering, but he didn't have any idea of what career he might pursue.

Tommy worked hard and proved to his parents he could hack it in difficult courses. But at the end of his freshman year, he decided to change schools and maybe change majors. It was at that point that William asked if I thought an assessment might be of any help. Naturally I thought it would.

The assessment pointed out Tommy's strengths and indicated two general career directions with associated majors. Tommy looked over the reports and did some follow-up research. Soon he knew what he really wanted to do. When William and Betty studied the reports, they saw the same thing Tommy had seen and were able to encourage him much more effectively than before.

The career direction given by the reports was clearly very helpful to Tommy. Perhaps one of the greatest benefits of the assessment was that it had come from an objective third party who had no emotional stake in the outcome. It enabled William and Betty and their son to view Tommy's future from an objective viewpoint, thus eliminating a layer of tension that had been present before.

It was about this same time that Tommy's sister Jenny, a senior in high school, began making plans for college. Again, there seemed to be some tension over what Jenny should do with her life. We tested her, and when I saw that she had some non-traditional career aspirations, I understood some of her parents' concern. William and Betty thought she was well suited to be a veterinarian, and she was, but her tests also showed she had a strong desire to serve in the military.

During her freshman year in college, Jenny got a part-time job working in a vet's office. She enjoyed it a lot and was considering becoming a veterinarian, but she still had a yearning to be in the military.

One day William stopped by to tell me he had been helping Jenny apply to the Army Reserves. His excitement for her future was genuine, and I know it was a big encouragement to her to know her dad and mom were giving their blessing to her plans. Again the assessment had helped them to be a positive influence in Jenny's career planning.

Although they haven't taken their place in the world of work yet, I think Tommy and Jenny are going to enjoy their future careers. They know their talents and their interests, and they have strong support from their parents to be what God designed them to be.

For families like the one just described, an assessment can make a big difference. It gave encouragement and direction to the children and helped their parents to use the powerful influence parents naturally have in a very positive way.

TWELVE STEPS FOR INFLUENCING YOUR CHILD'S CAREER DECISION

Obviously there are many areas of parenting that will affect your children's development into adults. But some of the key steps that will enable you to have a positive influence on their career choices are listed below. You'll see that these relate to attitude, values, and faith. If you can get those right, you won't feel the urge to manipulate, and the other steps will fall into place naturally.

Step 1.

Pray that God will help you understand and trust His values about work and success and that you'll understand the difference in being an owner and a steward. Ask him to show you your children's bent and how you can encourage them in the way they should go.

Step 2.

Model the character traits that will yield responsible work habits: discipline, respect, honesty, and concern for others.

Step 3.

Recognize that your children are unique individuals and not clones of yourself. God has given them motivations and talents for a purpose, and he has chosen you as their steward, not their owner. You'll find it liberating to realize that you are responsible only for the process of stewardship, not the results of God's design and their choices. They're His children first. Our job is to encourage and develop the bent He has given them—not to force them into our mold.

Become an objective observer of your children, and rejoice in who God has made them.

Step 4.

Help your children see the value of work as an opportunity to express their talents and to contribute practically and spiritually to the kingdom of God. This is difficult when they are young, and we assign them chores that don't relate to their interests and talents. It's important to allow them the freedom to do some of their tasks in "their way" rather than the way you would do it. Also include some assignments that will require them to use their special interests and talents.

Step 5.

Remember that children are children and *not* small adults. They will not be capable of working to the standards you set for yourself, so have realistic expectations for them.

Step 6.

Find out your children's interests and talents and then encourage them in their use and development. Become an objective observer of your children, and rejoice in who God has made them. Make it clear to them that they have your blessing to be who they are. (See *The Blessing* by Gary Smalley and John Trent.) You'll find it much easier to push them in the direction God naturally gave them rather than to try to constantly pull them into what you want them do. (Keep reminding yourself that they are not you.)

Get involved in the hobbies they like rather than always trying to make them do what you like. This is tough for many of us; we tend to be selfish about our time. Remember, you'll have plenty of that when the nest is empty.

Step 7.

Help them discover the various career opportunities available in the world of work. The more you can expose them to the actual work performed in different jobs, the better their decisions will be.

Step 8.

Help them get part-time and summer-time employment in various jobs. It is especially helpful if they can get into jobs that will use and develop their key strengths. It's also important for them to learn what they don't like, but probably there will be plenty of that in almost any job a teenager gets.

Step 9.

By late high school they should go through some sort of career guidance or assessment program, and the more objective the better. The fact that it is not coming from the parents will take away some of the natural temptation to do the exact opposite of what the parents are suggesting. This is very important because they are in the period of "individuation" or breaking away from their parents and becoming individuals. Confirmation of their unique talents and interests will be a big encouragement and give them confidence to face adulthood.

Step 10.

Help them learn about specific occupations that match their interests and talents. You want them to have as much reality in their thinking as possible. Try to arrange for an interview or a half-day shadow program with a friend who is in an occupation they are considering. Also see if they can get an internship or apprentice job in this field.

Step 11.

Help them develop a plan for their education and training. First, they need to find out what kind of preparation will be required for the occupations they are considering. Encourage them by reminding them that post high-school courses will be different and they will be treated as adults.

Be sure to be open and honest with them about how much you will help them finance their education and training. The financial arrangements should be worked out and understood by both parties. This is the time to begin treating them like adults.

Step 12.

Your responsibilities are limited, and eventually you must turn them loose. You can't control what other people do, and it should be quite clear by this point that they are "other people." Each year you should have been playing a smaller role in their decision-making process. If they are to be well-adjusted adults, they must stand on their own and work it out for themselves.

But remember: Your encouragement (not to be confused with manipulation) and prayers should go on forever. I can assure you they will never live their lives exactly like you, so just accept their choices and give them your blessing at every opportunity,

These 12 steps outline a process that will help you to have a positive influence in the career decisions of your children. The very fact that you acknowledge that they are unique and a special creation from God will increase their self-confidence and respect for your opinions. It also will show them you love them unconditionally and believe they have a special purpose in their future.

If you love your children unconditionally, you will not fail in your role as a steward and you will have a positive influence on their career choices.

Giving someone unconditional love and a vision of a special future is one of the most powerful concepts in leadership. You'll recall that Jesus' interactions with people were often based on this principle.

"Love is patient, love is kind, and is not jealous; love does not brag and is not arrogant, does not act unbecomingly; it does not seek its own, is not provoked, does not take into account a wrong suffered, does not rejoice in unrighteousness, but rejoices with the truth; bears all things, believes all things, hopes all things, endures all things. Love never fails" (1 Corinthians 13:4–8).

CHAPTER NINE
Planning for Retirement Career Decisions

Is Retirement Scriptural?

I am convinced that retirement, as we know it in our generation, is not scriptural. I'm not implying that someone who retires at age 62 or 65 is living in sin. There are some instances when retirement is a part of God's plan for a particular individual. But the basic concept of idling the majority of people at such an early age is a modern innovation, not a biblical principle.

There is actually only one direct reference to retirement in the Bible. *"This is what applies to the Levites: from twenty-five years old and upward they shall enter to perform service in the work of the tent of meeting. But at the age of fifty years they shall retire from service in the work and not work any more"* (Numbers 8:24–5).

Exactly why God directed that the priests should retire at 50 is not known. It is possible that they assisted in other functions but couldn't perform the ceremonies themselves. So if you're a Levite priest, according to God's Word your retirement decisions have been made. If you're not, read on.

Retirement, as we know it, is so new that most current retirees can still remember when practically no one retired. In my grandfather's generation certainly few, if any, ordinary citizens would have considered that they could stop working at age 65 (or before) and spend their time playing golf.

In the first place, few Americans made enough money to be able to retire to the golf course, and those who did were so committed to their careers they had little interest in retirement.

For our present system of retirement to function, two essential elements are required: first, a large class of workers who make sufficient incomes to save a sizeable portion for the future; and second, most of these workers must be so dissatisfied with their jobs that they're willing to quit at an early age.

Such a combination was found in two groups of workers during the fifties: union members and federal employees. As the labor unions grew in number and strength during the high employment period after World War II, their collective bargaining eventually took in long-term benefits, such as retirement. Companies were more than willing to negotiate for deferred benefits in lieu of current wage increases.

For the first time, retirement became an attainable goal for blue collar workers. The impact this idea was to have on American society was incalculable at that time. It would eventually give rise to a multibillion dollar investment industry in the sixties, and it would doom the Social Security system to failure as the majority of workers over age 60 decided they could retire.

Once the retirement "bandwagon" got rolling, millions of additional people joined it. Eventually American workers became convinced that retirement is a basic "right." During the sixties and seventies laws were passed *requiring* workers to retire by age 65. With more and more younger workers coming into the work force, retirement became a logical way to free up jobs. As I said earlier, several factors now have made that same notion illogical—not the least of which is the lack of gainfully employed people to support the Social Security system.

Workers who planned to retire in the sixties developed their retirement plans around Social Security and a modest company pension that would allow them a reasonably comfortable lifestyle. They had the best of all benefits: a growing economy, a growing labor force, low interest rates, and low inflation.

SOCIAL IN-SECURITY

Only three decades earlier, the Great Depression of the thirties had ended any thought of retirement for the average American worker of that day. Instead, for nearly 10 years the emphasis for most Americans shifted to basic survival. At the outset of the Great Depression in the early thirties, millions of hard-working older Americans had been wiped out financially by the collapsing economy. Those beyond the age of 50 were often unemployable and yet, outside of finding whatever work they could, they had no means of living. The New Deal established the Old Age Pension Plan, now known as Social Security, as a means to bridge the gap for these workers.

The Roosevelt administration never intended that Social Security would be used as anything but an old age *supplement.* Social Security remained a supplemental income plan until after World War II when politicians, vying for public favor, began to expand the system to match benefits in the private sector, including workers' disability, survivors' benefits, and more extensive retirement benefits.

Based on much of the material I have read from that era, it's quite possible the enhancement of the Social Security system was motivated by guilt over an ever-expanding federal retirement system. In an economy with nearly full employment, low-cost credit, and worldwide exports, little thought was given to the future costs of funding such a massive system.

By the late sixties, most Americans viewed retirement as a foregone conclusion. At age 65, you retire. In the seventies, the average retirement age had dropped to 62. Unfortunately the assumptions upon which most Americans based their hopes for retirement in the fifties and sixties changed drastically in the seventies and eighties, including Social Security.

But I'm getting ahead of myself. The basic issue I'm addressing here is not the Social Security system; nor is it whether individuals can save enough to stop work at 62 and live comfortably. The real issue is: Is retirement itself a biblical principle God established for His people?

Since there is so little Scripture dealing with this subject, it would seem logical to make one of two assumptions: Either God forgot to discuss the subject of retirement, or it is not a part of His plan for us. I discovered long ago that God doesn't forget anything; therefore it has to be that our whole perspective of retirement is out of balance.

Having concluded that retirement (as we know it) is not scriptural, I would like to clarify what I mean. Although retirement is not biblical, it can't be placed in the same category as objective sins— adultery, lying, stealing. These are expressly prohibited by God.

Retirement is not *prohibited*; it simply isn't discussed to any degree. Therefore it's little more than an innovative way for modern society to escape the drudgery of workplace boredom. For some people it's a way to extend their useful years by seeking out new careers, supplemented by a retirement income. And for some, retirement is necessitated for health reasons. But, in general, retirement is not endorsed biblically.

We may not be able to do the same things at 70 or 80 that we could do at 30 or 40, but we can do something useful and meaningful.

If God's plan for most of us is not retirement, then what is it?

Any logical observer would agree that the vast majority of people who live beyond the age of 70 are not capable of doing the same amount or level of work they were able to do when they were younger. The aging process lowers physical stamina, reflexes, and sense (although not necessarily mental faculties).

Just look at professional athletes, for example. Few professional football players are gainfully employed as active athletes beyond the age of 35; none are beyond the age of 50. But since they're not employable as professional athletes, should they automatically conclude that their working careers are over? Hardly so.

I know of many ex-professional athletes who have started successful careers after retiring from their sports. Frank Gifford, Roger Staubach, Terry Bradshaw, and Fran Tarkenton are just a few. Bill Bradley, Jack Kemp, and Byron White have attained recognition in a career field totally removed from their athletic careers—politics.

The point is, just because they can no longer do what they had been doing doesn't mean they can't do something! The same principle holds true for the rest of us. We may not be able to do the same things at 70 or 80 that we could do at 30 or 40, but we can do something useful and meaningful.

Some good friends, Walt and Ralph Meloon, are walking examples of this truth. For many years Walt and Ralph ran the Correct Craft boat company in Orlando, Florida. Now well into their seventies, both men have turned the day-to-day operations of Correct Craft over to their children.

But Walt and Ralph have not settled down into their rocking chairs; nor do they spend their days on the golf courses of Florida. They're some of the most active men I know. Often when one or the other is passing through our area he'll stop over to have lunch. Usually, they are traveling around the country visiting some of the Correct Craft distributors as ambassadors for the company.

A few years ago the Meloons started a ministry to help business people who are in financial distress and, often, in imminent danger of bankruptcy. They sponsor weekend sessions, called Turn-Around Weekends, where couples can come for advice and counsel. At these sessions both Walt and Ralph spend endless hours counseling with hurting people and sharing their own experiences about when Correct Craft was forced into bankruptcy during the early fifties.

Age most certainly has been a limiting factor for these two men of God, but they simply have found a way to be useful within these limitations. Christian history is full of examples of those who knew the biblical truth about retirement: It begins in eternity.

Remember: God uniquely created each of us, including our endurance and durability and, as a result, not everyone will have the same ability to work at the various stages of life. Consequently, there will be varying degrees of retirement for all of us. The degree to which we slow down is not the fundamental issue here; ceasing all productive activity is.

Statistics indicate that retirement probably will not be possible for most Americans beyond the end of this century which, at the time of this writing, is less than 10 years away. There simply won't be enough active workers to support all the retirees.

This leads to some pretty sobering conclusions: Either the majority of workers will continue to stay gainfully employed or society will find a convenient way to lower the costs of maintaining the nonproductive ones. If you think euthanasia never can happen in America, just consider what those in their 20s and 30s are now doing to their unwanted offspring. This is the generation that will be in control of our country in the next century.

SABBATICALS

God in His infinite wisdom knew that His creation would need rest and relaxation. The method He chose to provide that rest and relaxation is called sabbatical—the resting time. The term sabbatical comes from sabbath, or the day of rest in each week.

In the fifth chapter of Deuteronomy the Lord told the Jews that they should work six days, but *"the seventh day is a sabbath. . . ."* The meaning behind the sabbath is twofold: The first is to set apart a day to honor the Lord; the second is to take a day a week to recover. This practice was extended to include a sabbath year, called the year of remission, described in Deuteronomy 15:1–11.

I say this about the sabbath to point out that God has provided a plan for His people to rest and recover during their working lives. As best I can determine, God has not prescribed a time when we should retire. We have arbitrarily decided that at age 62, 65, or some later period, our active working careers should stop. Nothing could be further from the truth, and we should begin to adjust to a saner and more reasonable philosophy.

Storing some funds during the most productive years of your life for the later years is both logical and biblical. As Proverbs 6:6 says, *"Go to the ant, O sluggard, observe her ways and be wise, which, having no chief, officer or ruler, prepares her food in the summer, and gathers her provision in the harvest."*

Having some reserve allows you to take more frequent sabbaticals later in life or to volunteer your services to ministries without the necessity of being paid. But if you want to live the long, happy, healthy life that God has prescribed for you, don't retire!

(Adapted from *Preparing for Retirement* by Larry Burkett, Moody, 1992.)

*   *   *

As Larry has pointed out, retirement as we know it is a passing fad. Most of those who are under 50 will have to continue working at some level just to have a livable income. But even if supplanting your income is not a necessity, there are many reasons to keep active and productive.

Stay active.

Medical research shows that physical activity promotes better health and longer life. It basically boils down to the expression "use it or lose it" and many older people are losing their strength and mobility because they are not active. Our society has many poor role models for retirement, but we don't have to follow their example. There are some great examples to follow.

> *Everyone has a different situation, but no matter what your circumstances, the more active you stay, the better will be your quality of life.*

Think of the farmers in their 70s and 80s who still tend their land and animals. I know some of them, and they would never think about just quitting altogether. My neighbor Frank is over 70 and he raises beef cattle and trains bird dogs professionally.

At age 92 my great uncle still had a vegetable garden, lived alone, and took care of himself. I'm convinced the reason he was so healthy was that he never quit. He did slow down a little more every year, but he stayed active until he went to the nursing home at age 95.

Granted, everyone has a different situation, but no matter what your circumstances, the more active you stay, the better will be your quality of life. And as Larry has pointed out, there is no indication in Scripture that God intended for us to walk off the job He wants us to do. Our calling to serve in the kingdom has no expiration date and we won't get our real "gold watch" until we get to heaven.

Continue to use your talents.

We know that many people are using their golden years to move to a new career and do something they've always wanted to do. At Life Pathways we've assisted several who are retiring and are making career transitions. Through our career assessment program we've given them ideas for other careers, as well as areas where they can use their talents in Christian service.

I know many people who made a transition into ministry activities as their answer to retirement. Monty, a friend who introduced me to CFC materials, budgeting, and a prison ministry, is a good example of someone who continues to use his talents in retirement. After his children left home, Monty and his wife Penny continued to live simply and modestly with a definite plan for another career in retirement—a plan of being debt free so they could provide their services to ministry work.

Because they had always been good money managers and maintained a modest lifestyle, they had many options for service. When Monty was in his early 60s, he sold his construction business and made the transition.

Monty and Penny are not always easy to locate because they travel a lot. They go to Mexico during the summer months, where they do missionary work and Monty uses his engineering talents in supervising construction of churches. One time I called them and found they were in Texas doing volunteer work for Youth With a Mission.

The next time I called, I found them in Orlando working with Campus Crusade for Christ. Recently Monty called our office and said he was at a camp in Pennsylvania and needed some budget workbooks to use in teaching a class. Most of us might refer to this couple as being retired, but they haven't quit using their talents to serve the Lord and to help others.

Dave and Cynthia are also a good example of people combining their talents with paid work in ministry. Dave is a retired banker, but he works as much as anyone I know. He is our key instructor for the *Business by the Book* seminar; and Cynthia only recently gave up leadership of the local crisis pregnancy counseling center.

If we aren't careful, we can crawl into a cocoon of selfish activity and forget that we still have talents and that, with them, goes responsibility.

Bob is a good example of someone who retired but works full time in a ministry. Bob was president of a publishing company before he joined the CFC staff. When I interviewed him, prior to his coming to CFC, he said he would be glad to do anything we wanted him to do, even sweep floors; he just wanted to be a part of this ministry. Bob does have a real heart for ministry and with his background in publishing, financial management, and marketing, he hasn't had to sweep floors. He has been a blessing to us all and especially to those of us in Career Pathways, where he serves as our administrator and financial manager.

In relating these examples, I used the term retirement because it does communicate an age of transition and usually a time when people slow down. But these individuals are active and productive. Some are continuing to earn an income and all are making a difference in the kingdom. Not everyone will join a ministry-type activity when they reach retirement age, and that is fine. We desperately need mature Christians in the workplace, in community volunteer agencies, in politics, and in every walk of life.

The important thing is that we don't adopt a mind-set of "I've done my part; I deserve to quit and fulfil my dreams by doing whatever I feel like when I wake up today." If we aren't careful, we can crawl into a cocoon of selfish activity and forget that we still have talents and that, with them, goes responsibility.

Have a financial plan.

For those of you who will be making a transition to another career or a different level of activity, the best advice we can give is to plan thoroughly and realistically with your finances. If you haven't been building a surplus, you definitely should get started. It's a good idea to plan now for the skills you'll want to use even when you've lost some of your mobility and stamina, because you may need to supplement your income.

The one thing we can count on is that all economies go in cycles so, even in the best of circumstances, we'll have some lean years from time to time. Considering what we see on the horizon, it could get very lean for people on fixed incomes and pensions.

Live a simple lifestyle.

To go along with being debt free, we encourage a simple lifestyle. One of the new terms of the nineties is "downscaling," which describes what many families are doing to simplify their lives and cut their expenses. Downscaling is also an excellent technique for getting debt free, and that should be the goal for every individual approaching retirement age.

The examples I used above were all quite successful by the world's standards, yet they have chosen to live simple and modest lifestyles. By doing so, they have been able to pursue options for serving that many of their contemporaries would not have. I praise the Lord for these families who are committed to being active, productive, and good stewards of their talents and resources. Rather than just spending their time selfishly, they are investing it in the kingdom.

Seek God's will for your retirement.

We can't tell you what God wants you to do in your retirement years, but we encourage you to struggle with that question until you have an answer. Pray about it, and plan financially so you will have some options. If you are under 50, more than likely you'll have to have some employment just to provide basic needs. Rather than being disappointed at that, look on it as an opportunity for being a blessing to others.

Remember what we said earlier about process and results. God is not concerned with our results. He only asks us to be committed to the process of following Him.

In an era when many people say they want to escape work and go spend their children's inheritance, serving Jesus in retirement may sound like a real sacrifice. However, if you think you would have to give up something, think about the words of the missionary Jim Elliot who was killed by the Auca Indians in Ecuador.

"He is no fool who gives up what he cannot keep in order to gain what he cannot lose."[1]

SECTION THREE
Identifying Your Talents for Work

CHAPTER TEN

Discover Your Skills and Aptitudes

*I*n this section we are going to walk you through a process of self-assessment. It's an opportunity to learn about your strengths and how they can be used at work. This information will equip you to make good career decisions now, and the same process can be used to re-evaluate your career goals as you move through the seasons of life—even in retirement.

The experience of learning about yourself can be very exciting, but there are some cautions we should mention. Done with the wrong motives, self-discovery feeds our natural inclinations toward self-centeredness, so there are some legitimate concerns with the widespread "self-discovery" movement in America today.

Many people are trying to "find themselves" when what they really need is to find a personal relationship with Jesus Christ. As followers of Christ, we should be focusing our efforts on a lifestyle that models love for others and servanthood. It's our purpose to point you in that direction.

You'll need to be cautious in conducting a self-assessment. Question your motives. Are you trying to glorify yourself or just understand the talents you've been given and how you can use them?

There's a genuine need to evaluate honestly your talents and interests as you plan your career. As a steward (manager of the talents you've been given), you're a decision maker and, as such, need good information on which to base your decisions. So let's assume that already you have the proper motivation toward life and work and you're ready to find out about yourself. What do you need to know?

PATTERN OF TALENTS

God has given an assortment of talents to each of us. We have combinations of strengths, interests, and gifts that fit together in a general pattern. During our research at Career Pathways we found that there are four main areas that seem to define a person's pattern of talents for work:

I. skills and abilities
II. vocational interests
III. work priorities and values
IV. personality (temperament).

These four dimensions are independent; yet there is usually a significant amount of overlap among them. For instance, a person whose personality revolves around relating to people usually will have vocational interests in social occupations that involve helping, influencing, or counseling others. That same person probably would place a high value on helping others as a life goal, and we would see that he or she has strong verbal skills.

You can gain a fairly accurate picture of these four areas through either a self-survey or formal assessment. Then, by putting the four together, you can develop a good overall picture of your pattern of strengths and interests for work.

We have found it helpful to use the concept of patterns to illustrate how your talents and interests define good career matches. The following chart depicts two patterns and how they can be used to match a person with typical occupations.

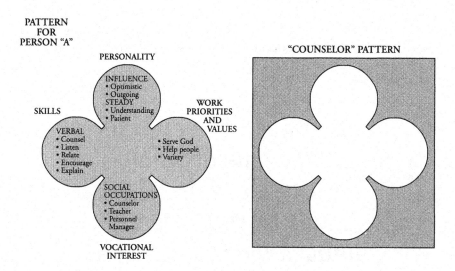

PATTERN
FOR
PERSON "A"

PERSONALITY

INFLUENCE
• Optimistic
• Outgoing
STEADY
• Understanding
• Patient

SKILLS

WORK
PRIORITIES
AND
VALUES

VERBAL
• Counsel
• Listen
• Relate
• Encourage
• Explain

• Serve God
• Help people
• Variety

SOCIAL
OCCUPATIONS
• Counselor
• Teacher
• Personnel
Manager

VOCATIONAL
INTEREST

"COUNSELOR" PATTERN

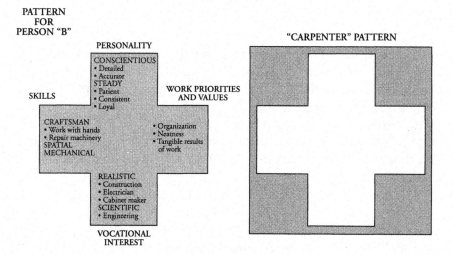

PATTERN
FOR
PERSON "B"

PERSONALITY

CONSCIENTIOUS
• Detailed
• Accurate
STEADY
• Patient
• Consistent
• Loyal

SKILLS

WORK PRIORITIES
AND VALUES

CRAFTSMAN
• Work with hands
• Repair machinery
SPATIAL
MECHANICAL

• Organization
• Neatness
• Tangible results
of work

REALISTIC
• Construction
• Electrician
• Cabinet maker
SCIENTIFIC
• Engineering

VOCATIONAL
INTEREST

"CARPENTER" PATTERN

MATCHING PATTERNS TO OCCUPATIONS

As you read the next two chapters, think about the four parts of your pattern. Then, as you begin to understand your basic design, try to envision how it might match your various career fields. If you can incorporate this concept of comparing your pattern of talents with the needs of various occupations, you'll be well equipped for making career decisions for the rest of your life.

> *Choosing a career is not a one-time decision; it's a series of decisions, made as you progress through the seasons and experiences of life.*

Most people who come to Life Pathways for the assessment want us to tell them an exact occupation that would be best for them. Trying to do that is more complicated than trying to predict the exact weather for next week. The human being is too complicated, and there are too many variables for anyone to tell you "this is the one job for you." What we can do, however, is give you some basic information and show you how to use it to evaluate your potential for various occupations.

Choosing a career is not a one-time decision; it's a series of decisions, made as you progress through the seasons and experiences of life. As the expression goes, we would rather teach you how to fish (make your own decisions) than give you a fish, (decide for you). In fact, if you can learn to fish (make good career decisions) and then teach someone else, maybe a lot of the employment, productivity, and even spiritual problems that Christians struggle with today could be resolved. Your first lesson in "fishing" is to learn how to evaluate your abilities.

YOUR SKILLS AND ABILITIES

Most people tend to use the terms *skills*, *abilities*, *talents*, and *aptitudes* almost interchangeably, and if you look at a dictionary you'll see their meaning is about the same. A *skill* is a proficiency or expertness in some area; a *talent* is a natural or acquired *ability* or *aptitude*.

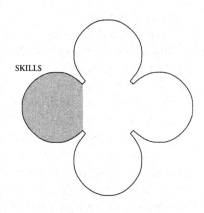

For example, an interior decorator needs to be skilled in picking the right colors, materials, and styles to give the right atmosphere and ambience to the room being decorated. Supporting that skill are several natural abilities, such as an eye for detail, an appreciation of color, a sense of perspective on spatial relations, and a strong artistic and creative bent.

Each of us has some abilities that develop easier and faster than others. Some people have an aptitude for math, others for certain sports; still others have a special potential for detail work, nurturing, or doing research. Developing a realistic evaluation of these strengths is not always easy, but it is essential for making good career decisions.

The best way to assess your skills is to put them to the test of experience, and the earlier you can do that the better. Athletic skills are usually evaluated this way. As young men, Larry and I both played high school sports and, over a period of time, we learned that our potential was very limited. We loved sports, but slow feet and average balance and strength made it clear we would never be able to succeed in the athletic world.

Wouldn't it be great if high school offered the opportunity to test your skills in other potential job areas? We probably could avoid much of the career frustration currently in the workplace.

Unfortunately, we don't always get a good assessment of our skills soon enough in life. One of our clients reported she had been fired from seven jobs. As we looked at her list of jobs, they couldn't have been a worse match for her strengths. She was a very bright, fast-paced, take-charge generalist. Yet all her work had focused on slow, repetitious, detailed work, where she had no opportunity to have control over her work. What a blessing it would have been if someone had identified her leadership skills and helped her develop them much earlier.

Regrettably, most people have neither the experience to evaluate their skills nor the required testing and assessment until they are already in an occupation.

Then how can you evaluate your strengths? First, look at your experience thus far. With all the testing in our school systems, most people know if they have strong abilities in basic academic areas— math, English composition, spelling, science, or foreign languages.

Furthermore, through school and church activities, there's an opportunity to experiment with drawing, music, and similar creative arts. I (Lee) remember art classes in the fourth grade. My drawings were so bad that I was embarrassed for my classmates to see them. When directed to draw a three-dimensional object on a piece of paper, I proved to be a spatial moron.

Interestingly enough, however, I have been good at visualizing and flying three-dimensional aerobatic maneuvers. As in sports, art, and many other areas, the best way to determine the strength of your skills is to use them and get feedback from others.

Probably the best method of evaluating your skills is to note how quickly you seem to master the processes involved. If you learn a skill much faster than the average person, you probably have a talent for it. This is the basic principle used by the military to screen for pilot aptitude.

In spite of 50 years of research, the Air Force has not been able to develop inexpensive tests that adequately identify the skills required of a military pilot. The primary method still used to identify those talents is to observe the learning rates of students during flying lessons.

As an instructor, it was clear to me that I could teach almost anyone to fly, given enough time. But to have the highest quality pilots for the limited cockpits available, we needed to weed out those who were marginally talented. By conducting training in accordance with a rigid syllabus requiring a set rate of progression, we could identify those with a high proficiency for flying.

Conversely, if a student wasn't able to master the increasingly difficult maneuvers by the specified lessons, he or she usually would be eliminated from training. Likewise, an honest look at how fast a skill is mastered will help to identify aptitude in that area.

If you ask people what their skills are, usually they can name only one or two areas where they feel strong. It's just not something they have thought about. However, we've found that most people are very accurate in evaluating their strengths if you ask they the right questions.

The Skills Search concept we use at Life Pathways divides skills into three areas: job skills, transferable skills, and self-management skills. You can use the same concept to gain a better understanding of your skills in these three areas.

JOB SKILLS

The following are skills that refer to specific job functions:

prepare income taxes	be a chef
lay bricks	teach a class
sell insurance	survey land
repair diesel engines	prepare payroll accounts
take x-rays	operate machinery
purchase supplies	alter clothing

> *God does not make mistakes; we know He has gifted everyone in some areas and for specific purposes.*

Most people can identify these job skills if they've done them in their work. Job skills are usually acquired through training and actual on-the-job experience. Sometimes these are strengths and sometimes they aren't. The truth is, we all do some things in our work that aren't our strengths. What we don't want is to be in a job that requires extensive use of skills that don't come easily.

When you're working in a job that requires skills that are not natural to your talents, it will be stressful and quickly become discouraging. One person who responded to the Life Pathways' survey put it this way: "When I worked in areas that required talents I didn't have, I experienced frustration, failure, and extreme stress, not to mention a blow to my self-esteem." This individual learned a valuable lesson through experience.

As mentioned earlier, actual work experience is one of the best ways to identify the level of your skills. For that reason, it's easier to identify the talents of an adult than a young person because adults have more experience. That's also why we encourage parents to help their children get work experience. Work helps teens develop maturity and independence, and it's especially helpful in bringing reality to career dreams. The more experience a person has, the more realistic the appraisal of skills.

Any time you start evaluating yourself, you run into the problems of being subjective. If you are totally honest, you may have to fact the fact you are not talented at some of the things you do; and that can be discouraging. On the other hand, to inflate your talents does not help because it deprives you of the accurate information you need for decision making.

You can prepare yourself for being subjective by acknowledging that we all do some things well and some things not as well. Your effort should be to discover talents God has given you. God does not make mistakes; we know He has gifted everyone in some areas and for specific purposes.

Your boss, co-workers, and instructors can be a big help in evaluating your talents. You can ask them to point out your strengths and weaknesses. Most supervisors will be able to tell you how well your job skills compare with the typical worker in your area.

In addition, probably you can gain good insights from the feedback you get from the organization and your peers. Have you won any awards or had any recognition for your performance? Do people look to you as the expert in a particular area? Have you been chosen to conduct training for new people in certain job skills? These are some indicators that will help you in you self-evaluation.

TRANSFERABLE SKILLS

When evaluating your potential for various career fields, we have found it's especially helpful to look at transferable skills. Transferable skills encompass activities that have broad application in several career areas. We include 120 transferable skills in our Skills Search, and probably there are many more.

Transferable skills include the following:

record facts/data	conduct research
speak in public	sell by phone
inspect products	write expressively
handle complaints	edit
work with hands	operate vehicles
negotiate	estimate
repair things	design
manage	coordinate

A good way to evaluate your strongest transferable skills is, first, to identify a large number of skills you have used in your work, hobbies, and volunteer work. It helps to brainstorm with someone who knows you well so you can come up with a good long list. Then go back and look at your life's successes and joys and see which ones of these skills you've used. Have you had a pattern of success at repairing things? Perhaps you were the one who could always negotiate an agreement that would allow people to work together?

If you look back, you'll see a pattern of repeated success in certain activities and environments. The results or rewards of your successes are not so important. Rather, it's the processes you used that you want to identify.

In their excellent book, *Finding a Job You Can Love*, Ralph Mattson and Arthur Miller confirm the importance of looking back at life experiences to identify what they call your "central motivational thrust." Their research shows that we are each gifted and motivated to operate in a unique and consistent way.

By looking at the processes you consistently enjoy using in your life and work, you'll be able to see your motif and identify your strongest transferable skills.

To illustrate how a knowledge of your skills can help you make good career decisions, let's look at one of our clients. Bill's strengths center on his ability to work with details. He is gifted in his abilities to assemble things, do skilled craft work, and complete most kinds of detail work. He is naturally patient, cooperative, and supportive.

We also learned in the assessment what is *not* part of Bill's pattern. He is not bold or assertive and generally prefers to avoid risks. Making big decisions that involve lots of people and money is not something he feels comfortable doing. Bill is very intelligent, has a masters degree, and has had a good career progression; yet he is very unhappy in his job. He invested over ten years in a military career, and now he's in a leadership position requiring talents that are not part of his pattern.

Knowing your strongest transferable skills will be very important because these are the processes you'll want to use in your work.

During the early years, Bill was more of a specialist, keeping up with the details of purchasing and supply. This matched many of his strengths and he handled his duties well. But as a leader he must be a generalist, a bold decision maker, and one who deals daily with conflict.

Bill came to us for the assessment because he knew things were not right. His promotions and job progression thus far looked good on paper, but the stress was eating away at his health and morale. Just by looking at Bill's strengths in the skills area, we could see a mis-match between his pattern and his work.

Knowing your strongest transferable skills will be very important because these are the processes you'll want to use in your work. In fact, if you're in a job search, you should develop your résumé to highlight these skills. In today's changing work environment, employers are especially interested in transferable skills; they indicate not just what you have done but your potential to grow as the needs of the organization change.

SELF-MANAGEMENT SKILLS

We have found it helpful to look at another area: Self-Management Skills. These encompass areas of character and maturity and mainly focus on qualities such as dependability and responsibility. Although they aren't what you normally think of as skills, they can be developed, and they are very important for success in your career.

People with self-management skills accept supervision and complete assignments, as well as being:

trustworthy	self-motivated
willing to learn	persistent
punctual	dependable
hard working	helpful
courteous	responsibile
efficient	cooperative

These areas sound almost too basic; yet they are essential traits for success at work. Including them in self-evaluation is valuable because it forces you to take a hard look at what you are offering your employer.

If you stop to think about it, these traits reflect the character of Christ. They require agape love, an attitude of service, and a commitment to integrity. We could change the world if all Christians would exhibit these characteristics in their workplaces. Growing in these areas should be our constant goal.

HIDDEN TALENTS

Clients sometimes ask if they have any "hidden talents." This is definitely a possibility but not something that likely will be revealed through testing. Encouragement from others, your inner desire, and firsthand experience will be the best indicators of hidden talents. If you have had a desire to do something, try it and see how it goes.

The following case study illustrates how hidden talents can emerge.

Angela had gone to college for a year and a half but was not sure of what she really wanted to do. She dropped out of school and took a job as a waitress to be nearer her boyfriend. She eventually left that job and took a clerical job just to have more stability and better working conditions. In her new job she worked a variety of tasks, such as data entry, record filing, and assembling packages for mailing. Very soon it became clear that Angela was exceptional at organizing clerical work and getting it done.

Angela was fast, not just at getting one job done but she could carry out as many as 15 different functions during the day and still keep everything neat, organized, and on schedule. Within a few months she had earned a reputation in the organization as being a whiz at her work. When management decided to consolidate several administrative functions of a key program and put them under one person, Angela was the person chosen.

You might say these were "hidden talents" because she had no experience or confidence in her ability to do such intricate clerical functions. Yet when we interviewed Angela to find out her strengths, we found she had always been very organized and a fast worker. Even as a child she'd kept her room neat and organized, so she knew exactly where things were.

> *What you are looking for is a work field that uses your strongest abilities.*

Angela reported a gift for house cleaning, saying she had the reputation for being able to put things in order quickly. She also reported a strong ability to learn step-by-step processes. For instance, she learned how to program a VCR before anyone else in her family. These same strengths allowed her to learn computer software programs quickly and to maintain order in what could have been a chaotic work environment.

Did she have hidden talents? In a way you could say yes but, in reality, she always had used these skills; she just transferred them from her personal life to her work. By operating with the motivations and gifts God had placed in her, she honored Him and found success in her work.

EMPLOYERS NEED SKILLED PEOPLE

During the "good times" many businesses enjoyed in the eighties, they often hired people at an average level of competence because the highly qualified were not available. But when the cutbacks started, a real talent evaluation process took over and those who were not in a job that fit them were usually the first to go. Of course, even some of the most talented eventually were cut during many of the downsizing actions. But as a rule, the closer your skill strengths match the job, the more secure your employment will be.

You'll also need to update your skills continually to meet the needs of the twenty-first century workplace. Today, it is not wise to "sit" on your current skills. The world of work is changing rapidly and we all must continue to develop personal strengths.

RELATE SKILLS TO INTERESTS

Before leaving the subject of skills and abilities, we should re-emphasize that just because you have the basic ability to do a job does not mean it would be a good match for you. The human being is very complex and has the ability to do many things. What you are looking for is a work field that uses your strongest abilities. As we indicated previously, usually these are the talents we most enjoy using.

Isn't it marvelous how God gives us not only the ability but also the desire to use these talents in our work? Vocational interests are definitely related to talents, as you'll see in the next step of the self-discovery process.

CHAPTER ELEVEN

Identify Your Vocational Interests, Work Priorities, and Values

*I*f you had nothing else to go on in making a career decision, you probably could get off to a good start just by following the desires of your heart. In considering various occupations, you'll find that some will appeal to you while others won't. It's helpful to look at groups of occupations you like, as well as those you don't like. By analyzing your likes and dislikes, you'll be able to identify the criteria that are important to your career choices.

Similar occupations are commonly grouped into vocational interests categories referred to as *clusters* (also called groups or themes). There are several clustering systems in use today.

We have shown three such systems to give you a good idea of the concept of occupational clusters. It will be helpful for you to read through them and develop a mental picture of various types of work and work environments. The more you know about the available occupations, the more likely you are to find occupations that match your pattern of talents and interests.

VOCATIONAL CLUSTERS

Dr. John Holland developed what is probably the most well-known clustering system in use today. His theory is that people who prefer the same types of occupational settings tend to share many similar personality traits. His clusters are the basis for several vocational interest inventories, including the *Self Directed Search*, *the Strong Interest Inventory*, and the *Career Assessment Inventory*.

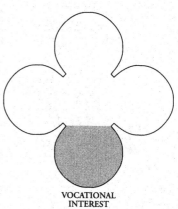

VOCATIONAL
INTEREST

Several other vocational interest inventories use the Holland system but with different names for the clusters. At some point, you'll probably encounter these occupational clusters, so we've included a description of them below. Possibly you'll be attracted to two or three of the groups.

Realistic (Outdoor/Skill Trades/Crafts)

Generally prefer outdoor and/or hands-on type activities . . . prefer working with things rather than people or ideas . . . frequently enjoy using tools or large equipment . . . often like physical activity, adventure, and variety . . . prefer tangible rather than abstract problems.

Typical occupations include construction, engineering, agriculture, forestry/wildlife, coaching sports, some military jobs, numerous technical jobs, and skilled trades.

Investigative (Scientific/Research)

Tend to be curious, creative, theoretical, studious, and often prefer to work by themselves . . . enjoy solving abstract problems . . . prefer to work with ideas rather than things or people . . . and often have a high potential for formal education. Typical occupations include design engineer, biologist, physicist, technical writer, medical technician, and other technical, scientific, or mathematical fields.

Artistic (The Arts)

Have a high interest in creative activities such as music, writing, art, and entertainment . . . aesthetic, . . . enjoy working with ideas more than things or people . . . often prefer a non-conforming unstructured lifestyle . . . value independence . . . actively seek opportunities for self-expression.

Typical occupations include musician, artist, interior decorator, actor/actress, scriptwriter, or producer.

Social (Social Service)

Prefer activities which involve interaction with others in order to train, develop, cure, enlighten, or encourage . . . usually are outgoing with strong verbal skills . . . get along well with others . . . are intuitive and prefer to solve problems through discussions or counseling . . . usually are cheerful and popular . . . prefer to deal with people more than things or ideas. Typical occupations include teacher, counselor, trainer, social worker, pastor, nurse, and medical service areas.

Enterprising (Business)

Good with words, especially in selling, leading, managing, and influencing . . . usually energetic, self-confident, adventurous, dominant . . . often are impatient with detail work . . . tend to seek status, power, and wealth . . . prefer to work with people rather than ideas or things.

Typical occupations include business executive, stock broker, real estate agent, manager, salesperson, promoter, and consultant.

Conventional (Clerical)

Prefer activities that are highly organized—the keeping of data or records, organizing materials, or operating business equipment such as a computer . . . generally choose to follow rather than lead . . . like to know exactly what's expected of them . . . typically stable and dependable . . . favor working with data or things, rather than people or ideas.

Typical occupations include accountant, tax expert, data systems operator, bank teller, inventory controller, bookkeeper, and office worker.[1]

Another widely used format for clustering vocational interests is the COPSystem developed by EdITS/Educational and Industrial Testing Service. Unlike the other groupings above, the COPSystem has levels of occupation—based generally on whether a college degree is required to do the work. The clusters are as follows:

science professional	business professional
science skilled	business skilled
technology professional	clerical
technology skilled	service professional
communication	service skilled
consumer economics	arts professional
outdoor	arts skilled

A lack of information is definitely one of the major obstacles people face in making good career choices.

The Guide for Occupational Exploration, a common reference book found in most libraries, uses another clustering system. It divides occupations into the following groups:

artistic	business detail
scientific	selling
plants and animals	accommodating (services)
protective	humanitarian
mechanical	leading, influencing
industrial	physical, performing

As you can see, the clustering systems are very similar. Each has some advantages and disadvantages. All of them are based on good logic, with their differences being the criteria established by the authors. Typically a person will be attracted to occupations in two or three of these groups.

Having read through the clusters above, select those that appeal to you most, and try to identify what it is about them that appeals to you.

Usually we are attracted to certain processes, such as working with details, operating machinery, working with art, working with math, or working with people. Identifying why certain occupations appeal to you will give you good decision-making information and help narrow your career focus.

INVESTIGATE VOCATIONAL INTERESTS

A lack of information is definitely one of the major obstacles people face in making good career choices. The information is available if you're willing to put forth a little effort. We can't encourage you strongly enough to do some research on several occupations associated with each of the clusters that appeal to you.

In almost any library or career center there are three commonly used sources for information on occupations. *The Guide for Occupational Exploration* provides a helpful guide for considering various career fields and also gives a description of hundreds of occupations. A companion book, *The Dictionary of Occupational Titles* gives a job description for over 30,000 occupational fields. Finally, *The Occupational Outlook Handbook* also describes general career areas and projects the outlook for employment in those fields. Larger libraries usually will have more specialized career information, such as *The Allied Health Education Directory.* It provides detailed information on 28 occupations in the health service and technology areas, including listings of schools that provide the prerequisite education and training. Careers covered range from *anesthesiologist's assistant* and *athletic trainer* to *radiographer* and *surgical technologist.* Similar books for other career fields are usually available in city and college libraries.

There's a lot of information available on occupations and associated careers for the person who's willing to exert a little effort in research. It's amazing how much time the average person will *spend* watching television or videos and, yet, so few actually invest time investigating occupational choices.

If you're going to "learn to fish," you'll have to go to the water and cast a line. Like most everything in life, your returns are directly related to your investments. Considering the changes in the workplace, I think you'll see the importance of investing time in learning about the emerging occupations that use your pattern of talents.

WHAT LEVEL OF JOB IS BEST

One of the decisions nearly everyone faces is what level of job to aim for. Before you get carried away with the prestige of a title that may go with a certain level of job, keep in mind what we've said about matching your strengths with those required for the job. As long as you can use your natural strengths in the primary activities of your work, go for the highest level possible that interests you. The level you choose will be determined primarily by the level of education and training you are willing and able to achieve.

The whole issue of career satisfaction and fulfillment in life hinges on combining our work and our faith.

For example, a brain surgeon and an electrician might have very similar talents and even the same level of natural intelligence. What would be the difference? Maybe one has a stronger confidence in academics while the other is attracted to the rigor of outside physical work. Or perhaps somewhere along the way one became fascinated with the nerve circuits of the human body and the other was intrigued by electricity.

Naturally, you'll have to start out at some entry level, but as you gain experience, probably you will want to go broader or deeper into your career field, depending on your personality. In either case, develop the talents you have; then, use them to the utmost. If you do that, you'll always be at or moving toward the right level.

Mentioned earlier was the concept of teaching you how to fish—meaning teaching you how to evaluate your talents and match them to appropriate occupations. Rather than listen to what everyone else would do, continue to use these techniques and you'll be equipped to find the levels where you can succeed and glorify God.

Remember, you are unique, and what everyone else does has no application to you; you have your own pattern of interests and talents. The challenge is to find occupations that will match.

WORK PRIORITIES AND VALUES

When we first began working on the Career Pathways' assessment program, it was clear that we had to include a section on values. Even the secular world is starting to recognize that values are important. A director of counseling and testing at a large university put it this way: "A look at values will be essential to any good career counseling program."

Also, from our interviews with people who were experiencing work stress, it was clear that conflicts in values were a major source of employment problems. Yet, interestingly enough, we found no existing survey adequate to help people identify their values. Part of the problem was the limited number of values covered by most surveys. Our major concern, however, was the omission of a Christian perspective on values.

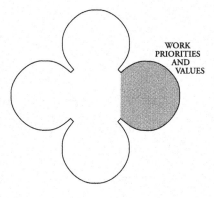

As previously discussed, many of the problems of job dissatisfaction are directly related to our society's attempt to separate our relationship with God from other areas of our lives. The whole issue of career satisfaction and fulfillment in life hinges on combining our work and our faith. Any good values survey must require people to evaluate how they are reconciling their core issues of life (values and purpose) with their needs in other areas (work, leisure, and finances).

To meet this need we developed our own Work Priorities Evaluation survey. As you would expect, development has been an evolutionary process; we are now in our third generation of this survey. Because the concept of values is so broad, we found it best to break it into four areas.

    I. What abilities do you want to use at work?
   II. What work environment do you prefer?
  III. What work activities do you desire to do?
  IV. What are the most important values in your life?

As you might imagine, there's a lot of overlap between Sections I through III above and the Vocational Interest area discussed earlier. This redundancy helps clients refine their thinking about what they really want to do at work. These added pieces of information also increase their confidence in the accuracy of the assessment. Shown below are the various areas included in the Work Priorities Evaluations. You can learn about your priorities by prioritizing the items in each section.

I. What abilities do you want to use at work?

verbal	artistic
written	craft-related
athletic	clerical
research	technical
creative	mechanical
performing	intellectual
leadership	

II. What work environment do you enjoy most?

stable	travel-oriented
outdoor	flexible hours
adventurous/risky	harmonious
varied	challenging
clean	well-organized
educational	

III. What work activities do you desire to do?

work with machinery	work with math/data
work in communication	work with hands
work with people	work with children
work with art	work with music

The final area in evaluating work priorities is what we call the Values section. It is also the area that deals with a person's life purpose. In many ways this is the most important part of your pattern for work. You can be matched perfectly to an occupation in every other area of your pattern, but if your values are being compromised or not being met, you won't find job satisfaction. In reviewing this section, I think you'll see how a values conflict can cause major life and work problems.

IV. What are the most important values in your life?

service to God	helping others
family	integrity/honesty
wealth (prosperity)	achievement
recognition	security

Most of us want to place some level of importance on several, or even all, of these values. The question is, which will take priority? For Christians, we believe the first four should be fairly easy to identify: serving God, family, helping others, integrity. Even these are not easy to keep in that priority. In fact, there were many years in my life when, for reasons of insecurity, pride, or whatever, I was not guided by such priorities.

For example, there were times when my actions showed that achievement, recognition, or helping others was more important than family. I find it takes a constant battle to keep my priorities lined up in a way that would honor God. But because I have purposed in my heart to serve the Lord, He keeps bringing my priorities back in focus. The Holy Spirit constantly prompts me to get back on track through prayer, godly counsel, and reading God's Word and hearing it taught and preached.

On the surface you might think it's not difficult to establish your priorities. But we challenge you to spend some time reviewing how you've lived your life and how you want to live it in the future. Here are some of the tough questions you'll want to ask yourself.

- Do my activities, time, money, and relationships reflect the priority of my values?
- Are my life and work decisions governed by a clearly defined set of values that will have eternal significance?
- By living the way I am living now, will I accomplish my life's purpose?

Dr. Joseph Stowell, president of Moody Bible Institute, addresses values in his excellent book *The Dawn's Early Light.*

> Our values must be biblically based if we are to reclaim our minds for Christ. Whereas some values are a matter of preference, such as choosing books over sports, other values are absolute and are clearly taught in Scripture.
>
> In direct contrast to our culture's values, authentic Christian values regard people above possessions, others above self, eternity above the present, righteousness above the temporary pleasure of sin, His will above my will, forgiveness above revenge, giving above receiving, children over careers, character above credentials, truth above falsehood, fact above feelings, commitment above comfort, and Christ above culture.
>
> Because our values determine how we organize facts and drive us toward decisions, clear biblical values help guarantee a thought process that is godly, beneficial, and eternally significant. All that remains is for the Christian to learn what those values are and to choose them over the prevalent systems of secular thinking and selfish desires.[2]

There will come a day when we'll all have to give an account of our lives, and we'll see that much of what we considered to be important has no value at all.

Take time now to look down your current pathway. If you see you're not headed in the right direction, we encourage you to follow Dr. Stowell's advice, which is really another way of saying what Jesus said on the subject of priorities and values: *"But seek first His kingdom and His righteousness; and all these things shall be added to you"* (Matthew 6:33). The values you honor with your work and life will ultimately lead you to the only destination that counts.

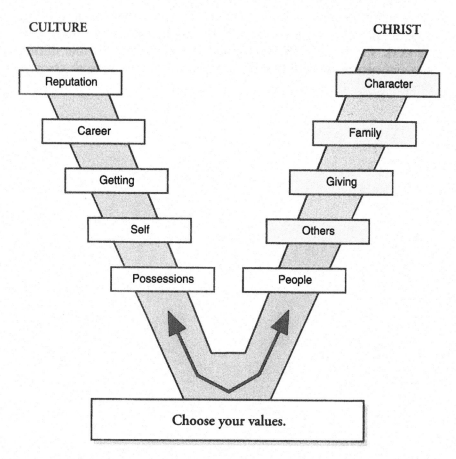

CULTURE

CHRIST

Reputation

Character

Career

Family

Getting

Giving

Self

Others

Possessions

People

Choose your values.

Adapted from *The Dawn's Early Light* by
Joseph M. Stowell, Moody Press, 1991.

We've covered three of the four areas of your pattern. The final area, personality, is so significant that we've devoted the next five chapters to covering it in detail. Chapter 12 will provide an in-depth explanation of personality and conclude with a section that brings together all four of the areas we've discussed that form your pattern for work. In Chapters 13, 14, 15, and 16, we'll cover the four dimensions of personality (D, I, S, C) and relate them to the work environment.

CHAPTER TWELVE
Understand Your Personality Strengths

Of the four areas that define your pattern for work, personality is the most intriguing and probably the most useful in helping you choose your basic line of work. As you gain an insight into your personality profile, you'll understand why some abilities come naturally and why entering some career fields would be like dragging a ball and chain.

This chapter gives a general overview of personality. The four subsequent chapters will elaborate on the four primary personality dimensions.

The use of personality (or temperament) surveys has gained widespread acceptance in recent years. Personality profiles and temperament "type" indicators are being used extensively in churches and in the corporate world. They can be very beneficial if used in the proper context.

These surveys are generally self-interpreting and can be used without the benefit of a trained counselor. However, it's important that you understand what the survey is designed to do and how the results should be used.

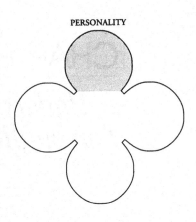

PERSONALITY

First, let's clarify exactly what is meant by *personality*. It includes all the behavioral traits of an individual. For our purposes, personality defines the way a person normally functions. It includes behaviors that are affected by emotions, temperament, and thought processes, and it describes the way energy is directed. It encompasses the motivation and the means through which you exercise all your talents.

Personality includes a number of dimensions: traits such as assertiveness, sociability, patience, confidence, accuracy, compassion, enthusiasm, independence, and flexibility. Generally, we think of these as positive traits but, remember, there's a time for each and too much of any of them can be just as bad as too little.

A personality survey indicates the levels or strengths of these traits in a person's typical behavior. It also is important to emphasize that the personality surveys we're talking about are designed to be used by normal, stable, emotionally healthy people.

A clear understanding of the natural levels of your personality traits can be helpful in finding a good occupational match. If you know your personality traits and the behaviors or traits needed to succeed in a particular occupation, you'll be equipped to make an informed judgment about whether it will be a good fit.

If you are experiencing job stress, you may be able to identify the source of the problem just by understanding this one area. Moreover, we believe that coming to grips with who we are, personality-wise, forces us to confront much of the "flesh" that must be stripped away if we are to walk with the mind of Christ.

Remember, personality surveys provide feedback on people in general so you must validate the results to decide what applies specifically to you. (Our experience is that 80 percent or more will apply directly.) Since everyone has blind spots, it's best to validate the feedback with someone who knows you well and will be totally honest. There's an expression used in writing classes: "Fight for feedback." We think that's the major value of the personality survey. It provides a framework for looking objectively at yourself—good and bad—and offers a structured way for you to gain feedback from others on your effectiveness in various dimensions.

Learning to balance the extremes of your personality is part of maturity.

Keep in mind, the results of personality surveys are descriptive and not prescriptive. You are the one who decides how to use the information. More than anything else, personality surveys are educational. Validating the information gives you an opportunity to consider how you affect others positively and negatively.

The whole idea of the personality survey is to help you understand how you operate and, thus, understand your strengths and limitations. With that information you can make decisions on how to maximize your talents while minimizing the negative aspects of undeveloped or overused areas.

As you would expect, learning to balance the extremes of your personality is part of maturity. If you have a naturally motivated ability to talk, that can be a strength. But if you talk so much that you're never quiet enough to listen to others, you're out of balance in this dimension, and your effectiveness will be reduced. Your goal, therefore, would be to have a Spirit-controlled personality so that all your actions would evidence a Spirit-filled life.

DISC SURVEYS

There are several good personality surveys on the market today. We favor those that use the four dimensions of D, I, S, C. DISC was developed by William Marston in the early 1900s and his book, *Emotions of Normal People*, is the basis for various DISC models. (The

four dimensions of DISC will be explained in detail later.) DISC surveys are simple to administer and score. The basic concepts are relatively easy to understand and, therefore, almost everyone can relate
to them. There are a number of companies using DISC surveys. We
probably have seen 10 different versions, but they are basically the
same, with variations in the words used in the survey and the format
of the feedback.

After assessing over 7,000 people with DISC personality surveys,
we are convinced they are an excellent tool for identifying a person's
strengths and weaknesses for work. Over and over again clients veri-
fy the helpfulness and accuracy of the information. One client put it
this way: "There is no way you could have known this much about
me without having lived in my house." Spouses of those who take the
survey say such things as "I've been telling him (her) this for years
but he (she) wouldn't listen to me."

We think that a knowledge of the DISC concept can benefit you
in many ways for the rest of your life. (It's like adding another lure to
your tackle box.) We find that, as people gain a better understanding
of themselves, they also relate better to others at work and at home.
Those who learn about the DISC system of understanding personalities usually report an immediate improvement in their understanding
of their spouses, their children, employers, employees, and friends.

WHAT IS DISC?

DISC stands for four major behavioral tendencies. *Dominant*,
Influencing, *Steady*, and *Conscientious*. In reading through the definitions of D, I, S, and C below, you'll probably be able to relate to a
primary and secondary dimension of DISC. (For instance, my profile
is High D/High I.)

Dominant: People who have a high level of dominance (High
D) are naturally motivated to control their environments. They are
usually assertive, direct, and strong willed. They are typically bold
and not afraid to take strong action to get the desired results. They
function best in a challenging environment.

Influencing: People who are highly influencing (High I) are
driven naturally to relate to others. Usually they are verbal, friendly,
persuasive, and optimistic. They are typically enthusiastic motivators
and will seek out others to help them accomplish results. Tending to
be more emotional, they function best in a favorable environment.

System and Author	D	I	S	C
Career Pathways, Ellis:	Dominant	Influencing	Steady	Conscientious
DiSC Personal Profile System™ (©Carlson Learning Company), Geier:	Dominance	Influencing	Steadiness	Cautiousness
Personal DISCernment™ Inventory (©Team Resources Inc.), Mohler:	Dominance	Influence	Steadiness	Compliance
CARD Personality Style, Rickerson:	Dominant D ←	Relational R ←	Amiable A ←	Conscientious C (CARD)
Personal Styles, Merrill/Reid:	Driver	Expressive	Amiable	Analytical
Greek, Hippocrates, LaHaye/Littaur:	Choleric	Sanguine	Phlegmatic	Melancholy
Animal, Smalley/Trent:	Lion	Otter	Golden Retriever	Beaver

Steady: People who have a high level of steadiness (High S) are naturally motivated to cooperate with and support others. They are usually patient, consistent, and very dependable. Being pleasant and easygoing makes them excellent team players. They are especially productive when working in a supportive environment.

Conscientious: People who have a high level of conscientiousness (also called cautiousness) are focused on doing things right. Usually they are detailed oriented and find it easy to follow prescribed guidelines. Typically they strive for accuracy and quality and, therefore, set high standards for themselves and others. They function best in a structured environment.

OTHER NAMES FOR DISC FACTORS

As mentioned earlier, there are several versions of the four-dimension theory of personality, and most of them use different terminology for the four dimensions of DISC. Since you may be more familiar with some of these other surveys, on page 169 we have provided a chart relating them to DISC.

UNDERSTANDING A DISC GRAPH

Since we talk so much about the "Highs" and "Lows" of DISC, we should explain the reference for High and Low. Personality surveys typically use graphs, such as the following, to reflect the intensity level of a particular dimension. Keep in mind that even though most people talk about the highs, the lows are also important and have strengths and limitations as well. Most people will have high levels of two of these dimensions (a primary and a secondary) and low levels of the other two. Some people will have high levels of three, and a few people will have only one high dimension. The first graph shows the most common way of depicting DISC.

The second is another version of a DISC graph. It differs from the previous one in that it charts lows and highs from left to right instead of bottom to top. (If you rotate the page 90 degrees left, the graphs will have the same general shape.) The advantage of this format is that it treats highs and lows as equally important and makes it easier to comprehend the range of behaviors between the extremes.

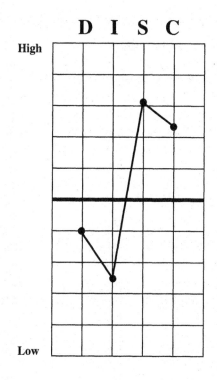

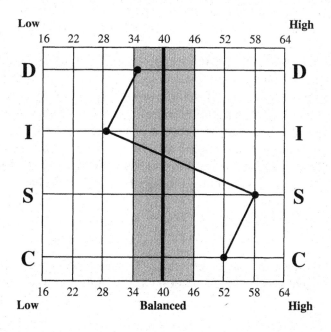

SOME CHARACTERISTICS OF THE DISC

If you are not already familiar with your particular profile, the list below of adjectives or traits will help you envision where you might fall on each dimension. Keep in mind that it is common to be balanced (neither high nor low but mid-range) in one or two of the four dimensions. A survey that indicates balance in all four, with no highs or lows, reflects a period of transition or stress and should be considered inconclusive. For more accurate results, the survey should be taken when the period of stress has passed.

DOMINANT	INFLUENCING	STEADY	CONSCIENTIOUS
High D	*High I*	*High S*	*High C*
assertive	cheerful	steady	accurate
independent	talkative	considerate	detailed
goal-driven	fun-loving	easygoing	disciplined
confident	high-spirited	patient	careful
pioneering	popular	loyal	reserved
Low D	*Low I*	*Low S*	*Low C*
peaceful	factual	spontaneous	independent
team player	serious	energetic	freethinking
humble	realistic	quick	adventurous
supportive	works alone	active	flexible
composed	earnest	impatient	intuitive

Each of these dimensions shares some commonalities with one of the others. For instance, people with High D or I tend to be extroverted (outwardly focused) in their thought patterns; those with High S or High C tend to be more introverted (inwardly focused).

The following graphic shows several areas in which *Dominant* and *Influencing* are similar; *Conscientious* and *Steady* personalities share many of the opposite traits. It may surprise you to see that D and C also have some common characteristics, as do I and S personalities.

THERE ARE NO GOOD OR BAD PROFILES

A point we will stress repeatedly: Certain profiles are better suited for some occupations than others. On the other hand, we could give

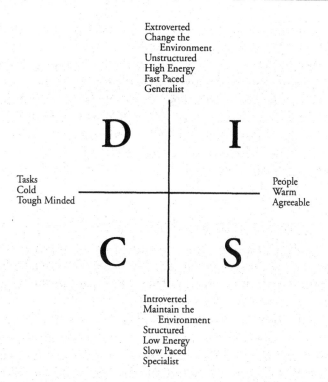

you many examples of individuals with totally different profiles succeeding in the same career field. Probably the most important point about the relationship of DISC and job success is that people succeed best when they use their motivated style.

From corporate executives to assembly-line workers, we've seen people succeed who were high in each of the four dimensions. They were successful because they found a way to do their work by using their natural strengths.

A *Conscientious* personality will manage a company quite differently than an *Influencing* personality, but both can be successful. Likewise, the *Influencing* person can be happy as an assembly-line worker if he or she is able to talk to others on the job and maybe do some sharing, counseling, or union organizing during the lunch breaks.

It also is true that people can stretch their behavior to meet the needs of the situation. Most of us can do anything for a while, but stretching requires energy. For example, requiring a High C to work in an unstructured, chaotic, and undisciplined environment, causes stress and, eventually, burnout. With the erosion of discipline in our schools, is it any wonder so many of our best teachers are bailing (burning) out of a profession they love?

We should also point out: With extensive training, indoctrination, and experience, people develop skills to offset their limitations. Consequently, managers who lack detail skills (accounting for instance) will learn the basics, then find someone they can trust in that area and delegate those duties. Likewise, managers who are not naturally sensitive to the needs of other people may depend on employees in the organization to keep them informed about the personal problems of workers.

FOUR LEADERS WITH FOUR DIFFERENT STYLES

During World War II some of our most famous generals had radically different personality styles; yet they were very successful. It is important to note how they gravitated to positions and work environments that used their major strengths.

General Eisenhower was a High I/High S. People with his profile are usually popular and can get along with almost anyone. The record shows that Eisenhower was one of the most popular cadets in his class at West Point. His popularity continued during his military career.

Ike was a logical choice to be commander in chief of the allied forces because that job required someone who could be *Influencing*, *Steady*, and political.

Ike's personality was ideal to lead a coalition warfare campaign requiring cooperation of strong-willed military and political leaders from several countries. In 1952 the Republican Party chose him as their presidential nominee. With his High I/High S personality, he seemed a pleasant and confident candidate, and it was easy for many Americans to wear an "I Like Ike" button.

General Patton, a High D, always had one goal in mind—to win military battles—and he didn't want anyone to get in his way. Patton was so blunt and outspoken about his ideas that General Eisenhower had to get him out of England so he wouldn't offend the politicians and the King. But Patton's *Dominant* style was perfect for leading the Third Army through Europe. His fearless, aggressive, and commanding leadership brought incredible military conquests.

General Bradley, a High C, was one of the most effective generals of his time. He was always diplomatic, polite, and disciplined.

His high integrity and sound thinking earned him great respect from his officers and soldiers. Bradley's squeaky clean, conscientious reputation also gave him a lot of influence with his superiors. It was Bradley who convinced Ike to give Patton another command after Patton had been in hot water with military and political leaders.

Back in Washington, General Marshall was perfectly matched to his job as chief of staff. His profile, High S/High C/Mid-line D, is probably the ideal profile for an administrator—*Steady*, *Conscientious*, with enough drive to be results-oriented. Marshall was an outstanding success in managing the people and resources to carry out a worldwide conflict. After the war Marshall continued to serve his country as secretary of state; he created and guided the Marshall Plan for the rebuilding of Germany.

As you can see, we had four senior generals who were very successful; yet they operated from completely different personality styles. During the course of their careers they learned to capitalize on their strengths and they found their niche. They also had leaders with the wisdom to put them in positions where their true talents could be used.

Patton would have been miserable in Washington as chief of staff (not enough action for him). And certainly he would not have been a good choice for General Eisenhower's job, in which a sensitivity to politics was so critical. Ideally suited as a field general, Patton needed someone over him that could control his impetuous nature. Marshall selected the disciplined, diplomatic, unassuming Omar Bradley to be his immediate superior—a very unlikely team. However, it worked because both Patton and Bradley chose to respect each other's complementary strengths and understand each other's weaknesses and limitations.[1]

Our research and experience shows that you can be very successful with any profile as long as you have the opportunity to use your strengths as a major part of your work. That should not be a surprise because our personalities are just part of our gifts from God; and we know He gave them to us for a purpose.

There is no good or bad profile. They all have strengths and they all have weaknesses. Be happy with the profile God has given you and develop it to the maximum.

GENERALIST OR SPECIALIST

We have acknowledged that people with various profiles can be successful at any level of the organization. On the other hand, we have observed that people with different profiles will operate differently and, therefore, will tend to be a better fit for some types of work than others.

We all have to carry out some generalist and some specialist duties, but most of us are "wired" to excel one way or the other.

In subsequent chapters, we'll cover these differences in more detail. Before concluding this overview on DISC, however, we would like to make a broad comparison to show some of the major differences between D/I profiles and S/C profiles. Experience shows that profiles primarily driven by D or I behaviors tend to be generalists, and those driven by S or C behaviors tend to be specialists.

Generalists are concerned with knowing the big picture and then influencing others to bring about the work that gets the results. They usually have a hard time following repetitive processes. They tend to be conceptual, wanting to understand the high points and envision how the project or concept will come together, but they don't want to get tied up in a lot of details. However, they are quick at picking out someone else's errors in details because they view them from a distance.

If you really want to lose generalists (High D or High I personalities), just start leading them through a thoroughly detailed explanation of something. You can watch their eyes glaze over and pretty soon you'll know they are no longer listening; they are trying to figure out how they can get control of the conversation and get it moving back to the big picture. Part of the problem is that they have a hard time listening (it's one of their key weaknesses), but it's also that their minds resist slowing down long enough to process details.

Generalists like pictures and resist reading instructions. They usually think that, if they can just figure out the basic idea, they'll figure out the details as they go along. (Give me a couple of landmarks and I'll find my way.) Sometimes they do; sometimes they don't.

Generalists tend to estimate rather than calculate, and they are frequently "close enough" to make good broad decisions. They sometimes become impatient with specialists, whom they think tend to over-calculate and over-analyze every detail before making a decision.

Specialists, on the other hand, are more concerned with going deep to find out the how and the why. Details and accuracy are important to them because they don't come to conclusions lightly. It's important for specialists to have the right answer and to know exactly why it's right. As the name would imply, specialists often provide the core of expertise in a specific area for their organization.

Specialists are patient and will move more slowly in order to get the depth of information they need. They are good at staying with one task or one idea for an extended period of time. They usually can sit still longer and can keep their attention focused on one area; thus they also are good listeners. Specialists are often annoyed with generalists who act as if they know the answers even though they can't tell you how or why they know.

It's true that we all have to carry out some generalist and some specialist duties, but most of us are "wired" to excel one way or the other. You can see that putting a generalist in a specialist career field, or vice versa, for an extended period of time could be stressful. This one concept could save many people from making bad career choices.

BE CAREFUL ABOUT LABELING

Larry and I have a tendency to speak in terms of High D or High C. Many churches also are using a variety of spiritual gift tests, temperament surveys, and type indicators that tend to generate labels for different groups. However, there's a real danger in "labeling" ourselves and others as being "this" type or "that" profile. In order to communicate ideas, we sometimes generalize and use terms as labels. Using terms to communicate general ideas is a good way to explain and teach, but "labeling" people as a "this" or "that" can have very harmful effects. It can deny the complexity of God's creation; it can deny the power of the Holy Spirit to work at His discretion; and it can unintentionally wound a spirit.

Larry is definitely a High D (*Dominant*) person, and he does have many of those characteristics. However, from that label you might miss the fact that he also is considerate, nurturing, cautious, and patient. Those characteristics are not natural to the High D; therefore, in Larry they are clear evidence of the Holy Spirit working in him. So when we use terms and labels, let's use them for a positive purpose, and don't let them restrict your faith in what God can do through a person.

It can be a great encouragement to know your pattern of talents, but you can't stop there.

We must use caution also not to use general characteristics associated with labels as excuses for our sinful habits. It's not okay to say "That's just the way I am because I'm a (this or that)." We are called to confess our shortcomings and allow the Holy Spirit to work in us to make us new creations in Christ. When the apostle Paul had his Damascus road experience, his assertive nature was not changed, but his motivation to serve Christ brought new direction and control to his strong personality.

HONOR GOD WITH YOUR PERSONALITY

As in every other area of our lives, we need to lay our personalities on the altar as sacrifices to be used in honoring the Lord. If you have been given five talents worth of High S skills, develop and invest them in your work. Likewise, develop the other dimensions so you can use them when the situation warrants. Then, identify the limitations of your profile and submit them to the work of the Holy Spirit.

In subsequent chapters, we will elaborate on the natural strengths and limitations of D, I, S, and C profiles. Study them and identify which ones apply to you. Then, make a commitment to allow the Holy Spirit to change you and bring these core elements of your being under His control.

Dr. Timothy LaHaye's *Spirit Controlled Temperament* is an excellent book that addresses this subject. Without the power of the Holy Spirit controlling your personality, you will be of little use to the Lord. It is through your personality that you demonstrate that Christ is alive in you. Will others see your motivated behavior as selfish (all four profiles can be selfish) or service? As you yield your rights and focus on service, you will be a powerful witness in the workplace.

RECAPPING THE FOUR PARTS OF YOUR PATTERN

By reflecting on the four parts of your pattern for work, you should have gained a good idea of the interests and strengths God has given you. Now it's time to put them together so you can see the whole pattern at once. If you were to fit them all together, they might look something like the following pattern.

It can be a great encouragement to know your pattern of talents, but you can't stop there. You have to put the information to use by relating it to work, and that can be work in itself. A career quest is never easy. Exploring occupations to find a good match will require you to do some broad brainstorming (generalist work) and some research (specialist work). It will require you to be aggressive and positive, yet patient, detailed, and cautious.

Since most of us have not mastered all of these traits, we highly recommend you recruit a partner or coach to assist you. Find someone who is different from you in personality. Your helper or coach should be an encourager and someone to

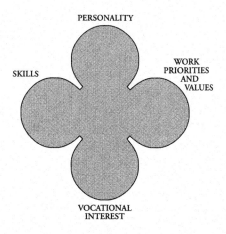

PERSONALITY

SKILLS

WORK PRIORITIES AND VALUES

VOCATIONAL INTEREST

bring accountability to your ideas and actions. The biggest problem we see in those who seek career counseling is a lack of follow-through. Most people want someone to test them and then recommend the perfect job for them. Rarely will that ever work out successfully. As we've already seen, each person is unique and complex and cannot be measured to that level of accuracy.

We believe you can gain some very important insights through an assessment. But ultimately you, the individual, must take responsibility for investigating potential occupations to see how they match with your pattern. Only you can put that "individual spin and personal touch" into the final choice of an occupation. Although you must make the decision, there's a lot of help available. Throughout this book we have tried to offer tips and resources to guide you through the process that will lead to a wise decision.

The next four chapters will give an in-depth explanation of the four dimensions of personality (DISC) and use a number of client examples to explain further how personality is a major determinant in finding a good occupational match.

CHAPTER THIRTEEN
The Dominant Personality

*T*his chapter and the next three will elaborate on some of the strengths and weaknesses associated with each of the four basic personality dimensions (DISC). Included are some real life examples that demonstrate the characteristics of each. Remember that broad, general terms are used, so don't expect every characteristic to fit every person with that profile. However, based on feedback from Career Pathways clients, these descriptions are significantly accurate.

Let's review what is meant by being *Dominant*. As you would suspect from the name of this dimension, those with a high level of dominance like to be in control of the situation. Also, you'll recall from the definitions in the previous chapter, these people are very results-oriented. When counseling High D clients, we view these two characteristics, control and results, as keys to finding work satisfaction.

High D personalities will have difficulty working in jobs where they are not allowed a lot of control over their work. They can work well for others as long as they are given broad responsibilities, a challenging mission, and minimum detailed instruction or supervision. Ultimately, finding a balance between autonomy and accountability will be the key to success for the High D profile.

As stated earlier, every profile has strengths and related limitations. A strength out of control can be a person's greatest weakness. Learn to recognize your strengths and then develop the potential God has invested in you. The following are some of the major strengths of the High D profile.

HIGH D PERSONALITY STRENGTHS

Independent: High D personalities make their own decisions rather than wait to see what the "popular" decision will be.

Results-oriented: Activity alone is not enough. They are interested in accomplishing goals, in getting things done.

Confident: They have little doubt about their abilities and believe they can make a difference.

Direct: People in this profile "tell it like it is" and move straight toward the critical path.

Problem solvers: When faced with a challenge, they will figure out a way to "fix it."

Entrepreneurial: High D personalities are not afraid of risks, like to initiate things, and have a strong ability to bounce back from rejection and failure.

Visionary: Good at long-range planning, they tend to be futuristic and big-picture-oriented.

Competitive: High Ds expect to win every competition; they hate to lose at anything they undertake.

Ambitious: Being very achievement-oriented, they have high goals.

Bold: Undaunted by opposition or criticism, they will move forward when others would hesitate.

With these strengths, you can see why Gary Smalley and John Trent call High Ds "the lions."[1] They often are the leaders or the king or queen of their domain.

MATCHING THE HIGH D WITH WORK

In general, High D people need the autonomy we've spoken of earlier. They won't find much job satisfaction when they are closely supervised. They especially need the opportunity to build, develop, create, initiate, control, drive, manage, supervise, lead, teach, or sell. Ultimately they want to be responsible for the results or outcome of the effort. They are not afraid to take risks and, when they fail, they usually bounce back quickly.

High D personalities tend to be visionaries.

In looking at the strengths of the High D profile, you'd think people in this group would be good in leadership and management positions, and this has been our experience. Entrepreneurs usually have many of the strengths listed above, as do truck drivers, surgeons, military leaders, religious leaders, administrators, builders, heavy equipment operators, salespeople, attorneys, reporters, and supervisors. As we've already indicated, people in this group tend to be broad generalists, as opposed to specialists. We've worked with some who started out as specialists (engineers, accountants, crafts people, secretaries), but once they mastered the challenge of their trade they were driven to have breadth and variety in their work.

High D personalities tend to be visionaries. They are good at conceptual thinking, and they have a natural ability to see the big picture. These gifts make them good long-range planners, and it probably accounts for their tendency to ignore immediate details.

In the long run, we think the High D's success at work will hinge on his or her ability to use these God-given strengths and still deal with the need for control (power). The High D needs accountability and, like everyone else, needs to answer to someone, whether it's a supervisor, manager, or board of directors.

With such strong personalities, High Ds are attracted to power and are the least likely to be challenged. As Lord Acton said, "Power corrupts and absolute power corrupts absolutely." No matter what the position, being under the control of the Holy Spirit and being accountable to other people or groups will protect High D personalities from the worst aspect of their sinful natures—the abuse of power.

HIGH D PERSONALITY LIMITATIONS

People in each of the profiles also have weaknesses. The list below gives some of the key problem areas.

Act first and think second: They need to think things through and seek advice before making decisions.

Insensitive to others (overbearing): They need more consideration for others' feelings. (Tending to be left brained, they don't like to acknowledge feelings.)

Underestimate amount of detail required: They need to be more realistic in their projections of time and effort required.

Don't like to maintain: Though they are good starters, they get bored with details. They need to finish current projects instead of constantly jumping to something new.

Poor listeners: They enjoy talking and forget that others have something important to say; should be more sensitive.

Impatient: They want results quickly and can be overly demanding; they need to remember people are human beings, not machines.

Remember this general rule for all four profiles: Strengths overdone become flaws and undermine effectiveness.

Being ambitious, bold, and competitive may be appropriate in some environments but, as in most other areas of life, too much of a good thing can be harmful. No matter what your profile, you'll want to monitor your strengths to be sure you're not using them to excess.

That may be about all the limitations the High D personalities reading this can handle, though probably our spouses could think of a few more. Thank the Lord for Judy (Burkett) and Mary (Ellis), whose love and patience have been used by the Holy Spirit to help us recognize and deal with these and other weaknesses in our lives.

HIGH D PROBLEMS AT WORK

By now it's likely you have thought of some of the problems High Ds have at work. The following are examples from clients and our own personal experiences. One lady who came to us had been fired from almost every job she'd ever had. Her jobs had been repetitious and closely supervised. One look at her DISC graph explained a lot of her problem; her D was so high it could hardly fit on the chart. When things didn't go the way she thought they should, she tried to take control through words or actions. Although she probably had some good ideas, she usually came on too strong and lost her job. Apparently her dominance was overused or out of control; her jobs gave her no control. She needed to modify her behavior some, but she also needed a different work environment.

Since both Larry and I have high levels of dominance, we can relate to many of the problems associated with this profile. You may have heard Larry say that High D people are "often wrong but never in doubt."

We also have found it common for people in this profile to enjoy driving or operating machinery (probably the control factor).

He relates the story of one of his early jobs as an electrician's helper. Larry boldly corrected his supervisor several times in front of the big boss. When the boss left, the supervisor fired Larry. That's one lesson Larry says he's never forgotten.

I have a similar story. I was disappointed by my commander's skimpy praise for the unit's "outstanding" inspection rating and the hard work by the troops that made it possible. When the boss finished his remarks, I stood up and proceeded to pass out the praise I felt the commander should have given. A few minutes later he had me on the carpet for a "don't you ever do that again" speech. He also reminded me I was the deputy commander and that he was the commander.

The moral of the story for all three of these examples: Even High D personalities must respect the authority of their superiors. Those in the High D profile would do well to remember that even though they are sure they're right, there's a time, a place, and a way to express opinions. And sometimes it's better just to withhold them.

As bold, visionary, problem solvers, these people are often quite creative and somewhat driven to initiate. They like to start new programs or launch new ideas. For that reason they usually don't make good accountants, or at least they don't stay in the actual accounting jobs very long. Accounting is really about accuracy and following prescribed procedures, not winging it with new ideas.

We remember one High D accountant who seemed to be in hot water constantly because of his "new ideas." Eventually he saw how he could combine his knowledge of finances and his initiative and put them to use as a financial planner. This occupation was a good match for his talents and he was very successful.

OTHER INSIGHTS ON HIGH D PERSONALITIES

We also have found it common for people in this profile to enjoy driving or operating machinery (probably the control factor). They learn to drive at an earlier age than their siblings and will want to drive tractors, trucks, race cars, airplanes, boats, motorcycles (especially), and anything else that moves.

If you play golf with a High D, you can expect that person will want to drive the cart. If you're going on a trip, the High D will want to do most of the driving. We're not sure what it says about this personality group, but we've noted these people often have a latent desire to drive a bulldozer.

High D personalities are high-energy people who usually rise early and tend to require less sleep than people in the other profiles. They are predisposed to be driven people, and when they are forced to slow down at work, they're likely to transfer that energy into their hobbies.

A business friend of ours is a good example. Jim's doctor told him he had to quit working so hard and recommended that he take up golf as a way to relax. Initially that turned out to be a mistake because golf is one of those ultimate challenges that attracts the competitive High D like steel to a magnet. After a few months, Jim was just as compulsive about his golf as he had been about his work. Finally, he saw what had happened and began to deal with his driven behaviors.

In some of the other personality surveys, the High D is also called a *choleric*—a term meaning easily angered—and that's one of the weaknesses of the profile. Some have conjectured that the source of much of the aggressive and tenacious nature of High D people comes from a deep-seated anger.[2]

Whatever the cause, the solution is for the High D to truly know the unconditional love and forgiveness of God and then begin to radiate those same attributes toward others.

High Ds can be very effective people, but they are greatly mistaken if they think they can "go it alone." There are no one-man teams, and without a supporting cast to balance their weaknesses, High Ds usually produce catastrophic failures that affect large numbers of people.

When counseling High D personalities, we encourage them to recruit an individual or develop a system to help cover their weaknesses. Usually that means someone who will patiently handle the details and stay with the task until the project is finished.

High Ds problem-solve by making gut reactions and moving ahead. They would be more effective if they would seek counsel from people who move cautiously and analyze every detail before making a decision (usually High Cs).

This is a hard match to make work effectively, because both personality profiles tend to get frustrated with the style of the other. (One wants to take action now; the other wants to think about it a while.) When these two can work together with respect for each other's strengths and weaknesses, it produces a great team and capitalizes on the principle of unity described by Paul in his references to the body in 1 Corinthians 12.

WHAT ABOUT LOW D PERSONALITIES?

Though much emphasis is given to the highs of each dimension, we do think it's important to discuss the lows also. What was a weakness for the highs will be a strength for the lows and vice versa. A look at the strengths and weaknesses of the Low D personality will illustrate that point.

Too often the Low D person avoids speaking out rather than run the risk of being rejected.

Low D profiles are not driven to be in control, and they tend to be good team players. Their motivation is to cooperate and to be more diplomatic than their High D counterparts. Shown below are some of the strengths of the Low D.

LOW D PERSONALITY STRENGTHS

Cooperative: They are motivated to work in harmony with the group or organization.

Gentle: These people are naturally motivated to be kind and considerate of others.

Mild: Because they are easygoing, it's easy for them to adjust to the needs of others.

Trusting: Low D people generally expect others to keep their commitments.

Patient: They are willing to wait on the results, especially if they think waiting will produce a better product.

MATCHING THE LOW D WITH WORK

As you would suspect from their strengths, people in the Low D profile are predisposed to be excellent team players. They also work well alone. Although they don't exactly fit the image of a dynamic leader, they can be very effective leaders in structured organizations where tasks and missions are clearly defined.

LOW D PERSONALITY LIMITATIONS

There are some typical problems that can affect them in their work. As we said earlier, by identifying weaknesses and using a combination of working around them and improving them, Low Ds can be more effective in the workplace.

Unassertive: They need to believe in their own ideas and communicate them more.

Too sensitive: People in this group need to develop thicker skins to deal with criticism and rejection.

Too timid: They need to develop confidence, believe in themselves, then step out in areas of expertise.

Take mistakes too personally: They need to realize that mistakes are part of the learning process; they should make them and move on.

Too dependent on others for direction: They need to trust their own plans and take action accordingly.

We have observed that too often the Low D person avoids speaking out rather than run the risk of being rejected. The end result is that the entire team misses out on an important input and the Low D's talents go unnoticed. With the increasing focus on empowering all workers to contribute to goals and methods of operation, everyone will be expected to initiate ideas.

We encourage the Low D personalities to accept some risks and practice expressing their ideas verbally and in writing. It might be helpful to find ways in the established structure to do this comfortably.

While it's true that the High D people are more likely to claw their way to the top—building empires, companies, and large bank-rolls—it is also true that those things have an absolute zero relevance one second after death.

Jesus was very clear about who will inherit the Kingdom of Heaven (the poor in spirit) and who will be blessed (the sensitive, those who mourn, the gentle, the merciful, and the peacemakers). High Ds need to realize they will never truly be in control. God is. And Low Ds need to be bold and confident because of who they are in Christ.

In reviewing all the characteristics of the *Dominant* dimension, balance is the key: the confidence of the High D to pioneer new fields and the humility of the Low D to have a servant's heart and be sensitive to others.

CHAPTER FOURTEEN
The Influencing Personality

*Y*ou will recall that the *Influencing* dimension reflects the motivation that a person has for relating to others. Those high in influence are typically friendly, enthusiastic, and outgoing. They are drawn to others and thrive on social contact. Influencers are probably the easiest to recognize of the four dimensions. They are so expressive that their smiles, hand movements, and generally bubbly personalities stand out in any crowd. The higher the I dimension, the closer people are to being true extroverts. Their "batteries are charged" by being around people. They can go to a party every night for a week and hardly slow down.

On the other hand, Low I personalities may enjoy and love people, but extensive social contact, especially with strangers, will drain their energy quickly. Some Low I people literally have to go to bed and rest for a day or two after they've had two successive nights of social events.

It's almost impossible to keep High I people from talking, so they need to be in jobs where they can relate to others. They are also "fun" people to be around. They find it natural to laugh and joke and, basically, just have a good time no matter what they are doing.

Once, while leading a team-building seminar, I noticed two people who were constantly giggling and joking while taking the DISC personality survey. After everyone had finished the survey, I covered the basic characteristics of DISC and then asked the group of about 30 people to identify the classic High I personalities in the crowd. Naturally everyone pointed to the two who had been having so much fun. And they were right. As we've already indicated, High I personalities usually are some of the most visible people in an organization, so their talents are not difficult to see. Let's take a look at their strengths.

HIGH I PERSONALITY STRENGTHS

Socially outgoing: They can talk with anyone, anywhere, at any time, about almost anything.

Enthusiastic: They get excited about what they're doing and their enthusiasm motivates others.

Optimistic: Very positive about the future, they expect good outcomes from situations and from people.

Inspiring: Using their passion for a cause and strong verbal abilities, these people can move an audience.

Cheerful and fun-loving: Their sense of humor can break up serious moments.

Persuasive: Using their verbal strengths, High I people can be very convincing.

Change oriented: They prefer flexibility and adapt easily to new situations.

Trusting: Able to see the best in others, they overlook weaknesses.

With these talents, this group is very effective at influencing all kinds of people, and they certainly help any organization by brightening up the environment with their cheerful dispositions. You can see why John Trent and Gary Smalley call this fun-loving group the "otters."[1]

MATCHING THE HIGH I WITH WORK

Think of High I personalities as natural promoters. They are especially good at exhorting others to their point of view; and they can do it endlessly. You will recall President Ronald Reagan was dubbed "the great communicator" because of his ability to verbally influence the entire country.

Those who observed presidential candidate Bill Clinton were amazed at his ability to talk and talk and keep on talking. He never seemed to be at a loss for words. Since his inauguration, he seems to have spent the majority of his time doing what he likes to do best—promote his programs.

High I people love to entertain, perform, and carry on similar activities where they are the center of attention.

Other prominent figures who demonstrate High I characteristics are John Madden, Goldie Hawn, Kathie Lee Gifford, Florence Littaur, and Chuck Swindoll.

People in this group frequently become politicians, preachers, salespeople, and teachers, because they enjoy inspiring others to see their point of view. Public relations is an ideal field for a High I, as well as any occupation at any level where there's a need to relate frequently with the public.

Other good matches for this group include managers, coaches, travel agents, waiters, and people working in medical services, customer relations, telemarketing, the chamber of commerce, and some areas of human resource management. With their enthusiasm and strong verbal skills, High I personalities make excellent corporate trainers and seminar leaders. Their desire for variety and adventure makes it easy for them to travel to different cities to make presentations.

High I people love to entertain, perform, and carry on similar activities where they are the center of attention. They generally are not intimidated by being up front; in fact, they enjoy "show time."

Dion Sanders, a national sports celebrity in two professional sports, reflects many of the extremes of the High I profile. Sanders has been appropriately nicknamed "Neon Dion" and "Prime Time," reflecting his ability to capture attention both on and off the field. He's definitely flashy and a big talker but, like most High I people, when the spotlight comes on, he's ready to perform. In 1992, he batted over .300 for the Atlanta Braves in the World Series. Then the next week, playing for the NFL Atlanta Falcons, he electrified the crowd with a long kick return for a touchdown.

People in this group enjoy recognition and the risk and drama that will put them at center stage. Their need for attention can be disruptive to the overall team effort unless they are controlled by the Holy Spirit.

Those who have High I personality traits are consummate networkers. They know people everywhere, and are not shy about namedropping. They remember and cultivate their contacts and don't hesitate to call on them when they need help. In fact, High I personalities are great at thinking of someone who can do the work.

A typical example of a High I involved in networking was the New Testament character Barnabas. He was the one who went to Tarsus and got Paul involved in doing the work needed to expand the early church. If you have a job opening or some work that needs to be done, just ask a High I. He or she will have plenty of suggestions as to who would be a good choice.

Before making a job choice, a High I needs to evaluate accurately the amount of personal interaction involved. If the job requires someone who has strong verbal and interpersonal skills, the High I likely will be a good fit. Also, the High I typically functions best in environments calling for a lot of physical energy, movement, and interaction.

HIGH I PERSONALITY LIMITATIONS

Because they are so outgoing and so up-front, this group probably gets told their weaknesses more than the others. For most of them, working on these shortcomings is an ongoing battle. Let's look at some of the problem areas.

Too talkative: They need to listen more, give others a chance to talk, and practice being quiet.

Too optimistic: They need to plan more realistically by expecting some things to go wrong.

Disorganized: People in this group need to write things down and take time for in-depth planning.

Inattention to details: High I personalities should pay more attention to the small things that add up to be "big deals."

Easily distracted: They need to keep focused on the project at hand until the job is finished.

Poor money managers: They need to be more realistic about income projections, be organized, and keep up with details.

As you can see, some of the limitations for each personality group come from not controlling natural strengths. The first step to being in control of your personality is to be aware. If you're not sure what your strengths and weaknesses are, find someone who knows you well and will provide objective feedback. You could start the discussion by using the lists of strengths and limitations included in these four chapters on the D,I,S, and C dimensions.

HIGH I PROBLEMS AT WORK

The most obvious problem for High I personalities is to be in jobs that don't use their ability to relate to people. This group is *going* to talk. In fact, they generally can't *not* talk, so if they are given a task of adding numbers all morning you can expect they will be out visiting in other offices or at the coffee bar or on the phone. High I people can have many vocational interests, derived from the environment in which they grew up but, ultimately, they will need to be primarily communicators. We've seen people in this profile become farmers, accountants, computer operators, and crafts people, but usually they don't stay with such confining occupations for very long. They may be motivated by some aspects of detailed and solitary work but, ultimately, they won't enjoy working alone for eight or ten hours a day.

High I personalities will find an outlet for their social needs one way or another. Farmers will get in their trucks and go to the feed store to visit with their buddies for a while. Accountants will be up and down the halls at work, counseling everyone with problems.

Success at work will be directly related to their ability to narrow their focus to a specific area of expertise.

Keep in mind that influencers tend to problem-solve by verbalizing their thoughts and feelings and they generally expect others to do likewise.

Environments that require long periods of focused, serious attention will be stressful. They can do that for short periods of time but, basically, they are change-oriented. On the other hand, to be effective everyone has to learn to focus to some degree. The High I brain seems not only to project high energy, but it also has a hard time keeping focused on one area. One client described it this way: "New thoughts and ideas just seem to sweep through my head." This is understandable because everything seems interesting, important, and exciting to High I personalities. Their antennas are constantly searching the environment for inputs, especially those that relate to people and exciting situations. Their thought patterns and involvements tend to spread so widely they have difficulty following through with the important tasks.

High I personalities would do well to learn to set their sights on the key issues of their work and pursue them relentlessly to completion. In fact we could say that, in the early part of their careers, *success at work will be directly related to their ability to narrow their focus to a specific area of expertise and then focus, focus, focus on the task at hand.*

With strong needs for recognition and approval, this group performs best in a friendly environment. A lack of attention can cause them to become discouraged at work. The same is true when an autocratic or hostile supervisor consistently or rudely restricts talking.

Also, their approval needs can make it hard for them to challenge others or say no. They function best when they can encourage and help rather than confront. (Remember the difficulty President Reagan had in firing people.) Interestingly, we've never seen a High I working as a customs agent or IRS auditor. Those jobs require objectivity and thick skin, which generally are Low I, not High I, characteristics. The following is an example of how a friend of ours used his knowledge of High I traits to get help when he really needed it.

Brad was on a business trip when he heard that a big snow storm was headed toward his hometown, Atlanta. It was Saturday and Brad had finished all his work so he was ready to go home, but he had a discounted ticket, which required him to stay over Saturday night. Normally he would have had to pay a penalty to adjust the ticket for an early return. Brad knew that requesting an early departure was not unreasonable, considering the weather approaching his destination; however, he wanted to minimize the risk of being turned down by a no-exception-to-the-rule ticket agent.

Brad and his friend who brought him to the airport were both well schooled in DISC, so they decided to use this knowledge to increase Brad's chances of getting on an earlier flight. They decided to look for a High I ticket agent. They stood back and studied the three people working the counter. After a couple of minutes, it was obvious that one of the agents was a High I. She had a smile for everyone and seemed happy to interact with each customer. The serious, stoic faces of the other two agents seemed to reveal they were probably Low Is and cautious High Cs who would not like deviating from the normal procedures. Brad timed the line so that he could approach the High I agent who, as expected, was very happy to approve the request. Brad got home Saturday afternoon, just ahead of the ice and snow, thanks to the adjusted schedule facilitated by a helpful, flexible High I.

The bottom line for High I personalities is to use your God-given social and verbal skills in your work. Look for occupations in which you can use your talents to entertain, influence, help, train, inform, and network with others. To be successful, you'll need to shore up some of the problem areas mentioned in the next section.

OTHER INSIGHTS ON HIGH I PERSONALITIES

High I people tend to be poor money managers and, more than other profiles, are likely to be unreliable about paying their bills. Their optimism can be a liability, especially when it is not offset with caution and attention to details. Assuming that "everything will work out" and "the money will come in" causes this personality type more than its share of financial difficulties.

"Cutting a wide swath" is an expression that probably was created especially for this group.

With maturity and learning experiences, they learn to put some reality (things don't usually work out as planned) into their thinking. As with the other dimensions, we encourage influencers to seek counsel from someone opposite from them—in this case, a High C.

Impressing others is a natural desire for most High I personalities, and this also can cause serious financial trouble. "Cutting a wide swath" is an expression that probably was created especially for this group. If it's the "in thing" and somewhat flashy, they want it. Being impulsive, they usually are easy marks for an enthusiastic sales pitch. Unfortunately, many of this group never stop to think about how they will pay for the things they "have to have."

Because of the very nature of Christian Financial Concepts, the issue of finances comes up a lot. Our banker friends share with us that many exhorting Christians are their worst customers when it comes to paying their bills. Sadly, this group includes many pastor friends we've known over the years.

Another way High I personalities get into trouble is by not keeping their commitments. This group has a need to be accepted and will find it hard to say no when someone asks them to do something. At the same time, they're often unrealistic about what they reasonably can get done. Pretty soon they are overcommitted, and since writing things down is not a strength, they are prone to forget what they've promised. Even when they do write things down, sometimes they forget to check their notes.

Being a secondary I personality, I can relate to some of these problems. I once agreed to speak to a church group on Friday evening. My talk was planned and prepared a week in advance, but I didn't check my schedule on the day of the event. At 6:45 that evening the pastor of the church called to ask if I was coming (I was already fifteen minutes late for the start of the dinner). I was just about to cut the grass but I assured the pastor I would be there in 20 minutes. Fortunately, the church was only 15 minutes away. Since then, my fear of missing an engagement has prompted me to check my schedule more frequently. I also make sure my commitments are on the schedules of my secretary and my wife Mary.

WHAT ABOUT LOW I PERSONALITIES?

We're not focusing quite as much on the low elements of each dimension, but there are some valuable insights to be gained by looking at these areas. Basically the opposite of High I personalities, they are quiet and mostly keep to themselves. Sober and thoughtful, Low I personalities tend to be on totally different frequencies from their flashy opposites. You can see from the following strengths that certain work environments are ideal for the Low I.

LOW I PERSONALITY STRENGTHS

Work well alone: They don't need constant interaction in order to enjoy their work.

Focused: Not easily distracted by the environment, they like to concentrate on the problem at hand.

Realistic: They are good at anticipating the unexpected and the problems that will arise.

Earnest and reliable: This group generally remembers what they say and the commitments they make.

Reserved: Usually they are thoughtful of others, don't try to dominate the conversation, but have very good dry humor.

Factual: They try to be accurate and rarely exaggerate.

Good listeners: Being interested in what others have to say, they listen carefully rather than reflecting on what to say next.

Good money managers: Their realistic and somewhat pessimistic outlook helps them monitor expenses.

The Low I profile obviously has many strengths. Matching these strengths with the work environment will be a key element to finding job satisfaction.

MATCHING THE LOW I WITH WORK

Being alone not only doesn't bother this group, many actually prefer it because they want to work without the interruption of others. Consequently, Low I people prefer to work with things, data, and ideas, rather than people. They like quiet environments where they can concentrate (focus) on their work.

Typical career fields include artistic areas, such as design, sculpture, architecture, and drafting. In business, fields such as accounting, underwriting, actuary, and operations research provide a good setting for them. Of course, the majority of occupations in the sciences, skilled crafts, and many in the engineering and technology areas call for Low I strengths.

Obviously everyone has some versatility and can adapt to the work environment to some degree, but we keep coming back to the basic premise: You function best when you work in environments that match your natural personality. An honest evaluation of yourself and of what is required in potential jobs is the best insurance against stress in the workplace. To make that objective evaluation, you'll need to know some of the Low I limitations.

LOW I PERSONALITY LIMITATIONS

Seem to be curt and unfriendly: They should smile more and find something interesting about others.

Shy: They need to open up and share more; they do have a lot to offer others.

Too pessimistic: People in this group need to develop positive attitudes to inspire themselves and others to overcome roadblocks.

Out of touch with what others are thinking, feeling, doing: Should be more perceptive and more sensitive.

Low I personalities are never going to behave like High I personalities and that's good; we need both. But they will enhance their performances by being aware of their weaknesses and working to improve them.

LOW I PROBLEMS AT WORK

At some point every job requires some socializing and this can be a problem for the Low I. They prefer to skip socials or come late and leave early, and this can make them stand out. Some supervisors don't understand and will even question the loyalty of the unsocial employee, especially if that supervisor has an *Influencing* personality.

We are all part of the body. We may be different, but we were designed by our Maker to be a part of the lives of others in our sphere of influence.

In many organizations, camaraderie is an important part of building a cohesive team. The trust that can be so important in critical situations is developed as teammates get to know each other. Yet there's often little time at work for small talk or getting to know the other employees.

Often it is during the social activities (which Low I people typically dread and avoid) that unit bonding begins to take place. Low I people would increase their potential for personal and career growth by becoming more transparent in their relationships with others. To a Low I, that sounds like being political, which they detest, but these relationships are important.

Those in this profile usually isolate themselves from support systems that could provide encouragement for and insight into how the job could be done better. We would all do well to remember the principle of unity: We are all part of the body. We may be different, but we were designed by our Maker to be a part of the lives of others in our sphere of influence.

Finally, the Low I would do well to remember the results of a study conducted by *Communications Briefings* newsletter, which discloses the number one characteristic employees want in their new hires: the ability to get along with others. That doesn't mean everyone needs to act like a High I, but it does require an ability to be sensitive to the needs of others. Low I personalities should drop their guard more and be open to others.

Before leaving this group, we should re-emphasize how Low I people need privacy and intimacy with those they know and trust. Also, they should not be made to feel guilty for needing time alone to recharge after events where they've had to be good social mixers.

We keep saying and will continue to say: Don't expect others to be like you. We must learn to accept differences in personalities as being by design.

CHAPTER FIFTEEN
The Steady Personality

*I*n this chapter we move to the *Steady* profile. This dimension reflects the ability to work patiently and thoroughly to complete a task. *Steady* personalities also like stability and harmony and are good at cooperating with others to get results.

As you look at the characteristics associated with the High S (and later High C in Chapter 16), you'll recall that these two personalities are identified as the specialist—mentioned in Chapter 12. In reviewing the High S strengths below, you'll see why these folks are the glue that hold an organization together. More often than not, they're the ones who actually accomplish much of the detailed work that gets done.

HIGH S PERSONALITY STRENGTHS

Patient: Having a realistic view of the time required for activities, they can stay on task until the job is complete.

Dependable: They usually remember their commitments and follow through with them.

Consistent: Because they enjoy routine, their day-to-day performance hardly varies; they aren't distracted with every new idea that comes up.

Good listeners: They are good at actively listening to others without interrupting to give their own ideas.

Cooperative: Generally agreeable and good at working with others, they will adapt to meet the needs of others.

Loyal: They keep faith in others and have strong commitments to their families and employers.

Sympathetic: Because they truly care about others, they have strong feelings and are easily moved.

Tolerant: High S people can work with almost anyone and don't have to have their way about things.

You can see why Gary Smalley and John Trent have labeled this steady, loyal, and consistent group the "golden retrievers."[1] As Christians, we note that this group naturally seems to reflect the fruit of the spirit that we read about in Galatians 5:22–23 (love, joy, peace, patience, kindness, goodness, faithfulness, gentleness, and self-control). We all would do well to adopt the strengths of the High S profile.

MATCHING THE HIGH S WITH WORK

As previously indicated, High S personalities are likely to feel more comfortable as specialists than generalists. This group is motivated to become thoroughly familiar with a subject, activity, or process, and then use that knowledge over and over.

Think of this group as being like a potter's wheel or a flywheel on an engine: They just keep turning, and their steady performance provides smoothness and consistency to any operation. Day in and day out they tend to keep on producing.

High S people are usually quite adaptable and can work well with people, things, ideas, or data. The key to a good occupational match for Steady people hinges on their particular occupational interests being matched with consistent, harmonious work environments. High S personalities do not do well where there is frequent change, turmoil, and conflict. High S profiles are especially well suited for counseling and similar helping occupations. Their empathy and strong listening skills give them high acceptance and creditability with clients. They also have the patience to maintain a helping relationship for an extended period of time.

Probably the most difficult work situation for the High S involves handling conflict.

You'll find High S people flourishing in occupations such as technology, science, medicine, accounting, underwriting, administration, clerical, art, counseling, teaching, production, crafts, and many other areas. People in this group are very versatile and can do well in any field that allows them to use the strengths (already described), while avoiding the following weaknesses.

HIGH S PERSONALITY LIMITATIONS

Compromise too much in order to avoid disagreement: They need to take a stand more often.

Non-assertive: High S people may need to speak up or take action. Good ideas may go to waste if not advanced.

Don't look for the big picture: They can get too focused in day-to-day details and miss potential breakthroughs.

Slow to accept change in procedures: This personality type needs to recognize when it's time to discard outdated methods.

Low pioneering skills: These people need to get excited, step out, and take more calculated risks.

Can be lazy: They often need to light a fire and get moving toward personal and professional goals.

High S Problems at Work

As previously stated, this group can work well in many occupational fields, as long as the environment has harmony and stability. Going back to the analysis of the potter's wheel, inertia makes it difficult for these *Steady* personalities to deviate from their established routines. Traveling jobs will be difficult for this group and particularly after they have a family. High S personalities generally prefer to work at the same building every day, family is especially important to them, and they want to be in their own homes when the sun goes down.

Early in our Life Career Pathways experience, a man in his 30s stopped in to talk about his work situation. He said he worked for a great company, had a great product and a great boss, but did not find satisfaction in his work. He was a traveling salesman, selling a top-rated product that had little competition and really sold itself. After a few minutes of conversation, we determined he was a High S profile and suggested he find a more stable position where he could be at home with his family every night and go to the same office every day. A few months later we received a note fro him saying he had followed our advice and now is experiencing the peace in his work that had been missing earlier.

Probably the most difficult work situation for the High S involves handling conflict. This conflict can come from dealing with unhappy customers, a nasty boss, or critical co-workers. High S people are naturally motivated by harmony, they are sensitive, and they take affronts very personally. When this profile is exposed day after day to conflict at work, you can expect them to have health problems.

The stress is evidenced in some through stomach and digestive problems, while others will experience pain in the lower back, shoulder, and neck areas. The basic problem is that the central nervous system is stressed out and the symptoms can appear in any number of areas.

We have observed a strong trend when comparing the High D and High I (which tend to be introverted) with the High S and High C profiles (which tend to be introverted). Whereas the extroverts tend to get angry and blame others, the introverts are prone to internalize conflict and often blame themselves.

People in the D and I profile seem to be healthier because they tend to express their feelings, but their relationships do suffer as they explode on others. It is Christ in us that brings these issues under control. He gives humility to the proud and confidence to the reserved.

Another area of conflict for the High S is frequent new situations requiring on-the-spot decisions. *Steady* personalities like to do things the way they've always been done: the tried and true. They need to process information and get used to the change—to see it as positive and beneficial rather than a threat.

Facing new problems every day is energizing for the High D and High I, but the High S and High C do not thrive in such turmoil. High S profiles would do well to place stability as a high priority in choosing their lines of work. They will be much happier operating the established rather than establishing a new operation.

OTHER INSIGHTS ON HIGH S PERSONALITIES

After having said so much about the High S avoiding conflict, we would like to share an interesting discovery which, on the surface, seems to contradict what we have just said.

High S personalities can become very aggressive when defending their homes and families or their turf.

Larry and I have had the opportunity to share biblical principles of finances and career planning with the Christian professional athlete group called Pro Athletes Outreach (PAO). These athletes have spent their lives in sports, and for the most part never even considered any other career. What makes them unique is that, on the average, they have to make a complete career change before they reach their late 20s. We knew if we could help this group we could help virtually anyone our career assessment materials. During one of their conferences we tested a number of the athletes with our Life Pathways assessment.

The unusual discovery we made was that many of the great linebackers in the NFL have a High S profile. In fact, the majority of the 16 linebackers we tested were High S personalities. At first this didn't correspond to our knowledge of the Steady dimension, but as we began to analyze what linebackers do, we developed a theory.

First of all, football is a complicated Same that takes years of practice to master. It requires tremendous dedication to run the same drills over and over, and doing something over and over is a strength of the High S profile. Linebackers usually are the leading tacklers and the backbone to any good defense. Their assignment is to follow the ball, yet the offense is always trying to fake them out. So the linebacker has to be patient as the play develops, in order not to commit too early and go for the wrong man.

Because of their key position, linebackers have to be the most dependable people on the team. Play after play, they have to be ready and totally focused on the action. They have to pay attention to all the details and they have to follow a step-by-step process in carrying out their assignment. Linebackers operate the established plan rather than free lance as things develop.

But we wondered how a High S can be so fierce, so aggressive? Then we remembered that High S personalities can become very aggressive when defending their homes and families or their turf. In the case of football, that's exactly what they are doing—protecting the turf on their side of the line of scrimmage. Of course they tend to be soft-spoken, pleasant, polite, and quite peaceful when they are out of uniform.

In counseling these athletes for their next career, we tried to steer them toward occupations that would capitalize on their consistency and dependability and still fit within their vocational interests.

Two years ago we began giving the DISC survey at CFC's Teacher Counselor Training workshops (TCTs). As we suspected, the majority of those taking the training were High S profiles. We were pleased with this because it takes a lot of consistency and patience to stay with a client in budget counseling.

The patience factor is of prime importance when considering High S people at work. They need work that allows them to exercise their natural drive to maintain a steady, patient rate of work. The

High S group is also better than any other profile at being able to sit still. They generally excel in environments which require a lot of sitting, such as computers, accounting, or drafting.

Unlike the High D and High I people, who possess high energy and operate well on limited sleep, High S and High C profiles seem to need more sleep in order to function at full speed. Our theory is that there may be a difference in the brain that causes the D and I profiles to operate at a near-manic pace, giving them what we typically think of as "type A" or "driven" personalities. They are energized by change and challenge. The S and C seem to operate at a slower pace and seem to be more likely to be "type B" or "laid back" personalities.

WHAT ABOUT LOW S PERSONALITIES?

This group is active, and when mixed with High D or I they approach hyperactivity. Low S people need movement, a fast pace, and lots of variety and change. Let's look at some of their strengths.

LOW S PERSONALITY STRENGTHS

Action-oriented: More doers than thinkers, if nothing is happening, they will start something.

Energetic: They enjoy physical activity and will move around a lot in their work and have a lot of endurance.

Spontaneous: Always ready to respond, they don't need a lot of plans in order to take action.

Change-oriented: Because they like to do things differently, they have a hard time doing things the same way twice.

Flexible: Low S people adapt easily to new conditions and are not upset by last minute or frequent changes.

Fast-paced: They like to live and work in an atmosphere of excitement and challenge.

If you will think of a bundle of energy in motion, you'll have a good picture of the Low S profile. The real challenge for this group is to find a work environment that will allow them the activity and diversity they need.

MATCHING THE LOW S WITH WORK

Ideally this group would like to be in action continuously and facing something new all the time. Obviously there aren't many jobs that will allow that amount of activity and diversity so, as with all the other profiles, some compromise will be required. The success of the Low S at work will depend on getting as close a match as possible and then working to develop some High S behaviors.

Since we are both Low S personalities, we understand very well the struggles and the triumphs of this profile. We both like to write, but it's stressful for us to sit still and type on the computer. Sitting still and staying focused on one area is a discipline that we have learned in order to be effective in what we feel called to do.

> *Usually they are good travelers because they can adjust to new situations easily and can recuperate quickly from being out of their normal routine.*

Larry uses the term "compartmentalizing" as a way to describe the mind-set we use to block out distractions. By shutting off everything—phone calls, radio, visitors—for blocks of time, we're able to adopt High S characteristics and stay with a writing project long enough to get something done.

Low S personalities can delay their need for action through disciplined commitment to a goal, but it does cause stress. Ultimately they need something they really enjoy, such as physical activity, to unwind and recharge. Typically, Larry relaxes by walking and restoring old cars; I play basketball and do yard work.

As you can see from their strengths, Low S people need diversity, variety, and action in their work. They can work with almost any product or setting as long as they have an environment that will capitalize on their need to be active. Low S profiles can be dynamic speakers, teachers, and salespeople. Participating in business and other enterprising activities also seems to suit the Low S quite well. Usually they are good travelers because they can adjust to new situations easily and can recuperate quickly from being out of their normal routine.

Low S people do not operate by routines naturally and, to a large extent, their successes will depend on developing good habit patterns and regular schedules. As in all the other profiles, if Low S people can have a work environment that uses their strengths and, at the same time, modify their behaviors to control weaknesses, they have the potential to be very effective.

LOW S PERSONALITY LIMITATIONS

It's interesting that many of the Low S weaknesses are similar to High D and High I weaknesses. This probably relates to a shared high energy level and a need for action. Let's look at the struggles of the Low S personalities.

Can't be still: They need to slow down, concentrate more on the issues at hand, and learn to rest more.

Do not complete assignments: They need to stay with a project until it's finished before starting new ones.

Can be unreliable: Low S people need to develop routine procedures and written schedules to protect from oversights and over-commitment.

Too impatient: They need to slow down and develop realistic appraisals of time required for activities.

Easily distracted: Low S people need to keep focused on key events and details and separate the important from the urgent.

LOW S PROBLEMS AT WORK

The biggest problem Low S personalities face is being put into a job where they're required to sit for long periods of time and do repetitive work. They really need variety and activity. On the other hand, everyone has to stay put long enough to finish their work. Low S people need to learn to stick it out to see projects completed.

Low S people have a tendency to get involved in too many activities. At times, they pause to look at themselves and are reminded of a juggler trying to keep several balls in the air. It's fun and exciting, but occasionally it catches up with them and they realize there's a limit for everyone.

When working with their opposites, Low S profiles need to remember how stressful their style is for someone who likes to plan things out and prepare in advance. Accordingly, these whirling dervishes will do well to show a little consideration for those who move at a slower, more thoughtful pace.

After reading this chapter, many of you who are married will relate very well to the differences between High and Low S profiles. If you are opposites, as my wife and I are, you probably have a new understanding of your mate.

Since learning about DISC, I now understand why Mary enjoys movies and low-energy leisure activities. I'm learning to slow down and enjoy some of the things she likes to do. At the same time, she's started an exercise program, and we often walk together. We haven't changed our personalities, but we have accepted our differences and modified our lifestyles some so we can be together more. After all, opposites do attract.

CHAPTER SIXTEEN
The Conscientious Personality

*Y*ou may be familiar with this dimension as either Conscientious, Cautious, or Compliant. Originally the name was Compliant but, in today's environment, assertiveness is the "in thing," and compliance has become a politically incorrect term.

Actually the use of the term Compliant didn't mean to be subservient; it's what would be considered a good characteristic: the desire to comply with high standards.

The term Cautious is still in use, but it also has met with some resistance because many overly cautious people are trying to be more assertive. Perhaps *Conscientious* is the best term to describe the High C profile, because these people definitely strive to fulfill both the intent and the letter of that characteristic. The *Conscientious* dimension reflects the drive to be accurate and to achieve a high standard of quality in everything that is undertaken.

HIGH C PERSONALITY STRENGTHS

As you review the strengths of the High C profile, try to identify which strengths apply to you and which ones you would like to adopt. You will see that every organization (and even every individual) needs some degree of these characteristics.

Structure, procedures, and regulations give the High C standards with which to comply.

Accurate: Because they take pride in doing quality work, High Cs put a lot of emphasis on always being correct.

Focused: While concentrating on what they are doing, they stay on one project until it is completed and seek depth rather than breadth.

Organized: They like structure, discipline, and rules. "A place for everything and everything in its place."

Thorough: High C personalities leave no stone unturned in order to be sure every step is done properly.

Disciplined: They are controlled in their actions, follow the rules, and expect others to do likewise.

Analytical: By thinking things through carefully, they can mentally dissect issues and examine each element.

Cautious: Since they don't like taking risks, High Cs consider the consequences carefully before they make decisions.

Detailed: High C people pay attention to the small things and naturally see details that others miss.

Smalley and Trent call this group the "beavers" because of their neat and organized manner.[1] You may have recognized many of these characteristics in yourself or someone close to you. There's a High C person in almost every work team or marriage.

With all these characteristics, you'd think High Cs would do well at work. And, like all the other profiles, they do, as long as their strengths are used extensively in the work environment.

MATCHING THE HIGH C WITH WORK

High C personalities need structure in their work. In many ways they are similar to the High S in needing stability instead of "spontaneous" happenings every day. Structure, procedures, and regulations give the High C standards with which to comply. Whereas the Low C and High D would rebel and challenge the confinement of such a prescribed environment, the High C person feels insecure without it.

There's a saying in the military, "Good soldiers keep square corners square." The High C needs corners to keep square, "i"s to dot, and "t"s to cross. Working in a loose, unstructured environment, where people are cutting corners and "doing their thing," will cause unhealthy stress for the conscientious person.

The best job environments capitalize on the High C's attention to detail, thoroughness, and accuracy. Several areas where the High C profile matches well are accounting and finance, income tax, some legal areas, and most sciences. This profile seems to be a natural match for many areas of engineering, math, medicine, and technology. In our testing we also find that many High C people have a strong desire to work with their hands and probably are some of the most creative people in our society.

High Cs frequently have a genuine gift for teaching subjects dealing with absolutes, such as math and science. They like knowledge, and they enjoy doing the research to develop strong lesson plans.

Traditionally, many of our elementary and secondary teachers were High C people. But based on the evidence we see, large numbers of these excellent teachers are leaving the field because they are so stressed out by the school environment.

With the breakdown of discipline in the home, many classrooms have become a jungle where kids do whatever they please. In order to enforce good order and discipline, the teacher has to come across as a High D "Attila the Hun." Making such an extensive behavioral stretch requires tremendous energy and, eventually, it exhausts the High C teacher. Many take early retirement or transition to another profession.

Our counsel to High C personalities who are motivated to teach is to consider a vocational school or community college setting, where discipline is not such a problem. Perhaps at some point our society will realize the anarchy we have created and restore authority and respect for our institutions in general and for adults and teachers specifically. Until then, High Cs (who are low in dominance) are going to have a difficult life with youth in classrooms.

High C personalities should fit well in nearly any occupation that provides structure and requires a high concentration of the strengths listed above. As we've alluded to already, everyone has the ability to stretch to some of the needs in the work environment. For the sake of your health, if you are having to make a stretch, be sure that the stretch is not too encompassing and does not continue for long.

HIGH C PERSONALITY LIMITATIONS

Just as in the other profiles, High C weaknesses come primarily from overdoing what is potentially a good trait. As you can see, most High C weaknesses revolve around being too concerned about getting things right. Let's take a look at the negative aspects of being conscientious.

Too much a perfectionist: They set standards too high for practicality; need to develop more realistic expectations for self and others.

Too cautious: High Cs worry too much about making mistakes, especially in areas that aren't major; they need to expect some failures as part of the learning process.

Too slow: They need to realize there's not enough time to do everything perfectly and remember that some things only need a cursory effort.

Pessimistic: Even if things rarely turn out as planned, that's okay; adversity is often an opportunity—not the end of the world.

Too critical of self and others: They need to remember that perfection is not needed or even possible in many areas.

Too sensitive: High Cs should not take every transgression so seriously and should forgive, forget, and rest in God's love.

THE HIGH C OFTEN WAITS FOR THE PERFECT JOB

This group seems to have the most difficulty in making career choices. Over 60 percent of our clients have a High C as part of their profile, and a big part of the problem is their desire to find the perfect work situation. Some of them tell us they will not make a move until they are 100 percent sure they know exactly what God wants them to do. Sometimes that can be only an excuse to avoid risks, because even when they can see what to do they may hesitate. The Hebrew leader, Moses, serves as a good example.

High Cs should be aware of their need to validate information.

You may recall that Moses had some very clear guidance from God as to what His will was for Moses' career. He was to boldly step out and confront Pharaoh; yet Moses had all sorts of reasons why he wasn't the perfect match for the job. Moses didn't follow through exactly as God had planned, yet He still used him and blessed him.

Few people ever get as clear an insight regarding their career direction as Moses received from God. Searching for God's will can be frustrating unless it's taken in a broad context.

The High C profile has a hard time stepping out into risks or uncertainty and tends to become tied up in what we call "paralysis by analysis." High Cs should be aware of their need to validate information. It can be a big help to High Cs to have someone listen to their ideas and give them encouragement (or permission) to make a decision.

Usually, our advice to the High C is to seek God's will, develop a plan, work the process, and then "step out," "get moving," "wade in," or "double your rate of failure." These exhortations to action are necessary; otherwise the High C will plan, study, plan some more, then study some more, and never take action to secure a job.

I've heard it said that it's much easier for God to direct a person already in motion than to get someone moving who is sitting still.

HIGH C PROBLEMS AT WORK

As with all the other dimensions, the biggest problems for High C personalities come in jobs that require them to use strengths that are not natural. It's not natural for them to be flexible, to have to perform without detailed preparation, or to have to hit the high spots and move on. Whenever the focus is changing rapidly, they will feel uncomfortable because they are naturally motivated for in-depth work, not shallow.

High Cs generally do not operate well in unstructured environments. A lack of structure will be very stressful for this group because they need to know what to expect every day. They don't respond very well to surprises or last minute changes in plans. If there's not a procedure or established plan of action, they will delay action while planning and wait for just the right moment. Probably one of the biggest complaints we hear from High Cs regarding their work is that they are pressured to work too fast. In today's production-oriented environment, everyone seems to want more work done, and that means employees must work faster. High Cs are concerned with depth and quality. They need time to be sure the work is done to high standards. Taking on jobs that don't allow time to work to this level of quality causes real problems for High C personalities.

Several High C accountants have asked us what they should do when they are pressured by their firm to increase their production (billing) rate. Our answer has several angles. First, to see if you might be able to speed up, ask people who work faster than you to show you their techniques.

Second, take a look at your work patterns. Perhaps you are being too cautious about checking and rechecking your work. Next, you should ask your employer for suggestions or ask if he or she can give you assignments requiring more accuracy and less speed. It's likely that both sides bear some of the blame and both can adjust some to make it work out.

Finally, you may have to find another organization that can live with your pace.

High Cs also have problems working in environments where they have to "wing it" (to act or perform without preparation or guidelines) as part of their work. Their natural drive is to be thorough and to plan all the details, so they don't adjust easily to spontaneous demands. This group wants plenty of time to plan and rehearse before they have to perform.

> *Naturally driven to avoid risks, High Cs who grow up in a threatening environment become overly focused on achieving perfection in order to avoid criticism, threats, or abuse.*

High C personalities tend to think more like specialists than generalists. If you ask a question, you can expect them to be hesitant to respond until they can think it through. They would prefer to calculate or study the issue in depth before offering an opinion. Being pushed for quick answers annoys them, yet their hesitation can provoke their High D or High I peers. As stated before, Larry says High D personalities are "often wrong, never in doubt." We could say High Cs are "often in doubt, but usually accurate." With these traits, High C people generally function best as detailed experts in their fields.

There probably was a time in society when the expert, the creative person, and the high quality "detailist" reigned supreme in the work environment. Unfortunately, modern management has lost a lot of its attention to detail and pushed workers to produce more while sacrificing quality. Our products and economy have been learning the hard way that things of lasting value usually require a commitment to excellence and a determination to do the little things right.

Too often the "successful" image has been portrayed as someone who can shake things up and produce a quick profit (High D) or someone who can sell any idea that pops up (High I). We now are beginning to rediscover a biblical principle that, over the long run, profits will depend on being able to produce a quality product, and quality products require time, effort, and attention to details.

Many of the qualities that motivate the High C profile are now emerging as the way of the future in management. Of course the qualities of all profiles are necessary to make any team successful, but it is exciting to see the terms "quality" and "excellence" back in vogue again. The talents of High C personalities are needed badly.

OTHER INSIGHTS ON HIGH C PROFILES

Since the majority of our clients have a High C in their profile, we have had the most experience with this group. We are not sure why such a high percentage are having problems finding the right occupation. It may be due primarily to the drive to find the perfect situation, as discussed earlier. If one has unrealistic expectations, he or she will always be searching for the perfect job. But it appears that perfectionism is really just a symptom of a deeper problem. Our personalities are determined primarily by inborn traits. Scripture tells us of twins wrestling in the womb. And most mothers will attest to the fact that their children displayed different personality traits from birth.

Yet, environment also has a large impact on how the basic personality design is ultimately shaped. Based on the feedback we get from High C clients and our own experiences in counseling with those of this profile, we find that these people carry a lot of scars from their environment. They seem to be more sensitive and introspective than the other profiles.

Naturally driven to avoid risks, High Cs who grow up in a threatening environment become overly focused on achieving perfection in order to avoid criticism, threats, or abuse. The same environment that would turn High D people into ego maniacs or send High I personalities into uncontrollable outbursts of emotion would drive High

Cs to perfectionism, self-doubt, and the inability to trust their own decisions.

The other profiles, especially D and I, typically mask their insecurities with bravado and big talk and are able to present themselves as being "in control," and "all together." They really do have scars, but their lives have been affected in different ways. High C and High S personalities' reactions to the stresses of childhood and life are generally internalized, thus affecting their outlook. These internalized feelings can cause moodiness, generate a lot of negativism, destroy their joy, and make it difficult for them to employ successfully the talents God has given them. This is likely the reason many temperament surveys call this dimension Melancholy.

Often High Cs will appear to agree by holding back their opinions; yet, later, they passively resist the decision and its proponents. A High C's passive aggressiveness can be just as undermining as a High D's blunt antagonism.

Our goal is not to single out the High C personalities, but the fact that we see them in such high numbers burdens our hearts for this group. We would like to help, and the best way we know is, first of all, to make this group aware of the common problems they share. Next, we encourage High Cs to continually give themselves permission not to be perfect when the situation doesn't demand it.

Also we would like to point out that many who suffer from perfectionism tendencies have received a great deal of help through Christian counseling and through reading Christian books on the subject.

Ultimately, the needed help comes when we realize that our adequacy is in Christ; we don't have to be perfect. As the Holy Spirit works in us, we are conformed to the image of Christ.

WHAT ABOUT LOW C PERSONALITIES?

Low C personalities are characterized by a natural tendency to avoid structure and rules. Basically they like to "wing it." Let's look at some of the strengths of the Low C profile.

LOW C PERSONALITY STRENGTHS

Independent: Low Cs can operate without a lot of guidance and are confident in stepping out into new areas.

Big-picture-oriented: They "see the forest" clearly because they don't pay much attention to little details like trees.

Unconventional: Rather than rely on established methods, they come up with new ways to solve problems.

Initiating; They don't wait to be told what to do; they implement their own ideas.

Generalist: They have broad knowledge and good conceptual understanding, prefer principles over specifics.

Confident: Low Cs are comfortable taking action or speaking without a lot of preparation.

Open-minded: Being flexible, they are willing to consider others' ideas.

Forgiving: Rather than hanging onto bad feelings, they tend to forget the bad and move on.

MATCHING THE LOW C WITH WORK

The best environment for this profile is one that capitalizes on their freewheeling, big-picture nature. Many of their strengths are well suited for sales and management. Obviously they need a lot of independence and room in which to operate.

---

*Working in a field
that does not match your
personality is usually
a ticket to burnout.*

Probably the most important thing to keep in mind is that Low C people are generalists, not specialists. They can have a special area of expertise and often will, but given an opportunity they will naturally try to use their expertise in a general way.

For example, engineers who happen to be Low C personalities (and there probably aren't many) will be happier as managers, developers, or salespeople in the engineering field, rather than functioning in the hands-on, detail-oriented engineering jobs.

Since they aren't naturally motivated for detail work, this group really needs work that does not require an in-depth focus. They also are not naturally organized and can function reasonably well in what would be considered absolute chaos by many of their High C counterparts. In fact, Low Cs can be quite comfortable in a sloppy or messy environment. And like Low S personalities, they can adjust quite easily to frequent changes in the work environment. Low C people, like High D and High I people, work well where there is variety and adventure. Much like the Low S profile, they don't enjoy doing the same thing over and over again and will unconsciously seek ways to vary the routine. Their willingness to take risks gives them good pioneering skills—similar to the High D profile. Low Cs need to be in jobs that will allow them to use their natural initiative and desire to take independent action.

LOW C PERSONALITY LIMITATIONS

Disorganized: Not being naturally structured, they need to put things in their proper places and develop habits and systems for repeated activities.

Unfocused: They are easily distracted and need to finish current projects before starting others.

Unscheduled: Low Cs need to develop a written schedule and then follow it to be sure commitments are kept.

Overlook key details: Before deciding or acting, they need to slow down and take an in-depth look at all the factors.

Reckless: These personalities need to carefully weigh the risks versus the rewards and seek counsel from someone more cautious.

Too independent, rebellious: They should remember that rules and accountability protect them from overstepping their bounds.

LOW C PROBLEMS AT WORK

From their weaknesses, it follows naturally that this group has trouble remembering their commitments and completing their assignments. They can get so strung out they loose track of what is due next. With their high level of independence, Low Cs tend to interpret the rules to suit their plans and go their own merry way. They don't need a lot of supervision, but they do need someone who is strong enough to confront them with accountability.

PUTTING PERSONALITY IN PERSPECTIVE

This concludes the discussion of the four personality dimensions (DISC). As you can see, understanding your levels in each of these four dimensions can be critical to success at work, as well as in the success of all your relationships.

No doubt there are some who would downplay the impact of personality by saying, "I can do anything." To that we would say, "You probably can—for a while—until the stress starts to have physical and mental consequences." Working in a field that does not match your personality is usually a ticket to burnout.

The purpose of using our strength in work should not be to exalt ourselves (results) but to exalt Christ (process).

We never would have started Life Pathways if there hadn't been a need to help so many who are miserable in their work. When we began, our intent was to focus on the youth. But immediately it became clear that parents wanted help for themselves first.

Thus far, 65 percent (4500) of our assessment clients have been adults. Most of them say they gave little thought to their talents when they started work. They assumed they could do anything, but as time passed they became miserable and burned out from not using the talents God had given them.

We have spent so much time on personality because it is the most important area of your talents; yet, traditionally, it has been the most overlooked factor in career planning. We hope this discussion of the four dimensions of DISC will help you consider this important area.

Let us reiterate one caution. There are no bad profiles; they all have their strengths and weaknesses. The critical issue is understanding how God has "wired you up" and applying that knowledge to career choices.

When you are making career decisions, look for work that requires the minimum development of your weak areas. Or, put another way, go with your strengths. You'll be enthusiastic and capable operating from your natural strengths, but you could spend a lifetime trying to develop your limitations and never reach even average abilities. Great athletes have natural (God-given) athletic ability; great pianists have natural musical talent. The title of a recent career book sums it up quite well: *Soar With Your Strengths.* We couldn't agree more.

As a footnote to this discussion on using strengths, let me respond to a question we get occasionally regarding Paul's comments in 2 Corinthians 12:9: *"My grace is sufficient for you, for power is perfected in weakness."*

The weakness that we must acknowledge every day is that we are not sufficient within ourselves. Apart from our Lord, we can do nothing of value. The greater our realization of this (weakness), the greater this power can be evidenced in our lives.

The issue being addressed here is: What do we use our talents for? Paul's thorn in the flesh (weakness) kept him from exalting himself. The purpose of using our strengths in work should not be to exalt ourselves (results) but to exalt Christ (process).

If you look at the lives of Peter and Paul, they both used their God-given abilities to serve the Kingdom, so they had no conflict in using their strengths at work.

OTHER RESOURCES ON THE DISC SYSTEM

We haven't covered everything relating to personality. For example, we haven't discussed the effect of a person being a blend of two conflicting motivations, such as High D and High C or High I and High C. But it isn't the purpose of this book to go into that much depth. Our goal is to make you aware of the importance personality plays in occupational choice, with the hope that you will consider at least the basics before making your vocational choices.

We encourage you to become more knowledgeable about the DISC personality theory. These concepts can be a big help in understanding your relationships with others, such as your spouse, children, and parents. In the Appendix you'll find a list of books that provide extensive information on the DISC system of personality.

SECTION FOUR
Preparing for Work and Finding a Job

CHAPTER SEVENTEEN
Preparing Through Education and Training

*I*n Section One we explained the need to prepare for the workplace of the future. An educated and trained work force will be essential if Americans want to develop and maintain a viable economy.

From an individual perspective, preparation will be key to your employability. Sound decisions regarding your initial education and training will be important, but you actually need to continue learning throughout your lifetime.

In writing this book we assume that most of you are adults who are either in a career transition or think you might be in one soon. We've tried to focus the discussion on education so that it will apply to you. However, the information in this chapter is intended to get both youth and adults thinking about educational and training opportunities.

STUDY TO SHOW THYSELF APPROVED

Education and training are very important for individual progress and also for the future of society. More importantly, one of the consistent messages of the Bible is that Christians are to be diligent, skilled, and faithful in developing their talents.

Education and training are two of the primary ways we become good stewards of our talents. This type of preparation also equips us to be excellent in our work and examples to others. Scripture has many exhortations regarding the need to be diligent in preparing for and carrying out our work.

"He who tills his land will have plenty of bread, but he who pursues vain things lacks sense" (Proverbs 12:11).

"Do you see a man skilled in his work? He will stand before kings; he will not stand before obscure men" (Proverbs 22:29).

"Let your light shine before men in such a way that they may see your good works, and glorify your Father who is in heaven" (Matthew 5:16). Concurrently, many Scriptures caution against being slothful with time and wasteful with talents.

"The soul of the sluggard craves and gets nothing, but the soul of the diligent is made fat" (Proverbs 13:4).

"If you are slack in the day of distress, your strength is limited" (Proverbs 24:10).

For the adults reading this book (we assume that's about 95 percent of you), further education and training may not seem like an option, or at least not one of your interests. Even if you don't have a need to take formal courses, we want to encourage you to develop a thirst for knowledge and a keen interest in developing your God-given talents. Obviously, everyone won't have the same interest in learning, but expanding your knowledge daily should be the goal for those who want to develop and use their talents in the workplace. Many of the career- and work-related articles now being published strongly make the point that unless people continue to develop their skills, they're likely to find themselves left out of the workplace.

In *The 100 Best Jobs for the 1990s & Beyond*, Carol Kleiman, business columnist for the *Chicago Tribune*, even goes so far as to say: "By the year 2000 three out of every four workers currently employed will need retraining for the new jobs of the next century."[1] The changing workplace and the competition for good jobs indicate that she has a good point.

There's a high probability that your job may change due to changes in technology, and you may need new knowledge and skills. Perhaps an equal likelihood is that your job may be eliminated and you'll have to find a new one. In either case, employers are going to be looking for those who have the education and training to fill not only their immediate needs but who can continue to grow as the workplace changes.

EDUCATION, TRAINING, OR BOTH

Educators sometimes get upset when education is referred to as training. There probably is a subtle difference in the two, but there is also a lot of overlap. For purposes of discussion, we like to think of education as referring to the learning of general knowledge that enhances a person's ability to think, to solve problems, and to make decisions. Education usually has broad applications. For instance, when students learn about the Roman Empire, or memorize a poem, or learn Newton's laws of motion, they never know when, if, or how that knowledge will affect a future decision. However, an understanding of history, literature, and science does enhance our overall thinking processes. You can see that many areas of knowledge have such broad application that they can't be limited to a specific skill.

On the other hand, many things taught in educational institutions are clearly oriented toward training a person to accomplish specific skills. Surgeons, architects, marketers, broadcasters, teachers, and almost every field of endeavor requires the learning of a number of skills.

Twenty years ago colleges would not think of teaching typing because that was really "vocational training," not education. Now "keyboard" is one of the most attended classes on many campuses because so much of our education requires the use of computers. It's not an either/or proposition; we all need both education and training to fully develop our potential.

Research shows that education actually accelerates a person's ability to accept training. A study by the U.S. Department of Labor revealed that more educated workers have a higher aptitude for training.[2] You might think of education as a framework for learning. An analogy might be the building of a house in which education would provide rooms that are easily adapted to special functions. In the discussion of education and training, there are some deeper issues involved. First, many adults are still turned off to education because of a bad experience they had in school. Second, many people are not interested in training because they don't see it as the way to a "professional" (usually they mean intellectual or high-income) occupation. And, there are people who don't consider skilled labor appropriate for people of their social standing.

Without a perceived need
to prepare for the future,
students naturally focus
their attention toward
the fun and pleasure
of today at the expense
of preparing for tomorrow.

If you stop and think about it, you probably were on one side of this fence or the other at some point in your life. Neither of these attitudes reflects a biblical viewpoint, and both are doing considerable damage to our people. Let's examine them and see why.

TURNED OFF TO EDUCATION

Unfortunately many people in our society want nothing to do with further education. For some, high school was like imprisonment. They didn't want to be there, they didn't see any benefit from it at the time, and so it seemed that nothing good could come out of it. Without the motivating spark to learn, education had little meaning other than drudgery. For many Americans, several issues have combined to relegate learning to the same desirability as going to jail. First of all, our affluent and "great" societies have encouraged slothfulness. There is no wolf at the door to help motivate students; the realities of life are far removed from most young people. Without a perceived need to prepare for the future, students naturally focus their attention toward the fun and pleasure of today at the expense of preparing for tomorrow.

The truth is that most people need to understand the use for what they are learning in order to be motivated to learn. Since there has been almost no career counseling or program to correlate courses to occupations, students are not able to grasp the value of the material to be learned.

Rather than students taking a refreshing drink from the fountains of knowledge, we are having to force-feed it to them in the same way farmers give medicine to cows.

It's also true that many people went through high school in a state of rebellion. No matter how much parents and teachers tried to help, they were not interested.

If you happened to be one of those people who missed out on a good education the first time through, don't despair; all is not lost. Attitudes can change and environments that at one time may have been a nightmare can turn into exciting frontiers. One of our Career Pathways' clients described her experience as following.

> I must share with you: In High School, I was not the best of students. I made a 700 on my SAT. I made As, Bs, Cs and Ds on my report card. I didn't care, didn't have much incentive, or even an understanding of the importance of school. Unfortunately, the past has left a scar on my files, but with God's grace, I have made up for it.
>
> I am standing with a 3.90 on a 4.0 scale. I have made only two Bs with 62 credit hours and the rest As. I never thought I could do that. Every test I do well on I must stop and thank Jesus. I never did well on tests when I was younger. When I got out of high school, I never wanted to step foot in school again, but now I find I'm enjoying it and it is challenging. —TLF

EDUCATION AS A SOURCE OF SELF-WORTH

There are those who are so focused on the perceived "status" conveyed by educational degrees that they won't consider "vocational training" for occupations where they might use their hands as well as their minds. We've had a number of clients who in every way are motivated and talented to work in skilled crafts, such as woodwork, mechanical repair, carpentry, or plumbing. Yet they are afraid of what others will think of them if they pursue a training program to learn "manual labor."

One of our clients who has a college degree received much criticism from her parents when she went to cooking school to become a chef. Somehow it didn't matter to her family what her talents and interests were. For the sake of their own pride, they preferred that she work as a third-rate accountant rather than as the excellent chef God had gifted her to be. Too often in our society pride is the real motivator for those who are pursuing a degree. Rather than rejoice in the talents they have been given, many students only want to achieve degrees, positions, and incomes that will symbolize success.

The decision whether to pursue vocational training or a college degree or both should be based on good stewardship of your talents, not on what is socially acceptable.

As mentioned earlier, people's career choices should enable them to fulfill their needs and values. Be sure that your educational and training choices are guided by these same motivations.

Sometimes it takes a lot of faith and courage to choose to use your pattern of gifts and follow the desires God has put in your heart. There will always be others around to tell you about the great future and high income offered by the latest "hot jobs."

As is the case in most spiritual issues, God's way may take a different path (usually the opposite direction) from the latest social trends. That's because God's economy does not place primary value on pride or material rewards. His purpose is that we be ambassadors for him (see 2 Corinthians 5:20) and that we be His instrument of reconciliation to a fallen world.

The decision whether to pursue vocational training or a college degree or both should be based on good stewardship of your talents, not on what is socially acceptable. We must trust that God will be with us and will faithfully guide us as we seek to use our talents to serve Him. Let's be strong in our faith as we choose training and educational programs.

"If God is for us, who is against us?" (Romans 8:31).

SOURCES OF TRAINING AND EDUCATION

Assuming that you have chosen your path and decided that you need more training or education, what are some ways you can make it happen?

1. Do-it-yourself learning.

Many smaller companies either can't afford to assist employees or just haven't seen the need to upgrade the skills of their employees, so the responsibility for your education and training may fall solely on your shoulders. Don't let that discourage you. There is much you can do on your own to enhance your abilities.

If you stop and think about it, most of what we know is acquired through unstructured learning. We read magazines and books; we ask questions; we get involved in group and hobby activities that give practical experiences in areas of interests. Why not make it a hobby to expand your knowledge in areas related to your work, your company, and your occupational field? By doing so you will become a lifelong learner.

If you are well matched to your career field, learning more about it should become almost a passion. Larry and I spend a lot of our spare time reading articles and new books and surveying materials related to our areas of work.

Make it a habit to read the trade journals of your field so you can stay abreast of changes. Identify some areas where you can improve your skills, set some goals, and move to a higher level of expertise and knowledge.

There is an old saying: "Things never stand still for very long. You are either progressing or falling behind." We think that idea applies to your expertise at work, especially in light of the changes currently taking place in the workplace. Those who are pro-active toward improving their skills and knowledge will keep pace. Those who react only after conditions change may be left out in the cold. As Christians our goal should be to excel in our work, and that will require continuous learning.

2. On the job training.

Many companies offer training to their employees. In *Control Your Destiny Or Someone Else Will*, a new book on corporate competitiveness, Jack Welch, CEO of General Electric, singles out education and training as key to future success: "What we've got to do is educate our people. . . . Within GE, we've got to upgrade workers' skills through intense and continuous training. Companies can't promise lifetime employment, but by constant training and education we may be able to guarantee lifetime employability. We've got to invest totally in our people."[3]

Find out if your organization offers training programs or tuition assistance; then let it be known that you are interested in upgrading your skills. If they don't have a program, they might start one and you may be the first to benefit.

3. Apprenticeships.

The great value of apprenticeships is that they allow people to get hands-on experience in the occupational field they're considering. All too often people choose a field of work with little or no idea of what is involved. One individual who wrote us points out the need for apprentice-type programs.

I know that the manner in which I chose a music career was all wrong and that my training was inadequate at best (although three moves and an inclination to not practice certainly didn't help).

Worse still, I was not exposed to the 'real world' soon enough to make an informed decision. Unlike a close friend of mine, who worked for both the high school newspaper and the local city paper (which he eventually returned to after working at a large metropolitan paper and is now business editor) before college (and never finished his degree), I remained sheltered all the way through college from the bumps and bruises of life that bring maturity and sound judgment.

If it were possible to travel back in time and apply my present knowledge and maturity to the circumstances I faced fifteen or twenty years ago—perhaps even as early as the fifth grade—one thing I would have done is set up some type of 'music apprenticeship' or other practical, actual work-while-I-learned experience that would have exposed me to 'real world' experiences. Such an 'apprenticeship' would have enabled me to better judge what I would be facing in my prospective career and what would be required of me to get where I wanted to go.   —D.D.

The armed services offer some great opportunities for leadership and technical training.

In case you haven't heard, the concept of apprenticeships is being revived. With a new emphasis on quality, companies realize that quality does not come without experience and training. If you are in transition to a new occupation, check to see if there are apprentice programs available. If there's nothing formally organized for the area you want to pursue, ask specific companies if they would be willing to design a program for your field.

4. Internships.

Internships provide academic orientation and training in a work environment. Minimum qualifications can vary from high school diploma to graduate degree, depending on the field. Benefits from internships vary widely. Some pay a salary, while others offer only room and board, and some may only provide the opportunity for on-the-job experience and training.

5. Cooperative Education.

Cooperative education (Co-op) programs are structured programs that alternate terms of work with terms of instruction. They are sponsored by companies, non-profit organizations, and governmental institutions. Co-op programs are especially good because they allow students to gain experience in a field of work or an insight into a particular company. Co-op programs often pay well, especially considering that the employee is still a student ($1400 per month would not be unusual).

6. Military education and training.

Even though the military will be cutting back significantly over the next four years, they still will be bringing in a sizeable number of new people. The armed services offer some great opportunities for leadership and technical training. Tuition assistance programs are available for everyone, and college classes are available on most installations. The military option isn't for everyone, but for those who are young and want to serve their country, it is a great place to start.

7. Vocational and technical schools.

Nearly every community in America has a technical school within reasonable driving distance, and some offer dormitory facilities for resident programs. Most vo-tech schools are government sponsored and therefore are relatively inexpensive. They also offer both day and evening classes so students can work and attend class during off hours.

Generally, vo-tech schools will have a testing and counseling department to assist you in determining your aptitudes for various courses of study. If you already have a good idea of your talents, they will be able to help you narrow your choices. Also, they typically have good relationships with local companies and know what specific occupations are needed in the local economy.

There are also private career schools offering training in more than 120 career fields. Many of these provide excellent specialized training that leads to good paying jobs. Check out these schools very carefully since not all are accredited. For more information on accreditation, contact the National Association of Trade and Technical Schools (NATTS), 2251 Wisconsin Ave NW, Washington, DC 20007.

8. Community colleges.

Community colleges are one of the great resources of our country and offer a tremendous bargain in education. They offer a wide range of education and training courses at a relatively inexpensive tuition and within easy driving distance of most people. Like the vo-tech schools, they offer evening classes so students can attend while maintaining their jobs.

Community colleges typically have good career counseling and testing departments to assist students in choosing fields of study. They may be a good source of information but, remember, they're not likely to understand as much about making good career decisions as you will when you finish this book. It is unlikely that these counselors will look at career planning from a biblical perspective, so seek their input and then make your own decision, based on your values and life goals.

Because they have such a close relationship with local businesses, community colleges will be able to help you learn about specific occupations that are available in your area. The placement division and many instructors should be able to assist you in your search for career information.

9. Four year colleges and universities.

Because college costs are escalating rapidly and jobs for college grads are decreasing, we encourage you to carefully consider all the other options before you enroll in a four year course of study. In addition to the financial commitment, the fact is that many people who go to college do so for the wrong reasons and end up having wasted time and money.

Statistics from the Bureau of Labor show that about 63 percent of recent high school graduates enrolled in college. About half leave before receiving a degree, so we need to ask the question: Is it the right thing for so many to go into an environment for which they either are not prepared or are not committed enough to succeed?

Considering the high attrition rates and the forecast that 70 percent of our future workers will not need a four-year college degree, our society needs to rethink the idea that a four-year college degree is the way to go. We are speaking out on this idea because we're trying to break some of you from the old mind-set about how to prepare for work.

As you can tell, we consider education and training absolutely essential, but we think times are changing. Rather than automatically thinking of a bachelors degree, we recommend you consider education and training in light of the realities of affordability, return on investment, and the needs of the workplace.

Having said all that, however, we know that a four year degree will be very appropriate for many of you.

In many fields, employers will be more impressed by skills and technical expertise than by an advanced degree.

---

10. *Graduate school.*

For certain professions, graduate school will be mandatory. Many of our clients are going back to school to get advanced degrees and, with the competition for professional jobs, this may be a good way to improve your résumé. We would caution against pinning your hopes for employment on another degree. In many fields, employers will be more impressed by skills and technical expertise than by an advanced degree.

11. *Non-traditional ways of getting more education/training.*

Schools are offering more and more options for people to take education and training courses. For instance, many schools offer college courses on Saturday, which works well for people who must work during the week.

Another option is to take a two-week short course during a vacation period or leave of absence. Most schools offer workshops, continuing education courses, and self-directed or correspondence courses. There are even some very good masters programs now offered through correspondence. These are especially good for adults who, for reasons of geography, work, or family commitments, can't attend a resident program.

We know two people who are completing their masters degrees in counseling from Liberty University via correspondence. My wife Mary is one of them, and I've seen firsthand the advantage of this program.

The advent of video taped lessons has allowed correspondence students to enjoy beneficial instruction right in their own living rooms. Testing is conducted through an arrangement with a local agency, church, or community college. Some resident work is required and is accomplished in one- or two-week blocks, so there is minimal disruption to home life. Practicum work can be done right in the student's community through local agencies.

Most of the readers of this book will be adults and many will be women who are considering entry or re-entry into the workplace. From our counseling we also know that many of you are concerned about ways to upgrade your skills. Our message is that there are many non-traditional ways of getting more education and training. It is up to you to investigate and locate opportunities that will suit your needs. Generally, where there is a will, there is a way, so be persistent.

FACTORS TO CONSIDER IN PURSUING EDUCATION AND TRAINING

As you contemplate further education and training, you'll want to consider carefully the following factors.

1. What do you want to study?

Your answer to this question should be directly related to your vocational interests, your values, your skills, and your personality strengths. Be sure your choice matches your pattern of strengths.

2. How much education do you really need or want?

We have been advocating more education and training, but you may not need to get it all at once.

For some people, a good career plan would be to develop a vocational skill, gain experience, then go back to college to broaden their education. Later they may go through some company-sponsored training to further refine their skills.

Be realistic and be a good steward. Tailor your education to your specific needs; don't just follow the crowd.

3. What is your level of motivation/commitment?

If you aren't going to apply yourself fully, why bother? As a steward of God's resources (time, talents, and money), are you willing to be the best student possible considering your personal situation?

4. How much will your education/training cost, and can you afford it?

What are the options, and what will be the best buy for your money spent? Consider your schooling as an investment and be sure you are making a wise choice. Again, every situation is different, so evaluate your situation based on your circumstances, not on what everyone else is doing.

5. How will you pay for the education?

Since finances so often are a critical factor, we'd like to offer some ideas on how to pay for your education. In today's society, many people think first of an educational loan. Generally we don't think it's a good idea to borrow to pay for education and we'll explain why.

> *Perhaps one of the greatest reasons to avoid borrowing is that debt repayment often becomes a major factor in career decisions.*

FINANCING YOUR EDUCATION

Probably we all know someone who borrowed for an education and successfully repaid the loan(s). But, as a principle, it's not a good idea. Keep in mind that debt always puts an added stress on your life and can adversely affect marital relationships.

When you borrow, you don't avoid repayment, you merely delay the obligation. It's easy to borrow because the repayment does not begin right away, but eventually the bills must be paid.

Our experience in financial counseling is that the debt on educational loans is much more difficult to repay than the borrower ever anticipated. With today's declining job opportunities and rapidly escalating costs of education, the risks of borrowing have increased. Department of Education figures confirm this because the total of the rapidly rising number of loan defaults is near $2.2 billion.

The usual tendency is to overestimate future incomes and underestimate future expenses. We've known too many people who are financially strapped, due in part to repayment of school loans.

Perhaps one of the greatest reasons to avoid borrowing is that debt repayment often becomes a major factor in career decisions. We see people choosing occupations that aren't really appropriate just because a certain income is needed to meet living expenses and keep the repayment schedule. It's sad, but true, that repayment of college loans keeps people from serving where the Lord might call them.

The following are some tips on how you may be able to get further education without borrowing.

1. Work and pay as you go.

This is the old fashioned way and, in fact, still the primary way people pay for education. Larry and I both paid for our undergraduate and graduate degrees by working before or after school each day. At the time it didn't seem so bad, but looking back now it's hard to believe that we actually got masters degrees by working all day and going to school at night.

The work and pay-as-you-go method usually stretches out your schooling somewhat, but if you keep at it graduation will come sooner than you think. Someday, you'll look back and be glad you did it this way rather than borrow.

2. Scholarships and grants.

These funds are provided by government and private sources. Many of these are based on need, while some are based on past accomplishments and future potential. Additionally some are targeted for very specific geographical locations and some are for specific majors. Check with the financial aid departments of the schools you are considering.

3. Tuition assistance.

Many companies and non-profit organizations assist employees by paying part or all of their tuition. Check with the personnel department of your organization for information. Also, the internship and co-op programs mentioned earlier usually offer financial incentives.

4. Parents and other family.

We think this is the most important financial inheritance a person can provide to children, grandchildren, and other family members. Sit down and discuss your situation with relatives who may be able to assist. Let them know your needs and ask them to consider investing in your future.

Remember, others will be more likely to assist if they see that you are being a good steward of what you already have. If you have a cavalier attitude about your own finances, they may not be so willing to help. By living on a budget, you would be able to demonstrate your needs and your commitment to being a good manager of what you have.

At Christian Financial Concepts, we hear from many who successfully achieve their educational goals debt free. Usually it can be done so, rather than borrowing, we encourage you to look at every other option.

EDUCATION IS A LONG-TERM INVESTMENT AND PERSISTENCE IS THE KEY

We live in a society that has grown accustomed to instant gratification. We can get almost anything—from coffee to copies to communications—on a near-instant basis. But you can't get education instantly. It takes time and effort to learn and to integrate that learning into your repertoire of skills and abilities. We'd do well to accept up front that education is a long-range investment, requiring commitment and persistence.

During the Vietnam war, I was an Air Force pilot flying combat missions to cut the flow of supplies into South Vietnam. About half-way through my tour of duty, my aircraft was shot down over North Vietnam and I was captured. As a prisoner of war during the next five and one-half years, I learned a lot about setting long-term goals for education.

Persistence is the secret to getting the education you need.

By nature, I am a very impatient person (my *Steady* dimension is near the bottom of the chart). Sitting in my little cell in Hanoi, I learned to wait. Initially I couldn't even comprehend six months of captivity, but eventually I was able to push the timetable for my release back as much as a year into the future and plan toward that. After three years I decided I could accept at least two more years of waiting (until the next presidential election).

I had several activities to pass the time, but the main one was learning languages. I had a roommate who knew French (which I had struggled through in college), one who knew Spanish, and another who knew German. For lack of anything else to do, we began language classes. My goals were to speak fluent Spanish and French, and to learn basic German by the time I was released.

We studied new words in the morning and spoke conversationally in each language for 20 minutes in the afternoon or evening. My progress was like the old joke "How do you eat an elephant? One bite at a time." Eventually a guy who once had hated every minute of his college French class became fluent in two languages and somewhat conversational in a third.

This didn't happen because of brilliance, but because I made a commitment to some educational goals and just kept at it day after day, year after year. Every day I took another "bite of the elephant." If you stop and think about it, that's really how we acquire knowledge about any subject. Persistence is the secret to getting the education you need.

So, it will be important to accept that achieving your educational goals may take a long time. If three or four years sounds like a long time, stop and remember where you were four years ago and realize how quickly the years have gone by.

For most people, the only thing that will keep them from getting the education and training they need is quitting.

If you persist long enough, you'll reach your goals. Just hang in there and "take another bite of the elephant." Someday you'll look back and be thankful you did—especially if workplace changes take a bite out of your career.

CHAPTER EIGHTEEN
Conducting a Job Search Part 1

*T*he biggest challenge facing those in a job search now and in the next five years is the restructuring of the American workplace. Of course, larger companies will always be hiring, but their overall situation will be a net decline as they continue downsizing (or as some companies call it, rightsizing).

Although the Fortune 500 companies once hired 20 percent of the labor force, their total now is down to 10 percent and is still shrinking.[1]

Smaller companies will be the major source of hiring and, due to their more transient nature, employment probably will be less secure in the future.

Considering our shaky economy, the changes in corporate America, and the impact of new technology on the workplace, the next five years will see more people than ever looking for new jobs. With the competition for jobs increasing, knowing how to carry out a well-planned job search will be an essential skill in our society.

To cover the job search process in detail, the information has been divided into two chapters (18 and 19), and Chapter 20 deals with résumés. We are indebted to Bob McKown, a Life Pathways Affiliate in Nashville, Tennessee for his input on these topics.

The following is an overview of the areas covered in this chapter.

- Have a Positive Attitude
- Determine an Objective
- Maximize Your Network
- Pursue Various Job Leads and Sources
- Make Your Job Search Your Job
- Join a Support Group

HAVE A POSITIVE ATTITUDE

Even though the job search itself tends to undermine the optimism of even the most accomplished, it will be essential that you maintain a positive attitude. Your greatest strength will be your absolute reliance on the Lord.

Some of the biggest problems our clients face are caused by their hesitation to do the work needed to research various occupations and job settings.

There is no question, you'll encounter some difficult situations, but with a childlike faith you must believe in His plan for you and that He will enable you to carry it out. Remember the discussion earlier about working the process and trusting God for the results.

Review the talents, motivations, and values you've been given and trust that they'll be more than adequate for what you are being called to do.

If your focus is on your weaknesses and shortcomings, your confidence can't help but weaken, and potential employers surely will notice. But if your confidence is in what God is doing through you, you will not be filled with doubts, but power. *"For God has not given us a spirit of timidity, but of power and love and discipline"* (2 Timothy 1:7).

DETERMINE AN OBJECTIVE

Keep foremost in your mind that your objective should be consistent with your talents (abilities and personality) and your interests (vocational interests, work priorities, and values). Also you need to consider the various factors that affect work satisfaction, previously mentioned.

Some of the biggest problems our clients face are caused by their hesitation to do the work needed to research various occupations and job settings. Granted, this can appear to be a challenge but, really, it isn't so difficult.

As you begin to identify actual companies that may have openings, you'll need to get more specific information. National companies can be researched through periodicals and professional publications.

For local companies, check with your Chamber of Commerce; they generally know the current status of businesses and community organizations. Likewise, your network of friends and business contacts should be helpful.

Of course the most obvious way to find out about an organization is to contact them directly. It's helpful if you have someone closely connected with the organization who can introduce you or assist you in scheduling an informational interview. Through such interviews you can learn detailed information that will help you identify occupations and organizations where you might like to work.

A list of typical questions you might want to use in an informational interview is included at the end of this chapter.

Wise counsel can help you trim away some of the options and get to the best choices. Counsel can come from many different sources, but be sure to get counsel from someone who is different in personality from you. That way you'll get a balance of views. Remember the biblical admonitions regarding counsel. Everyone needs counsel and several sources are better than one. (See Proverbs 11:14 and Proverbs 15:22.)

On the other hand, it's foolish to follow all the counsel you get. *"The naive believes everything, but the prudent man considers his steps"* (Proverbs 14:15). The bottom line is: You should seek counsel, listen, evaluate it, and apply it as appropriate for your situation. Ultimately, you must take responsibility for your own decision.

Your objective should include not only the occupation but the type of company you want to work for. Basically you'll be looking for companies and positions that would be a good match for your talents and interests.

At some point you should have a clear objective for your job search. You may not know the exact company, but you know your talents—what you have to offer—and you know the types of occupations and situations that would need someone like you.

The final step is to identify companies and organizations to which you could make a contribution. Make a list of them, set it aside for now, but add to it as new ideas come up.

MAXIMIZE YOUR NETWORK

Many people don't know it, but the majority of job openings are never published; they are filled by a recommendation of someone known to the hirer. As more of the labor force is employed in small companies, this type of networking will take on even greater importance because that's generally the way they find new people.

Your network is made up of those you know directly and those who come to know you indirectly through your primary network. It's important that networkers know enough about you to give a reasonable and legitimate input to their contacts; therefore, many of them will need a résumé or something to help them remember your talents and achievements.

One of the primary ways your network can help is by introducing or referring you to a third party who may be able to hire you. Anytime you can make contact with a potential employer through a mutual acquaintance, you're ahead in the game. From the employers perspective it's very risky to hire an unknown, so any information they can get firsthand about your character and talents usually is appreciated.

Network categories.

A good way to identify your network is to develop a list of names for each of the following categories.

family and friends	current or past employers
customers and clients	vendors and suppliers
job search support groups	church friends and neighbors
college placement offices	service clubs
professional associations	professional publications
other job seekers	boards and committees
boards and committees	community contacts
any other sources	

You also may want to volunteer your services with community non-profit organizations to broaden your network. A few years ago, I was asked to chair a drive to raise funds to build a veterans' memorial. The work was a lot of fun, and I met many wonderful people in the community. I wasn't looking for a job, but I did build an extensive network of contacts who knew my talents and character. If later I had needed a job, they would have been good sources for assistance.

Once you've completed your initial list, work through it to identify which contacts are:

- likely to be the most valuable and productive,
- the best ones to get in touch with immediately,
- easiest to contact,
- the best ones to postpone until later.

Use your network.

You'll need to determine how those in the network can help you. They may be able to provide information on an industry, a career field, an organization, or a specific job opening. You also may want to get names of other possible contacts from them or ask them to assist you directly with an introduction to someone who has hiring authority.

You're walking a thin line with your contacts by asking for their help, yet being sensitive not to push them into an embarrassing or precarious position. Finally, know your purpose for making the contact, and be sure to consider if what you are asking is within the person's ability to provide. Remember, do not ask a contact for a job.

Contacts are made over the phone, with a letter and, in some cases, you may want to set up a face-to-face meeting. In general, personal contacts are made over the phone because it's simpler, requires less time, and provides more immediate results. Phone conversations also tend to be more informal and usually are easier for both parties to express their true opinions.

Your typical approach to most contacts will be to ask for input because of their experience, knowledge, or position. To maximize your ability to reach contacts, remember to be persistent, polite, and brief. Know what you want to say and stay on the subject. You might even want to prepare a script to keep you on track. Follow up your contacts with a thank you note, no matter what the results of your conversation.

> *Follow-up confirms that you are both serious and enthusiastic about what you're doing.*

There are times when you may want to write rather than call a contact. Be sure to mention the name of your referring contact or any previous conversations with the addressee in the opening sentence of your letter. Generally, you shouldn't include a résumé, but you could ask for an appointment to discuss career opportunities in a general occupational field.

In your contact letter you should avoid discussing the possibility of employment, but stress that you are seeking information and input. It is acceptable to highlight your major achievements or credentials. Examples of contact letters are shown at the end of this chapter.

Follow up your contacts.

You should follow up in some way every contact you make during your job search. It could be just to say thanks for your time and help, or it could be to provide or seek more information. Follow-up confirms that you are both serious and enthusiastic about what you're doing.

PURSUE VARIOUS JOB LEADS AND SOURCES

The classified advertisements of newspapers usually are the first place most people look for employment. If you find a job through an ad, it certainly could be a good investment of your time. However, keep in mind that only about 15 percent of all positions available are advertised.

Specialty papers like the *National Business Employment Weekly* are also a good source of classified advertisements, as are professional and trade journals. Check with your library for career reference books that provide exclusive lists of associations and other resources.

Employment agencies and search firms are another good source to consider. They both tend to specialize in certain types of jobs, such as engineering, finance, marketing, or production.

Generally agencies are regulated and either are not allowed to charge clients for placement or not allowed to charge until after placement. Avoid those with up-front fees and be sure to check carefully any that you use.

Temporary employment services are becoming more and more popular and can be a good way to at least get a paycheck. They also are a good way to get your foot in the door and gain visibility that may lead to permanent employment. In fact it may surprise you to know that one third of temporaries are eventually hired permanently by their employer.[2]

MAKE YOUR JOB SEARCH YOUR JOB

One of the most difficult problems for the unemployed person is to stay focused on the task of getting the next job. First of all, it's a lot of hard work and not an easy challenge for anyone. Second, no matter what your strengths and talents, there will be parts of the job search that you won't enjoy doing.

For the outgoing personalities, the networking aspect will be fun because contacting people and enlisting their help is a natural thing to do. But keeping schedules, notes, and appointment times probably will be their achilles heel.

At the other extreme, reserved people usually dread making unfamiliar contacts because it's not a natural motivation; yet they enjoy getting organized, researching, and planning the job search.

Regardless of your personality strengths or limitations, you're going to have to do all the aspects of the job search. Your determination and discipline to stay on track and to do all the tasks will be very important in your success. Don't allow yourself to ignore or wish away some of the activities or responsibilities discussed in this chapter just because they don't sound exciting or because they sound threatening.

When faced with tasks you don't feel good about doing, first consider how you might adapt them to fit your natural strengths. Second, remember that others will accept you for who you are if you can be comfortable with yourself.

Finally, just do it! Most people who have gone through a job search will tell you that one of the biggest mistakes they made was putting things off.

Before you charge off in several directions at once, lay out an overall strategy.

I am reminded of the experiences we had with our kids at a place called Wildcat Creek in the mountains of North Georgia. They loved to slide down the slick rocks into the deep pool below, except initially it was hard to get them into the cold water. At first they would stick a toe in the water and then shiver and complain about how cold it was. Eventually, they would get enough courage just to jump in and start sliding, swimming, and climbing back up the rocks. An hour later they didn't want to leave because it was so much fun. Only then did they wish they hadn't wasted so much time getting in the water.

Certain aspects of the job search can be like that. Don't wait, and don't just "stick a toe in" and think about how cold the water is; just jump in and get busy.

Get organized.

To help you keep focused on your work and to remind you of just how important your activities are, try to set up an office. It could be at the local library, working out of your briefcase, or perhaps a friend or your former employer would allow you to use a desk and a phone.

Many people have an office at home or just use a corner of a room. Whatever the location, the more organized and businesslike you can make it, the more likely you are to perform your work of job search.

Before you charge off in several directions at once, lay out an overall strategy. We've offered a general outline in this and succeeding chapters, and you can adapt it to your specific situation.

Start with a skeleton outline so you can see the big picture of where you're going. Then put meat on the bones with a more detailed plan of what actions you need to take, as well as how and when you are going to do them. Organizing it all on paper will be a big help.

Keeping your materials organized also will make your search more efficient and give you confidence that you are on top of things. You'll need files for information on: career fields, specific companies, your network, references, and job leads. A sample tracking log is included at the end of this chapter.

Be sure to keep good records. Take time to organize and file notes from your research and memos of conversations with your network. Be sure to record the date, what was said, and who said it. These notes will be important for your follow-up.

Keep a regular schedule.

Being systematic in all your job search activities will be very important, and a schedule will help. If you're unemployed and not reporting to work every day, you'll have to set your own work hours and structure. Keep in mind, your new "job" is finding a job.

We recommend you keep a 40 hour work week and establish normal operating procedures, just as if you were working for someone else. You won't have the same pressure to perform as you would for a boss, so you'll have to find ways to motivate yourself.

It takes a lot of discipline not to cut corners on your 40 hour week when you are on your own. Be a taskmaster during work hours and then you can enjoy your family and leisure time with a clear conscience.

*Accept rejection as part
of the process and just
try to increase your
number of rejections—
they move you closer
to finding the job.*

You might be thinking, "What would I be doing in a job search that would take 40 hours a week?" Once you get your résumé done, you'll have plenty to do: researching, networking, seeking out new possibilities you hadn't thought about, reading books on job search, following up on leads, and trying to expand your network.

Set objectives and milestones.

Your overall goal is to get a job that fits your pattern of strengths and interests and meets the other needs of your specific life situation. Supporting that goal will be a number of objectives. To be sure you achieve your objectives, you'll need milestones that establish specific things to be accomplished in certain time periods. Let me illustrate this concept.

Our friend Gene has been a successful life insurance salesman for many years. He is intelligent, knowledgeable, and experienced; yet he still uses goals, objectives, and milestones to stay motivated and achieve success. He told me once how he does it.

First, he determines his goal for an annual income he can reasonably expect to earn. Second, he decides how many policies he needs to sell each month in order to make that income (objective). Then he calculates the number of contacts and appointments (milestones) needed to reach his monthly objective and annual goal.

From experience, Gene knows that ten qualified-lead phone calls will yield three appointments and, on average, he'll sell one policy for every three clients he meets with. So if he's going to sell two policies a week, in theory he needs to make twenty contacts and meet with six clients per week to meet his sales objectives.

From experience Gene knows he'll lose some days to holiday seasons, vacations, and illness, so he plans his year based on 40 weeks instead of 52. With this in mind, he sets his milestone at 26 contacts and 8 appointments per week. Some weeks it'll vary but, overall, he knows this will enable him to achieve his objectives and earn his overall income goal for the year.

It would be very easy to set up a similar management system for making contacts and other activities in your job search. One of the things I like best about Gene's method is that it plans for rejection as a natural part of the process. He doesn't take it personally when people don't buy a policy.

You should adopt the same attitude toward the rejections you'll get in your job search. Many people won't need a policy, no matter how good it is, and many people won't need your services, no matter what you can do. Accept rejection as part of the process and just try to increase your number of rejections—they move you closer to finding the job.

Identify sources of help.

There are many locations and agencies where you can get assistance in your job search. Of course the library, career guidance and placement centers at colleges and technical schools, state employment offices, and the local Department of Labor are ones that come to mind first. But there are many others.

Keep in mind that you'll need many sources of information, but genuine counsel should come from those who have a biblical perspective of work and the use of your talents. Be sure your counselors share your values or their counsel may not be helpful.

Job search networks are springing up in major cities across the country—many of them sponsored by churches. Our Career Pathways affiliates who assist people in the job search process tell us that their clients say that a good support system is essential.

JOIN A SUPPORT GROUP

Because of pride, people are sometimes hesitant to admit they need "support," but anyone who's been in a support group can tell you what an inspiration they can be. People who attend are generally transparent, admitting their weaknesses and seeking help for their problems.

In today's society, where most people pretend they have everything under control, you can start to feel inferior when faced with a problem. You'll find it a great encouragement to hear that others have been through what you are experiencing.

Support groups can be a great source of good information and help. You'll probably find someone to give you good feedback on your résumé, some tax advice, or the latest on the hiring situations of local companies. Fellow participants are also good sources to expand the branches of your network.

Christian support groups are becoming quite widespread and provide an excellent outreach to the community. Check your local newspaper under the classified employment section for weekly meeting times/places of these groups.

The most important thing you need in your job search is a strong trust in the Lord. When things are not going well, there's a tendency to think that He has forgotten you. The testimonies and the love of others with whom you develop a relationship in the group will be an important source of encouragement for you.

By now, you should be motivated, have your objectives set, be thinking about your network, be ready to get organized, and realize you'll need to join a support group. In the next chapter we will take you all the way to actually closing the deal on the new job.

CAREER INFORMATION INTERVIEW

You can learn a lot about a career field by interviewing someone who is happy and successful in a job. You'll want to schedule an interview in advance so the interviewee is expecting you. Also, it's good to mail them a list of questions (such as those below). This prepares them for your visit and helps you get the information in an efficient manner. Finally, be sure you write a thank you note to the one(s) who gave you time and assistance.

Suggested questions:

1. What is the product, purpose, or results desired from this job?
2. How do you like your job?
3. What is required for success in this job?
4. Are there any unique qualifications or skills required for this job?
5. On which duties do you spend most of your time, and what is a typical day for you?
6. Which duties do you like best?
7. Which duties do you like least?
8. How much do you travel in your job?
9. What are the opportunities for personal development in this job?
10. What are the working conditions like? the people with whom you work?
11. Are there seasonal peaks and valleys in this field?
12. How often do you move in this type of work?
13. Are there any social or professional obligations in this job?
14. How does this job affect your family life?
15. What is the typical salary range across the industry for this occupation?
16. Does this career field have a good future? Would you recommend it to someone like me?

Remember every company is different. . . .

Personal Contact Letter
(Phone follow-up)

1420 Glenview Rd
Brentwood TN 37027
January 5, 19--

Mr. John Archer
Vice President, Marketing Division
Petro Oil Inc
147 Tacoma Pl
Toledo OH 54321

Dear Mr. Archer: (Or, use first name when possible)

As you suggested during our telephone discussion yesterday, I am enclosing two copies of my résumé.

My goal is to become Project Manager of a medium-sized chemicals firm. I have almost 20 years of experience in process design, cost, and on-site construction engineering. My work has taken me to numerous parts of the world and involved me in many types of processes, mostly in petrochemicals. I believe I can contribute most effectively in a medium-sized company where there is a real need for a broad-based generalist.

I have BSChemE and MsChemE degrees from the University of Tennessee, and have taken accounting and organizational behavior courses in Vanderbilt's Owen MBA program. I have supervised as many as 50 people on recent $40 to $80 million projects in Tennessee and Canada. I will relocate and travel if required.

I look forward to hearing from you if you have any suggestions along the lines I've described above.

Sincerely,

Ralph Brown

Enclosure

Company Contact Letter
(Indirect approach)

September 11, 19--

Mr. John A. Davidson
Executive Vice President, Operations
Krypton Art Manufacturing Co
43901 Verde Blvd
Greenleaf MN 10532

Dear Mr. Davidson:

Although we're not personally acquainted, perhaps you could take a few moments to help me with my information search.

I have been an internal consulting engineer for large corporations in the area of process engineering for the past 20 years. I plan to leave my present employer and am seeking a new position with an organization in which I can apply my management background and engineering experience to produce key results for a progressive company.

I think you'll agree that the best way to find a new position in the "hidden job market" is through word-of-mouth, and I'm hoping you can provide me with some suggestions. May I count on your help? I will call in a week or so to answer any questions and to obtain any leads you would be kind enough to suggest. Once again, thanks for your assistance.

Very truly yours,

Joseph B. Keating

Enclosure

CONTACT TRACKING LOG

Date	Contact Name	Situation	Action Taken	Follow-Up	Outcome/ Future Action

This chart is for illustration purposes only and is not to scale.

CHAPTER NINETEEN

Conducting a Job Search, Part II

*T*he following are the topics we'll cover in this chapter as we continue discussing the process of job search.

- Keep Your Life in Balance
- Consider Alternate Sources of Employment
- Move Cautiously When Changing Career Fields
- Prepare for the Job Interview
- Negotiate the Job
- Begin Preparing for Your Next Job

KEEP YOUR LIFE IN BALANCE

Spend time with God.

Talk to Christians who've gone through a job search and they'll tell you of the importance of a quiet time for Bible study and prayer.

Usually periods of difficulty bring the greatest opportunity for spiritual growth, because we are willing to listen to God. (Have you noticed how easy it is to neglect God when everything is going well and you feel you're in control of your life?) Don't neglect your time alone with the Lord; He's waiting for you every day.

Spend time with your family.

As you can see, you need to attack your job search with a great deal of energy and commitment, but don't let it become an obsession. You also have other areas in your life that need your attention, especially if you have a family.

> *Most people who've gone through a job search single out regular exercise as a great way to relieve stress and clear the mind of problems.*

If you're married, keep your spouse informed but, at the same time, don't dump all your emotions on him or her. If you've planned your work and worked your plan, you should be able to schedule times to give focused attention to your family. They need to see you are confident that everything will work out in due time.

Take time to deal with your emotions.

A job search can be a very difficult experience causing emotions of anger, depression, bitterness, and fear. Be sure you deal with your emotions in a positive way. Find someone who really knows you and cares about you to be your confidante and prayer partner. If you are married, your spouse will be this kind of person, but you also need a friend of the same sex who will meet with you for prayer and counsel.

Take time for your health.

When we are under stress, it's easy to let good health habits fall by the wayside. Some people will unconsciously eat more than they need in order to feel better. Of course that never works, and as they gain weight they feel worse. Others may turn to alcohol or drugs to cope with stress; those things also only provide momentary relief while magnifying the problems later.

Most people who've gone through a job search single out regular exercise as a great way to relieve stress and clear the mind of problems. If you don't have a physical fitness program, there's no better time to start one than during a job search.

Take time for your hobbies.

Nearly everyone has some type of hobby or activity they enjoy doing in their spare time. If you happen to be one of those whose only hobby has been work, it could be that the Lord is allowing your unemployment to help you get your life back in balance.

If you've established a schedule for your job search, you should have some time for leisure. One of our clients pointed out that he used his spare time to fix up the house in case they had to sell and move to another city. He also found a used book store and traded for fresh titles to feed his reading hobby.

Keep in mind the primary purpose for your hobbies should be diversion and relaxation. If it becomes an occupation, you may have to find something else for your hobby.

Give of your time to help others.

We all need to have our own personal ministry through which we give at least a small part of our time to help someone else. God's overall plan is that we support one another. And the fascinating thing is that when we help someone else, we usually get more out of it than they do. Whenever you help someone out of true kindness and concern, agape love begins to operate. This type of unconditional love by one person for another is a powerful healing agent for emotions, stress, relationships, and even healing within the body.

CONSIDER ALTERNATIVE SOURCES OF EMPLOYMENT

Starting your own business.

Self employment is a good idea for some people, but certainly it's not for everyone. A business startup requires a tremendous amount of energy and drive to see it through.

Starting a business also requires a lot of knowledge, thought, and preparation. In a way it's like planning an invasion. Before entering into the fray, you really need to do your homework. First evaluate the capability of your own forces, what skills you have, and what you lack.

Then evaluate the competition: Are you really going to be able to advance into their territory? Next, consider the lay of the land: What is the need for products and services, and how will the economic outlook affect your operation?

Finally, and most important, count the cost. Do you have sufficient resources to sustain your initial push long enough to occupy the high ground and gain your piece of territory in the marketplace (turn a profit)?

The biggest causes of new business failures are lack of knowledge and experience, underestimating how long it will take to become profitable, and lack of capital. Obviously the more capital available, the more likely you are to overcome the first two hurdles.

If you already have extensive experience in a field, know the markets and customers, have profit and loss experience, and have a good reserve of capital, then you have the basic foundation for success. Getting good advice will be essential, so read some books, check with your nearest Small Business Development Center, develop a plan, and get counsel from other business people who know you and the field you are considering.

Consulting.

You also may want to consider consulting if you have an area of expertise. As companies cut back, they're beginning to sub-contract more of their specific services. This way they pay only for the projects they need, and they don't have to pay FICA (Social Security) and insurance benefits. Many people have been able to contract with their old company or some of its competitors or suppliers to perform consulting services.

Consulting is a two-edged sword in that it gives you many of the same benefits of being an entrepreneur, i.e., freedom and control over your destiny; but consulting means you pay all your own taxes and benefits.

MOVE CAUTIOUSLY WHEN CHANGING CAREER FIELDS

With the changes taking place in industry, many jobs are gone forever and some people will need to give serious consideration to retraining for a different field. Others may just want to find something they would enjoy more. Switching career fields may be good idea, but it should be preceded by careful consideration of all other alternatives.

Your first option should be to consider how you might use your current skills and experience in a related field. Take an inventory of your transferable skills as discussed previously and look for opportunities to use them.

> *No matter how much effort you've put into a résumé, research, or phone calls, it's the interview that probably will determine whether or not you get hired.*

On the other hand, some people have found a layoff an opportune time to make a transition they'd been considering for years. Unemployment just helped them make the decision.

If you've been in an occupation that really wasn't a good match for your talents and interests, a change in career fields could turn out to be a great blessing.

The decision to make a complete career change is a big one and should be weighed against such factors as your talents and interests, your financial situation, the amount of education or training required, and the realistic opportunities offered by all the options.

Most of all, you need to have a very strong attraction to the new field before pulling anchor and setting sail in that direction. If your motivation is strong enough, probably you'll make it through the turbulence that can come in a career change.

PREPARE FOR YOUR JOB INTERVIEW

All of the work behind your job search is oriented toward getting an interview. No matter how much effort you've put into a résumé, research, or phone calls, it's the interview that probably will determine whether or not you get hired.

Interviews generally fall into five phases, and it helps if you're aware when the transitions occur. Usually there's an *opening phase* for normal pleasantries—a time just to get a feel for each other. Be responsive and alert, but allow the interviewer to set the tone. You can tell you're entering the next phase, the *fact-finding phase*, when the questions shift more toward your background, experience, and skills. Be positive, brief, and to the point. This is a time to talk about your achievements and relate them to the mission of the company.

Before the interview, you should've done your homework on the company. You need to be familiar with its mission, products, environment, competition, current challenges, and general philosophy of management. You need to know a lot, but you don't want to show them you are a know-it-all. Your knowledge is primarily so you can look at the world from their perspective and position your answers in a light that shows you know who they are and what they're about.

At some point, the conversation will shift as the interviewer begins the *information-giving phase* about the company and the particular job they are trying to fill. Listen carefully to what is said and limit your questions during this phase. When the time comes for the *questioning phase*, ask about their expectations for the job, company goals, problems, and key elements needed for success.

When you see the interview is in the *closing phase*, be sure you find out what to expect. Ask when the decision will be made and when you'll hear from them. Arrange some sort of follow-up if they don't mention it. These details are normal and something you should be told as a matter of courtesy, but often this doesn't happen. You also should be courteous and not try to extend the interview. As soon as you sense it's over, thank the interviewer and be on your way.

Remember that first impressions are incredibly important. Be appropriately dressed for the job for which you're interviewing. If it is not a coat-and-tie-type job, it's still better to overdress a little for the interview. If it's a casual, construction-type job, clean, neatly pressed sport or work clothes would be appropriate.

During the interview you want to be confident, but you must also be yourself. I remember an incident when I was interviewing a lady for a secretarial job. She was quite nervous. In fact, she stopped at one point and said: "You know I get very nervous in these types of situations." I told her I understood and she completed the interview without any problems. I did hire her and she turned out to be a tremendous employee.

If you are a naturally shy person, a major part of your preparation for the interview should be just getting practice in meeting someone, looking them in the eye, and answering questions in an interview-type scenario. Start with using someone you know as the interviewer. A list of typical interview questions is included at the end of this chapter.

> *Don't expect to be perfect. Just trust that if you do your best that will be good enough.*

Once you are comfortable with your answers, recruit someone you don't know to interview you. Basically you are just conditioning yourself so you'll be able to relax when you go in for the real thing.

If you are a naturally talkative person, you need to practice giving short, succinct answers. I'd guess more people have lost a job opportunity by talking too much than by being shy. There's an old saying, which probably was derived from Proverbs: It's better to keep your mouth shut and have people wonder if you are a fool than to start talking and remove all doubt. *"The one who guards his mouth preserves his life; the one who opens wide his lips comes to ruin"* (Proverbs 13:3).

When you are being questioned, be sure you *listen* carefully to what is asked. Then *think* about it and *answer* only what is asked. The saying "engage brain before putting mouth in gear" is especially appropriate in interviews. It's easier to keep your foot out of your mouth than to have to remove it.

Good preparation will certainly increase your skill and confidence in pressure situations. And confidence will allow your brain to work significantly faster than when you are fearful or thinking negative thoughts.

As a flight instructor, I learned that students who had negative thoughts about their flying ability would soon be washed out of the program unless their confidence could be turned around. I saw the same thing as a teacher in higher education. Those who didn't believe in their ability in a subject were the ones who didn't do well on the test even when they knew the material.

Don't expect to be perfect. Just trust that if you do your best that will be good enough. If you still don't get the job, accept it as a blessing, thank the Lord, and start preparing for the next interview.

Don't forget to follow up your interview with a short thank you note, regardless of the outcome or even if you don't yet know the outcome. Your timely response shows that you appreciate their time and possess good social graces. It also gets you back in the mind of the decision maker one more time.

To keep up with your activities and be certain you have followed up, we recommend you use the log at the end of Chapter 18. This will contribute to your overall organization and effectiveness and help you see how well you're reaching the goals you've set.

NEGOTIATE THE JOB

The offer of a job can trigger some exhilarating emotions. After a long job search, it's okay to get a little excited about the possibilities, but you must keep your feet on the ground because there's still important business to do. In many ways this next stage is like negotiating and signing a contract. You need to know exactly what's being offered and what are the conditions and expectations.

Be sure you have an understanding of the basics: start date, working hours, supervisor, and working relationships. Both you and your employer should be clear about the job description and the benefits package. Also, this is a good time to ask for a copy of their employee policy manual and any brochures they might have detailing company benefits, such as insurance or retirement plans.

Depending on your status and the position, there may be some negotiable items. For example, if you are moving to a new location, there's nothing wrong with asking the new company if they would provide a relocation allowance. In some cases, you may be able to negotiate commissions, stock options, or bonus arrangements.

Throughout these discussions be sincere, businesslike, and unemotional. It doesn't hurt to ask for something that's reasonable for the position being offered. If you've done your homework, you should already know what is typical for the particular organization and position you are considering.

Read the situation carefully, and avoid coming in with a laundry list of perks that would apply to the CEO. Don't be like a person I knew who kept insisting on more season tickets and a bigger company car. Word got out about his demands and his image was tainted from the start with the other employees in the organization.

Once you've reached the negotiation stage, it's not the time to take foolish risks. A seemingly sure thing can slip through your fingers if you take too much for granted.

The following are some cautions that will help you keep on track until the job search is really over.

- Agree on a decision date and be sure to give your answer by that date.
- Don't cut off other options until you have actually started working. Until you're on the payroll, you don't have anything more than the employer's word.
- If possible, try to get the employer to "put it in writing" (in an agreement or letter).
- Be certain that no "contingencies" remain up in the air. For example, have all references and security checks been made? Have you passed the medical exam?

- Don't broadcast your good fortune to anyone until it's truly a closed deal. Premature celebrations have a way of backfiring.

- Once you've started on your new job, remember to write or call the other people with whom you were negotiating to thank them for their time and interest in you.

- Don't forget to thank the many individuals who were instrumental in helping you during your job search. You never know when you may be needing their help again.

BEGIN PREPARING FOR YOUR NEXT JOB SEARCH

With the fundamental restructuring of American businesses and the uncertainty of our economy, it's likely that most people will change jobs several times and many will change career fields entirely. With that thought in mind, you should always be preparing for your next job.

That doesn't mean that you're not loyal to your current or new employer. In fact, you want to be extremely loyal by being the best employee anyone ever could ask for.

It does mean honing your skills and staying on top of your field. If you're in a job that matches your talents and interests, it should be natural and motivating for you to be one of the best at what you do.

You should expect that your work and the tasks required in the workplace will change. By anticipating these changes, you'll be able to look over the horizon and see new branches and side trails for your career path. Through continuing education and training, you can be preparing for the detours that may occur.

One other key component of constant preparation will be your network. You must continue to expand this group who knows your character, your skills, and your achievements. If you are among the best at what you do, and you're always on the leading edge of your field, the word will get out.

And when it's time for your next job search, you may be able to go directly to the final step and negotiate the terms. It may not be quite that easy, but if you are always preparing for the future by increasing your skills, knowledge, and network, you'll have a good product to offer and a strong marketing team in place.

TYPICAL INTERVIEW QUESTIONS

Having a good understanding of how you are going to answer specific questions is crucial to presenting your unique background, knowledge, skills, and abilities to a prospective employer.

Shown below are some "hypothetical," often-asked interview questions for your review and for which you need to prepare written answers. Writing your answers will allow you to formulate your thoughts and ideas better. It also will provide a quick and easy way to review and refresh your memory prior to your interviews. Study each question before you start jotting down your answers, and do not underestimate its potential difficulty.

1. What were your duties, responsibilities, and accomplishments in your last job? (Be specific and show that you know what you're talking about. If your last job was not related to the job for which you are interviewing, answer the question, then relate your most recent job that does apply.)

2. Briefly describe your educational background. (Answer all questions the way they're asked. When an interviewer says briefly, that's what is meant.)

3. Would you briefly summarize your work history? (Again, answer the question—be specific, but not wordy.)

4. Why are you leaving your current job? Or . . . Why are you interested in a new position at this time? (Give an answer that does not reflect negatively on you, the company, or other individuals.)

5. Tell me about yourself. Or . . . Give me a thumbnail sketch of yourself. (Have a concise response ready. Exactly what you say is not usually as important as providing a clear, orderly, and logical response. Avoid rambling and needless detail.)

6. What are your career goals? (Phrase your response in a way the potential employer can relate to.)

7. What do you consider your major assets? Or . . . What are your strengths? (This isn't a time for you to be overly modest. Present your assets with assurance.)

8. Do you have any weak points? Or . . . What are your weaknesses? (Everybody has some, but indicate only something that has positive implications. For example, "Because I want to see a job done correctly, I tend to be somewhat of a perfectionist.")

9. To what do you most attribute your successes (or failures)? (This could be one or two questions. It deals with values and attitude. Your strategy for this question is to be both candid and positive. You should deal mainly with success, but if you must discuss a recent failure or disappointment, such as losing your job, emphasize what you've learned as a result. Remember, do not "bad mouth" your previous employers.)

10. What represents success to you? (This question directly asks you to express your values. It is essential not to try to answer this question based on what you think the prospective employer wants to hear, but you must answer what's in your heart. You may fool them, but you will not fool yourself. Not answering honestly, on this or any question, may mean you'll get a job where you will be miserable.)

11. What was your biggest accomplishment at your most recent job? (Tell what you have actually accomplished, not merely what tasks you have performed.)

12. What do you tend to do outside of work? (Give a rounded and balanced picture of yourself, but be honest.)

13. Is there anything else you'd like to say about yourself with regard to this job? (You may answer this question somewhat differently at each interview, but you should have an overall strategy for your answers. In most instances, this question is your opportunity to summarize and to sell yourself.)

CHAPTER TWENTY
Preparing a Résumé

One of the first and most important tasks you'll have as you begin a career transition is to get your résumé in good order. To write a good résumé, first you need a clear understanding of your purpose for writing it, who the recipients will be, and how they will view it.

Remember: The résumé does not get anyone a job; it merely presents a job candidate. Those who review résumés use them to screen applicants to narrow their pool to the best qualified candidates. In the interest of time and fairness, they must be somewhat impersonal and objective. They are looking for "just the facts" (as detective Joe Friday used to say). In the résumé, you want to give hard-hitting evidence that will convince the reader you have something to offer and are a good candidate for further consideration.

Keep in mind that those who review résumés usually have a system which enables them to move them quickly. They know what they are looking for, so your résumé must do its job in the first five to twenty seconds. That's all the time you have to "catch the eye" of the decision maker. Though that may not seem fair, it is realistic.

Target your résumé.

Before you begin to work on your résumé, you should have done your self-assessment and determined a career objective. Too often résumés are much too broad and after reading them it's difficult to tell what the person can do or even what they want to do.

Above all else, your résumé should focus on the strengths that support your ability to excel in your objective. The better your résumé can be targeted to your career objective, the more effective it will be.

As you begin to work on your résumé, it's a good idea to have a separate work sheet for each of the major headings of the format you elect to use. Fill in these work sheets with the information you'll be using to develop the résumé.

It's better to start out with more material than you need and then edit it to the really important, hard-hitting information that will quickly communicate your special attributes and achievements.

Your résumé should be no more than two pages long (one if possible), so make every word count.

High standards are important.

Most people underestimate the effort required to develop a good résumé, because they are not accustomed to doing things to the level of quality required in this important piece of paper. To get an acceptable product, the average résumé will take at least five drafts. Don't get discouraged when you've gone through three versions and it still isn't "right."

Also, don't be too confident in your ability to just "wing it." Errors or omissions will stand out like a sore thumb, so don't quit until you have a first class product.

The format and content of a résumé are evaluated by potential employers since both give a message about the candidate. Our preference is for résumés that are professional, yet personal—not too slick or glitzy.

Get help on your résumé.

In addition to being a unique format of communication, résumés are personally threatening to most of us. Writing in a positive, somewhat glowing style about our abilities and accomplishments is not easy. You can overdo it and sound like you have an inflated ego, or you can understate your case and sound like you are incompetent. Finding the right balance is the key and that often takes the help of someone who is a good writer and is knowledgeable about résumés.

Generally it's helpful to have someone interview you about your achievements. They will be able to help you recognize the importance of your contributions, as well as help you brainstorm ways to describe what you've done.

If you have good communication skills, you probably will be able to do most of your résumé yourself. However it would be helpful to have it critiqued by someone who sees a lot of résumés in the course of his or her work. You may know just such a person in your church or community who would be willing to assist you. If you are not a good writer and don't have help from someone who is, enlist some professional help. Professional assistance for a résumé only can cost from $60 to $150, depending on how much work has to be done and pricing in your area of the country. Many résumé services only format and present the information you provide the way you give it to them. Be sure you evaluate the services before hiring someone.

Almost all résumés are done on computers today because they offer unlimited flexibility for layout, font choices, and spacing. Computers also make it easy to change or update your résumé as the need arises. We recommend you have your résumé printed on a laser printer—to give it a professional look. Since the first-glance appearance of your résumé is such a critical factor, you can't afford anything less.

SPECIAL CASE RÉSUMÉS

Limited employment experience.

If you are a homemaker, with little public work experience, a résumé presents a special challenge: to adequately communicate strengths while being honest about limitations.

The purpose of any résumé is to communicate strengths you can bring to the workplace. It's a matter of identifying your strongest skills and giving evidence of your talents and achievements. For example: coordinating a car pool, volunteer work, president of the Women's Bible Study Group, Cub Scout den leader, counseling in a crisis pregnancy center, tutoring, or county chairperson of the Girl Scout cookie sale. These all indicate leadership skills and provide a platform for working with the public.

Don't let limited public work experience discourage you. Develop your résumé, get your foot in the door, and make your talents known.

Leaving military service.

With the current plans for significant cuts in our defense department, many service people will be returning to the civilian work force. As one who has made that transition, let me offer a few thoughts.

You'll find that the military gave you wonderful training: how to be a problem-solver, leadership training so you'd be able to take charge when called upon, and the importance of working as a team.

Employers are very skilled at spotting deceptions in résumés.

Your communication and staff skills probably will exceed those of your civilian contemporaries, so you'll be ahead of them in some ways. Your shortfall is that you may not have knowledge or current experience that applies directly to many jobs. However, from your military training it is likely that you'll have a good technical background and, in general, your overall experience will make you a trainable person if you have the right attitude: a team player who is eager to learn.

The challenge in writing your résumé is to highlight your skills and accomplishments in a way that will communicate to civilians. The military becomes so indoctrinated to its own language of acronyms and buzz words that many in uniform can't even imagine how unintelligible their expressions are to the outside world. Consequently, the safe thing to do is to strip every vestige of "military-ese" from your writing. That means no TDYs, no M-1As, no MK 82s, no COMNAVFORLANTs—not even any Bradleys or Falcons. The trick is to convert these terms into something civilians can relate to in terms of your responsibilities and levels of achievement.

Obviously your résumé will reflect that you're coming out of the military but, if done with the above guidelines, it can communicate your potential in a favorable light.

Choose a résumé format.

There are basically two kinds of résumés commonly used—the *chronological* résumé, and the *functional* (or skills) résumé. Examples of both are given at the end of this chapter.

The chronological résumé is usually the best when you are staying in your established career field. Employers who are familiar with the typical jobs and career progression would be able to relate quickly to your experience and see if you might fit into their organization.

The functional résumé highlights your skills, talents, and accomplishments under functional headings. It is good when you are changing career fields, when you don't have a work history, or for some reason you don't wish to call attention to your work history.

Keep in mind that employers are very skilled at spotting deceptions in résumés. If your work history has some holes in it, clarify that in the résumé, cover letter, or the job history section of the résumé. For instance, if there's a period in which you did part-time, temporary, or free lance work, indicate that.

The following are the headings you'll need to cover.

CHRONOLOGICAL RÉSUMÉ

Name, address, phone and fax number
This is vital information.

Career objective
Briefly state your objective. How specific you should be depends on your career field and the breadth of the audience you are addressing with the résumé.

Employment history
Begin with your latest employer and work backward. For a chronological résumé, this is where you detail any accomplishments and the impact they had on the company. Remember, it is not enough to say just what you did. Your résumé must specifically communicate your strengths and your achievements.

Education
Again, use the reverse chronological format to list your schools, locations, any degrees earned, and the graduation dates. Include any honors, such as "deans list" or "Summa cum laude," or "Phi Beta Kappa."

At the end of the résumé, type the statement:
References available upon request. Be certain you have references lined up *before* you send out résumés. More will be said about references later.

The following are optional categories you may or may not want to use, depending on your unique situation.

Affiliations
In this section you could list professional associations, certifications, or relevant non-profit or Christian organizations of which you are a member.

Honors
This is not included unless you have received exceptional or unusual honors that are not revealed in any other section of the résumé.

Personal
Be careful with this one. Use this category only for information that you know will be *relevant* to the reader. Knowing your audience will be very important.

Extra curricular activities
This category would be used only by a student or recent graduate who has had little work experience. Highlight responsibilities and achievements the same as you would for a job.

The functional résumé has the same basic purpose as the chronological format, but it takes a different approach. This format calls attention to your strongest talents and skills, so the headings are organized accordingly.

FUNCTIONAL RÉSUMÉ

Name, address, phone and fax number
This is vital information.

Career objective
Briefly state your objective, focusing on the types of activities you want to be involved in rather than a specific job title. This makes the résumé more flexible.

Highlights of qualifications
List four or five of your strongest qualifications.

Relevant skills and experience
Give evidence of your three or four strongest skills—the ones you want to use in your work.

Employment history
Give a reverse chronology listing of your employment.

Education
Use reverse chronological format to list your schools, locations, degrees earned, and graduation dates. Include honors.

References available on request.

Depending on the situation, you may want to use some of the optional categories listed earlier under the chronological résumé.

For some of you this brief coverage of the résumé will be sufficient, but many of you will need more in-depth instruction. There are several good books available on the subject, so check with your local library or bookstore.

Because the résumé is so important, just getting it done can cause stress and anxiety. Don't get so concerned about it that you put it off or work on it for weeks trying to perfect it. The best advice we can give is to get busy and get it finished. If you are anticipating a job search or you already are involved in one, you need your résumé done today.

USE A COVER LETTER

When sending your résumé via the mail or someone in your network, a cover letter is an accepted practice that serves several functions. First of all it enables you to communicate directly with the person who is going to read your résumé.

The brief letter allows you to explain why you are contacting them and indicates to the reader how your talents and experience might fit the needs of their particular organization. Most important, it allows you to make a direct connection with a potential employer. What will come of that connection? You don't know, but at least they will have seen a letter from you and that may help set you apart.

Your cover letters should be short (less than one page), grammatically correct, well organized, and tailored specifically to fit the company. A sample cover letter is included at the end of this chapter.

Line up your references.

The list of references you provide will allow potential employers to find out about your character, performance, or potential. Obviously you should choose references who will feel comfortable speaking positively about you.

Generally there are three groups you should consider as references:

1. Character references (someone who knows about your integrity, honesty, dependability, drive)
2. Job performance references (preceding supervisor or business colleague)
3. Professional expertise references (clients, professional peers, or competitors)

Make a list of several people in each group who are likely candidates; then contact them by phone or letter. Tell them you are looking for a job or are making a job change, and be clear about what specific position or employment situation you are seeking. If they seem comfortable in giving you a good recommendation, be sure you have permission to use their names as references.

Refine your reference list to about two in each of the above three categories and get them typed with the same quality and style as your résumé. Put your references on a separate sheet and *do not provide your list until someone asks you for it.*

Always send a thank you to those who have agreed to be references, and then send them a follow-up note after you get the job.

BE CONFIDENT, BE CONSCIENTIOUS

You can see that developing your résumé, your references, and a cover letter require a number of skills, some of which don't usually go together. You'll need to be confident and positive in clarifying your skills; you'll also need to be well organized, cautious, and conscientious to be sure these steps meet the highest standards.

As we've said often before, find someone who is your opposite in personality to be your coach or helper. Isn't it amazing how God planned it so that we need each other? When you are in a job search you'll recognize very quickly how difficult things are if you go through it alone. Our advice is to ask for help.

SAMPLE RÉSUMÉS

Example #1 (Experienced Professional)

James P. Smith
487 Cypress Lane
Wilmington, TX 88888
(512) 000-1010

OBJECTIVE

Responsibilities in administration—finance or operations—of a sound, growing financial institution or service company.

EMPLOYMENT HISTORY

Union Savings Association, Wilmington, Texas   1978–1989
Medium-sized thrift with nine locations.

President–Chief Executive Officer   1989

Senior Vice President–Chief Financial Officer   1989
  Supervision of accounts, treasury, human resources, and information resource management

Senior Vice President–Information Resource
Management and Human Resources   1983–1989
  Responsible for all computer resources and all personnel/payroll functions.

  • Coordinated two investigations of alternative mainframe systems, resulting in a decision to change processors.
  • Coordinated the design and installation of in-house item processing system, ATM system, and general ledger system.
  • Selected, installed, and managed a local area network of microcomputers serving 18 work stations.
  • Designed and implemented a corporate records management system including the physical facility and computerization.

  Also served in the following capacities as a senior officer:

  • Member of Senior Officer Committee, Chairman of Information Resource Management Steering Committee, Employee Involvement Committee, and Employee Stock Ownership Plan Committee.
  • Responsible for all corporate insurance—evaluation, purchases, and claims.
  • Designated liaison with state and federal regulators during examinations and with all potential acquisitors of the Association.

- Managed sale and liquidation of two wholly owned subsidiaries: an insurance agency and a lease financing company.
- Participated in or chaired task forces to
  1. Improve the quality of customer service,
  2. Design a formal structure for evaluating and compensating employees,
  3. Work out recurring problems with negotiable items, and
  4. Solicit proxies from stockholders for a tender offer for the Association's stock.

Senior Vice President–Chief Financial Officer   1982–1983
Vice President–Controller   1978–1982

Swift, Bridges and Company, Wilmington, Texas   1977–1978
Regional accounting firm serving Texas and New Mexico

Audit Manager
Complete engagement responsibility for all financial institution audits.
- Partner-level responsibilities in audit quality control program.
- Instructor for local office training programs.

Michael Drefuss & Co., Oakland, Texas   1970–1977
International accounting firm.

Audit Manager   1976–1977
Full engagement responsibility for banks, savings and loan association, a commercial finance company, and a regulated investment company.
- Served as firm's primary liaison with thrift executives in North Texas through involvement in industry organizations.

Audit Senior   1972–1976
Audit Staff   1970–1972

EDUCATION AND AFFILIATIONS

Stevens College, Abilene, Texas   1970
Bachelor of Business Administration

Certified Public Accountant, licensed in Texas   1971

East Point Chapel, Wilmington, Texas   1971
Treasurer and member of Finance Committee   1983–1989

Christian Financial Concepts, Gainesville, Georgia   1986–1989
Seminar leader and counselor in personal financial management

Example #2 (Young Professional)

JANE A. SMITH
4110 DOGWOOD STREET
ATLANTA, GEORGIA 00000
(404) 000-1919

OBJECTIVE

Writing/editing position, with opportunity to work with desktop publishing systems

HIGHLIGHTS OF QUALIFICATIONS

- Over three years experience in the publishing field
- Reputation for accuracy in writing and editing
- Skilled in research and organization of written articles
- Highly conscientious worker with experience in meeting deadlines while maintaining quality

RELEVANT SKILLS AND EXPERIENCE

Write/Edit/Proofread

- Organized, developed, and wrote factual articles for three well-respected regional food industry publications
- Edited news releases and other submitted materials to a suitable size
- Proofread copy for publications
- Collaborated with production manager in being sure advertisements were produced to specifications, ensuring client satisfaction
- Completed proofreading workshop sponsored by Superior Builders, 1989

Research/Interview

- Conducted research for articles utilizing various print media
- Interviewed food industry executives both by telephone and in person as part of research for articles

Computer Operation

- Over three years experience on IBM personal computer, utilizing WordStar and MicroSoft Word word-processing systems
- Trained on Macintosh Quark Xpress desktop publishing software system

EMPLOYMENT HISTORY

March–June 1992	Associate Editor
August 1988– February 1992	Business Writer/Reporter Detail Wrightsville Publishing Company, Inc. Wrightsville, GA
1985, 86, 87	Summer Day Camp Counselor Wrightsville Parks and Recreation Dept. Wrightsville, GA

EDUCATION

A.B., English, University of Georgia, Athens, 1988.
Summa cum laude, Phi Beta Kappa

A.A., Gainesville College, Gainesville, Georgia, 1986.
Dean's List

REFERENCES AVAILABLE UPON REQUEST

Example #3 (Clerical)

KATHERINE A. WILSON
1000 CHATTAHOOCHEE RD.
GAINESVILLE, GA 00000
(404) 000-4951

OBJECTIVE

Position in Administrative Services, with an opportunity for personal growth and career development.

HIGHLIGHTS OF ABILITIES

- Highly organized and detail oriented
- Excellent communication skills
- Supportive team worker; committed and responsible
- Reliable and adaptable; learn new processes quickly; and takes initiative

RELEVANT SKILLS AND EXPERIENCE

Office Experience

- Maintained folders and information for over 5,000 clients.
- Operated a wide range of office machines including copiers, printers, typewriters, voice mail.
- Processed incoming and outgoing mail.

Telephone and Communication Skills

- Managed inbound and outbound call activities to include:
  customer service
  customer and home office correspondence.
- Explained insurance policies to clients.

Computer Knowledge
- Operated various software applications: word processing, databases, statistical testing analysis. (IBM compatible).
- Processed and scanned test packages daily.

EMPLOYMENT HISTORY

Present	Administrative Assistant	Mountainview Nursing Home, Gainesville, GA
1991–92	Administrative Assistant	World Insurance, Athens, GA
1991	Scoring Technician	Career Pathways, Gainesville, GA
*1989–91	Waitress/Event Organizer	Columns Country Club, Athens, GA
*1988	Packaging/Customer Assistance	Bigg's Grocery Store, Athens, GA
*1987–88	Children's Clothing Specialist	Mall Dept. Store, Athens, GA
*1986–87	Banquet Waitress	University of Georgia, Athens, GA
*1986	Cashier	Flavers Dept. Store, Athens, GA

*Part-time jobs held during high school/college

EDUCATION

North Georgia College, Dahlonega, GA, 1988–89, Psychology Major.

REFERENCES AVAILABLE UPON REQUEST

Example #4 (Student)

James T. Wilson
234 Columns Drive
Athens, GA 00000

OBJECTIVE: A part-time position in sales or customer support. Desire to build an employment relationship that will continue throughout four years as a college student.

SUMMARY: A confident, outgoing individual who enjoys meeting people and presenting products or ideas. Personal strengths include:
  Enjoy selling, results-oriented
  Energetic with strong initiative
  Strong verbal skills
  Enjoy meeting people
  Dependable, seek responsibility

EDUCATION: Graduated Commercial High School,
  Commerce, GA, June 1992, top 25 percent of class.

EXTRACURRICULAR ACTIVITIES:
  Debate Team, two years
  Student Council, senior representative
  Baseball team, co-captain (shortstop)
  Fellowship for Christian Athletes, social chairman
  Peer counselor, teen hot-line

WORK EXPERIENCE:
  Customer Assistance/Stocker, 1990–1992. Sky-Mart, Commerce, Georgia. Fourteen hours per week. Outstanding attendance record. Started at bottom and moved up to weekend supervisor of sporting goods and auto accessories. Paid cash for first auto from earnings.
  Lawn Care, 1988–1990. Self-employed lawn business. Began with three customers and increased to nine. Gained experience in promotion, financial management, and customer relations. Never lost a customer. Saved $1500 for college expenses.
  Paper Route, 1986–1988. Self-employed. Serviced a forty-customer route, five days per week. Missed only three days in two years. Collected 95 percent of debits.

PERSONAL: Born March 15, 1974. Enjoy challenges and responsibility. Career goal is to be a certified planner and investment counselor.

REFERENCES AVAILABLE UPON REQUEST

COVER LETTER FORMULA

Your Name
Your Address
Your Telephone Number

Date

Contact Name (if available)
Title (if available)
Company
Address

Dear Mr./Ms. _____:

Refer to the advertisement and/or position for which your are applying.

Identify that your background and education make you an excellent candidate for the position. Indicate and describe why your qualifications make you the best person for the job. Give one or two specific accomplishments that most effectively highlight your match for the job.

Identify 2-3 personal qualities that represent you as an employee and how those qualities might benefit the organization.

Express appreciation for the attention to your information and request and interview. Provide your contact information (phone numbers, times to call).

Sincerely,

(Signature, if your name is Susan, but you are called Sue, sign, Sue)

Your Full Name (typed)
(as it appears on your heading)

FOLLOW-UP LETTER FORMULA

Your Name
Your Address
Your Telephone Number

Date

Contact Name
Title
Company
Address

Dear Mr./Ms. _____:

Identify the position for which you were interviewed and the date. Thank him/her for their time and the interview opportunity.

Express your interest in the position and the company. Refer to specific qualifications you have that will benefit the company and target any specifics that may have been discussed in the interview.

Close with suggestion of another meeting, if applicable, and/or a reference to a follow-up call in a designated time period. Provide your contact information (phone number, times to call). Repeat your appreciation.

Sincerely,

(Signature, if your name is William, but you are called Bill, sign, Bill)

Your Full Name (typed)
(as it appears on your heading)

CHAPTER TWENTY-ONE
Managing Your Finances

A financial plan is essential for career planning and will allow you to make career choices based on biblical principles, rather than just the need for a paycheck.

Many people aren't able to pursue a career that God has called them to because they're locked into repayment schedules that can be met only with a certain amount of income. Others could have much more career flexibility if they had managed their money and paid off their bills.

"The one on whom seed was sown among the thorns, this is the man who hears the word, and the worry of the world, and the deceitfulness of riches choke the word, and it becomes unfruitful" (Matthew 13:22).

Unless you are able to control your spending and live within your means, your career decisions will always be driven by the need for more money.

So even though your heart's desire and your God-given talents may be to lead and teach young people as a recreation director, you may feel pressured to be a sales person in order to make enough money to pay your bills.

Christian Financial Concepts has been teaching the concept of stewardship for over 17 years. Based on that experience, we know that most Christians struggle with finances. It seems that Jesus anticipated the depth of faith needed to surrender control of our finances to Him because He taught about money and possessions more than anything else.

Although financial management can be a struggle, we see many testimonies each month describing how people became debt free and achieved the blessings of financial freedom by living on a budget.

By first recognizing that "our" money and possessions are really the Lord's and then becoming good managers for Him, we become truly free to follow His calling.

Everyone Needs a Budget

"A prudent man sees evil and hides himself, the naive proceed and pay the penalty" (Proverbs 27:12).

Unemployed.

If you are out of a job, management of your funds will be especially critical. You'll need a budget for several reasons.

- To know the absolute minimum monthly income needed to support your family.
- To know how long you can last without a job.
- To know the bottom line needed for salary negotiation.
- If married, so husband and wife can both know exactly where they stand financially.

We often hear people who are living on a very low income say, "I don't make enough money to budget." Nothing could be further from the truth. They need to plan their spending more than anyone else. A budget is merely a written plan that reflects your spending priorities.

Career transition.

If you have a job but are planning a career transition, you'll need to be on a budget so you can build a surplus in case your income drops when you change jobs and also to pay for additional schooling to prepare for a new career.

Without a budget most young people entering the work force will be in debt within one year and have significant financial problems in three years.

Young people.

If you are going out on your own and entering the work force for the first time, you may have no idea how much things cost. When you've never had a regular paycheck, even a minimum salary seems like more money than a person could ever spend. Unfortunately many learn the hard way that you can spend it all and more very easily.

Without a budget most young people entering the work force will be in debt within one year and have significant financial problems in three years.

A budget will help you plan for the following.

- Fixed expenses such as housing, taxes, tithe, and insurance.

- Variable expenses such as food, utilities, medical, and entertainment.

- Children, savings, automobiles, down payment on house.

A budget is essential for everyone who wants to be a good manager of God's resources. By using a budget and the biblical principles of money management, you can break financial bondage and gain the freedom to pursue your calling.

This chapter will give you the basics for living on a budget. It's condensed from *The Financial Planning Workbook* by Larry Burkett. Refer to this workbook for a more complete guide to budgeting. Since the concept of "biblical" principles of money management is new to many people, we encourage you to work through the Bible study entitled *How to Manage Your Money.* Those who lack a thorough understanding of these principles are not prepared to withstand the lure of our society's materialistic value system.

As with careers, following the world's plan in your finances can only lead to more stress and, most of all, it denies the benefit of being in God's will and receiving His blessings.

SIX STEPS TO BECOMING DEBT FREE

The goal is to live within your means. What does this mean? It means to spend no more than you make each month. Ideally that means to live on a cash basis and not use credit or borrowed money to provide normal living expenses. It also means to use self-discipline to control spending and to keep needs, wants, and desires in their proper relationship.

1. Develop a written plan.

Show how you will spend income and the order of importance of each expense area. You must separate needs, wants, and desires.

Needs are the purchases necessary to provide your basic requirements such as food, clothing, home, medical coverage, and others. *"And if we have food and covering, with these we shall be content"* (1 Timothy 6:8).

Wants involve choices about the quality of goods to be used, such as dress clothes versus work clothes, steak versus hamburger, or a new car versus a used car. The following verse gives a point of reference for determining wants in a Christian's life: *"And let not your adornment be merely external . . . but let it be the hidden person of the heart, with the imperishable quality of a gentle and quiet spirit, which is precious in the sight of God"* (1 Peter 3:3–4).

Desires are choices according to God's plan that can be made only out of surplus funds after all other obligations have been met. *"Do not love the world, nor the things in the world. If anyone loves the world, the love of the Father is not in him. For all that is in the world, the lust of the flesh and the lust of the eyes and the boastful pride of life, is not from the Father, but is from the world"* (1 John 2:15–16).

Financial freedom is an essential step to being fully in God's will.

---

2. Focus on the essentials.

When in debt, stop any expenditure which is not absolutely essential for living. To conserve, you must avoid frivolities.

3. Think before buying.

Ask yourself: Is it a necessity? Does the purchase reflect my Christian ethics? Is this the best buy I can get? Is it a highly depreciative item? Will it lose value quickly? Does it require costly upkeep? *"By wisdom a house is built, and by understanding it is established"* (Proverbs 24:3).

4. Discontinue credit buying.

If you buy on a cash-only basis, you'll break the habit of spending what you don't have.

5. Avoid leverage (controlling a large asset with a small investment).

Borrowing to invest is very high risk. Leverage usually reflects get-rich-quick thinking.

6. Practice saving.

You can save regularly, even when you're in debt (saving even $5.00 a week will develop discipline).

STEPS TO FINANCIAL FREEDOM

Financial freedom is an essential step to being fully in God's will. If you make a commitment to achieve financial freedom, God will honor your commitment and work in a powerful way in your life to help you achieve that goal. There are several ways you can do this.

1. Transfer ownership to God.
2. Establish the tithe.
3. Become debt free.
4. Accept God's provision.
5. Keep a clear conscience.
6. Put others first.
7. Prioritize your time.
8. Avoid indulgence.
9. Seek Christian counseling.

CFC referral counselors provide free budget counseling. To locate a counselor in your area, write to CFC, PO Box 2377, Gainesville, GA 30503-2377.

STEPS TO MAKING A BUDGET

"He who neglects discipline despises himself, but he who listens to reproof acquires understanding" (Proverbs 15:32).

1. Determine current expenses.

Write down every expense for 30–60 days and put into categories (such as Housing, Auto, Food, Clothing, Recreation and Entertainment, Insurance, Medical). Determine fixed expenses—these are the continuing obligations you have each month. Determine variable expenses. Divide yearly expenses by 12 to get a monthly average for areas such as insurance, utilities, and medical. (Use check register and old bills for historical base.) Include all loans coming due.

2. List all available income.

Include salary, rental fees, notes, interest, dividends, bonuses, gifts, and tax refunds. (Note: If your income varies from month to month, as with commissioned sales or professional athletes, use a yearly average divided by 12 months.)

3. Determine net spendable income (NSI).

This is your monthly income minus tithe and taxes. Example: $25,000 annual income divided by 12 months = $2083/month, minus $208 tithe and minus $322 taxes = $1553/month net spendable income (NSI).

4. Compare income with expenses.

Expenses should not exceed income.

The Income and Expense form (on page 302) gives average percentages of NSI for a family of four earning $25,000 annually. (Percentage for each category may vary depending on your situation, but total must not exceed 100 percent of NSI.)

Gross Monthly Income equals $2083 ($25,000 annual).

1. **Tithe (10 percent of gross = $208)**
2. **Taxes (15.5 percent of gross = $322)** This is a typical amount. Use the total of your federal and state taxes plus FICA and Medicare. Net Spendable Income equals $1553. Expenses should not exceed Net Spendable Income (NSI).
3. **Housing (38 percent of NSI = $589)** This includes mortgage, taxes, insurance, utilities, and telephone. The most common problem of personal finances is buying a home that's too expensive. Spending over 40 percent of NSI usually brings financial bondage.
4. **Food (12 percent of NSI = $186)** Buying food requires careful planning and "list" shopping. You must eat mostly at the "need" level and avoid most wants and all desires.
5. **Automobile (15 percent of NSI = $232)** Overspending on cars is a major area of income loss. This category must cover payments or replacement, insurance, gas, and maintenance. Generally half of the total will be used for payments and half for gas, insurance, and maintenance. Most people cannot afford new cars.

6. **Insurance (5 percent of NSI = $78)** This is used as supplemental provision—not for protection or profit or for savings or retirement. It's always wise to learn about insurance before you buy. A trustworthy agent is a necessity.
7. **Debts (5 percent of NSI = $78)** If you have indebtedness, commit to paying off your debts. Stop buying on credit; buy on a cash basis and sacrifice wants and desires until you are current.
8. **Recreation/Entertainment (5 percent of NSI = $78)** Everyone must have some recreation, but you cannot use creditors' money to entertain yourself. Resist the urge to escape problems with entertainment.
9. **Clothing (5 percent of NSI = $78)** Be creative; use various resources. Buy basic clothing and avoid fads.
10. **Medical/Dental (5 percent of NSI = $78)** You must anticipate and set aside funds for this category or you can wreck your budget. Exercising and reducing stress can help reduce the amount spent in this category. Always question medical charges in advance. Shop around for best prescription prices.
11. **Savings (5 percent of NSI = $78)** Get in the habit of saving even a small amount. Saving lets you buy with cash and avoid paying interest. *"Go to the ant, O sluggard, observe her ways and be wise, which, having no chief, officer or ruler, prepares her food in the summer, and gathers her provision in the harvest"* (Proverbs 6:6–8).
12. **Miscellaneous (5 percent of NSI = $78)** Resourcefulness is the key. Budget limitations will help you control spending. Expensive gift giving can wreck your budget and is usually driven by pride, guilt, or your need for self-worth.

NOTE: People frequently are upset by the low amounts for housing, food, or autos, and say they are unrealistic. But as you can see, the figures add up to 100 percent—all of the income. You should personalize your budget to suit your needs, but remember, you can't spend more than you make and have financial freedom.

OPTIONAL CATEGORIES

Guidelines for the above categories add up to 100 percent of income. Categories 13, 14, and 15 are optional, and if they are used, categories 1 through 12 must be adjusted proportionally.

13. **School/Child Care (8 percent of NSI)**
14. **Investments (variable percentage)** As debt-free status is achieved and savings are established, more money can be diverted to this category.
15. **Unallocated Surplus Income** Unscheduled income, such as garage sales, bonuses, and gifts.

This chapter provides an introduction to present the basics of a financial plan. Once you have a written plan, you'll need *control* to live on it.

For a more in-depth explanation, refer to *How to Manage Your Money* and *The Financial Planning Workbook* by Larry Burkett, published by Moody Press.

MONTHLY INCOME & EXPENSES

GROSS INCOME PER MONTH 2083
- Salary   ——
- Interest   ——
- Dividends   ——
- Other   ——

LESS:
1. Tithe (10% of gross) 208
2. Tax (Est./Fed., State) 322
   (15.5% of gross)

NET SPENDABLE INCOME 1553

3. Housing (38%/NSI)   589
   - Mortgage (rent)   ——
   - Insurance   ——
   - Taxes   ——
   - Electricity   ——
   - Gas   ——
   - Water   ——
   - Sanitation   ——
   - Telephone   ——
   - Maintenance   ——
   - Other   ——

4. Food (12%/NSI)   186

5. Automobile(s) (15%/NSI) 232
   - Payments   ——
   - Gas & Oil   ——
   - Insurance   ——
   - License/Taxes   ——
   - Maint/Repair/Replace ——

6. Insurance (5%/NSI)   78
   - Life   ——
   - Medical   ——
   - Other   ——

7. Debts (5%/NSI)   78
   - Credit Card   ——
   - Loans & Notes   ——
   - Other   ——

8. Enter. & Recreation (5%/NSI) 78
   - Eating Out   ——
   - Baby Sitters   ——
   - Activities/Trips   ——
   - Vacation   ——

9. Clothing (5%/NSI) 78
10. Savings (5%/NSI) 78

11. Medical Expenses (5%/NSI) 78
    - Doctor   ——
    - Dentist   ——
    - Drugs   ——
    - Other   ——

12. Miscellaneous (5%/NSI) 78
    - Toiletry, cosmetics   ——
    - Beauty, barber   ——
    - Laundry, cleaning   ——
    - Allowances, lunches   ——
    - Subscriptions   ——
    - Gifts & Christmas   ——
    - Cash   ——
    - Other   ——

13. School/Child Care[1] (8%/NSI) ——
    - Tuition   ——
    - Materials   ——
    - Transportation   ——
    - Day Care   ——

14. Investments[2]   ——

TOTAL EXPENSES   1553

INCOME VS. EXPENSES
Net Spendable Income   1553
Less Expenses   1553
Income – Expenses   -0-

15. Unallocated Surplus
    Other Income[3]   ——

1. This percentage has not been factored into total percentages. If used, other areas must be decreased to offset.
2. No surplus for long-term investing at this income, given the obligations shown.
3. This category is used when surplus income is received. This would be kept in the checking account to be used within a few weeks; otherwise, it should be transferred to an allocated category.

CHAPTER TWENTY-TWO
Dealing with Discouragement

*N*o book on work and career planning could be complete without a section dealing with the issues of stress and discouragement. In recent years more and more attention has been devoted to these two issues as they relate to work, because they are having a major impact on our lives.

We have learned a lot about job stress and discouragement from the responses of our Life Pathways clients to our career questionnaire. This questionnaire has several questions that help clients evaluate the level of stress they are feeling and to help them identify the sources. As you would suspect, the sources include finances and relationships; but you'd be amazed at how many people are really stressed and discouraged over issues relating to their work.

Other agencies are finding that job stress is a major problem in our society. One day I received a call from a lady who had read one of our career articles in the *Money Matters* newsletter. She said that at a hospital staff meeting where she worked they had a discussion on the number of patients they were seeing who had health problems directly related to job stress. According to the caller, their staff agreed that job stress was the number one contributor to poor health.

About a year later Northwestern National Life Insurance Co. conducted a study, which revealed the following startling results.

- Seven of ten workers said job stress caused frequent health problems.
- Forty-six percent said their jobs are highly stressful.
- Thirty-four percent said they thought seriously of quitting their jobs last year because of workplace stress.
- Thirty-three percent said they expect to burn out from their job in the near future.[1]

Every indication is that stress at work and in our lives in general is increasing. The questions we should be asking are why and how should we deal with it.

Change is always stressful, and in the twentieth century we have experienced it in incredible proportions.

Although it isn't our purpose to delve deeply into the source of our stresses, we have alluded to the most likely possibilities. Many of the problems of work stress are related to job mis-matches: people being in jobs that don't match their natural talents and interests.

We have dedicated a large section of this book to help you solve that problem. But there are other issues causing stress in the workplace. The major one is change and, as Larry said at the outset of the book, it has been coming at an accelerating rate.

In my life, I went from riding a mule-drawn wagon to the grinding mill with my grandfather at age 7 to flying a supersonic jet at almost twice the speed of sound (1500 MPH) at age 22.

Change is always stressful, and in the twentieth century we have experienced it in incredible proportions. The increases in technology, information, transportation, and communication have had a tremendous impact on the way we work and what we have come to expect in the way of productivity. Have you noticed that even though we have automatic washers and dryers, electric can openers, microwave ovens, electric mixers, riding lawn mowers, and every other gadget imaginable to relieve the toil of labor, we actually have less free time than our parents and grandparents did. (Remember when people actually sat on front porches?)

The problem seems to be that we haven't adequately considered the human ability to adapt to the accelerating rate of change and the resulting complexity of life. Perhaps the industrial revolution has pushed us into thinking that people can operate like machines. But, as the study mentioned above would indicate, our central nervous systems were designed for more balanced lives than most of us are experiencing. We are not machines; we need rest, time to eat properly, time for relationships, time to emotionally recharge through recreation, and time to just sit on the front porch.

As a counselor, I have the opportunity to look closely and fairly objectively at the lives of others. What I often see is a life that is out of balance. In fact when we take an objective look, most of us can see that we have unrealistic expectations of what we can accomplish in a 24 hour day. We try to do more than is physically possible.

Have you ever said "If I just had a few more hours in the day, I could get every thing done"? I used to say that and then someone pointed out: That would not solve the problem. Eventually I saw they were right. It's exactly like those who overspend their incomes and then say, "If I just made a little more money I could make ends meet." After counseling tens of thousands of people, the staff of CFC has learned that isn't true either.

If the problem is one of spending without a plan and a prioritized way of allocating money, more money won't solve the problem. The inability to live within one's income and the inability to get it all done in 24 hours are both symptoms—not problems. The problem is one of priority and balance.

PREVENTIVE MEDICINE—LEARN TO SAY NO

Many years ago, Larry developed a budget to help people balance their financial ledgers so they could avoid overspending and going into debt. We need something similar to communicate the priorities necessary to maintain a balanced lifestyle. We don't have a lifestyle budget, but we have developed the following illustration to indicate some of the key categories of life that will need to be proportioned if we are to eliminate some of the stress.

As you probably remember, there are only 360 degrees in a circle. You might think of that as the total of your 24 hour day. In budgeting terms, it would be your total income. Just as with a budget, you must decide how to allocate your resources. You can't afford to buy everything, and you can't do everything.

If you are feeling a lot of stress in your life, consider your priority for each of the areas shown in the following diagram. Do your commitments add up to more than 100 percent of your time, energy, and finances? If so, you are running a deficit, and I can assure you that serious consequences will follow.

Unemployment certainly can cause some of the most discouraging times a person will ever face.

Whether you're currently employed or are looking for a job, you'll need to consider how you are allocating your time, money, and energy to the various sectors of your life. When cutting a pie, you can cut the pieces small or large, but there's only a limited amount of pie. Likewise, there is a limit to what you can do in a day.

Your allocations must be somewhat flexible, because they will vary with age, responsibilities, and situations that arise in your life. But you'll need to establish an allocation plan, based on your

Prioritizing Your 24-Hour Day

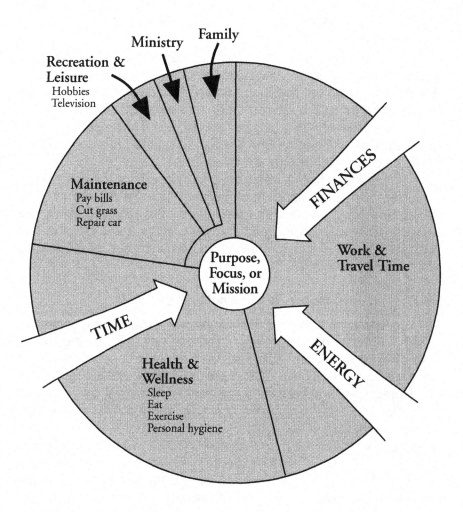

priorities, and then manage it accordingly to keep from living beyond your physical and emotional capabilities.

It's not easy to manage your life in the fast-paced environment of change in which we live. First of all, you have to recognize you can't do everything; there are just too many opportunities. Once you accept the idea that life in our era is like drinking from a fire hose, then you realize you must learn to say no. Saying no to some things we would really like to do can be painful unless you take a big picture approach.

For some people it will be easier to say no; by personality, they are more realistic about what can be done in a given period of time. For those who are optimistic and who like to please others, it can be much more difficult to set priorities and say "no" in order to live within a reasonable life plan. Our advice: Don't wait until you are a smoldering pile of plasma (burned out) to start to order your life. Do it while you are still healthy and in control.

When you're feeling pressure to withdraw from the plan you've set, stop and think about your purpose and the source of your strength. If you'll go back and read the psalms of David, you'll see how stressed and discouraged he became; yet he knew the source of his strength. Like David, in times of trouble we must trust in the Lord for our needs.

Defeat and discouragement are a natural part of life.

It should be accepted that we all will experience discouragement at times in our lives. We've seen that unemployment certainly can cause some of the most discouraging times a person will ever face. Yet life must go on. The question is: How can we overcome discouragement and get back in the battle?

The POWs in Vietnam learned a lot about defeat, discouragement, and bouncing back. Most of us were tortured at some time, either to give information or to comply in some way with our captors. Prior to capture, we all had thought we were as tough as John Wayne. The truth is, our captors were brutal enough to force the POWs to agree to do things against our will. We didn't do what they wanted us to do, but on a few occasions their torture forced us to do *something* to get relief from the pain.

I recall the time our interpreter came to the cell and demanded that we complete a biographical questionnaire. Of course we refused and were taken out and tortured. Eventually I agreed to do something, so I gave them a few truths, a lot of lies, and mostly I-don't-knows. Afterward, I was totally dejected. I felt ashamed that I hadn't been tough enough to defeat the communists.

Once I got back into the communication system in the compound, I learned that the others had done the same and knew what I'd been through physically and emotionally. The encouragement of my fellow POWs provided a big lift and helped me bounce back from what I felt was the greatest defeat of my life.

During our years of imprisonment we learned the importance of bouncing back from setbacks and discouragement. In fact, one of our policies directed all POWs to give maximum effort to communicate with and encourage those who were tortured or in solitary confinement. It was critical to get the individual back in good spirits and mentally prepared to resist the enemy again in the next round of the battle.

Although few people will ever be POWs, we all do experience adversity from time to time. In fact, the older we get, the more we realize that hardship and adversity are a normal part of life. Even so, it's hard to keep things in perspective when we are suffering. Usually it will be a big help if we can just adjust our focus.

If you'll think back to the hardships and disappointments you've suffered, you'll recall that, at some point, the discouragement began to pass, and you were able to view the world more optimistically. Your focus began to shift and you were able to see that life would go on in spite of the disappointment. The big picture became clear again. I believe the following illustration depicts how our problems can totally obscure our view of the big picture.

As a POW, I learned to see the big picture—I was alive, healthy, still engaged in the battle, and expected to return to my life as a free person. Many of my closest friends were buried in the hillsides of Southeast Asia. I was one of the fortunate ones who survived.

As a counselor, I try to help clients step back from the emotion of the problem and view the greater picture. If they can adjust their focus in this manner, they will have a more balanced view of life and be encouraged by the blessings they do have. They also will be able

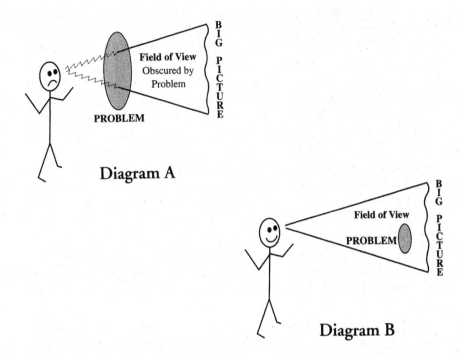

Diagram A

Diagram B

to see things more objectively and gain a better assessment of the problem and how to work a solution.

Role models are a big help.

It's always an encouragement to know that someone else has overcome a difficult problem. In the military we were encouraged to read biographies of great leaders and to learn from their experiences. As Christians we can read about our great heritage of role models who faced discouragement but remained faithful to the process.

Consider the examples of some of the familiar names of the Old and New Testaments.

Jacob's son Joseph certainly experienced some tribulations. After being sold into slavery by his brothers, he became an estate manager in Egypt, was thrown in jail for an offense he didn't commit, only to go to the Pharaoh's court and become the chief executive of the land. The words he spoke when he later confronted his brothers indicated he had the big picture in focus: *"Now, therefore, it was not you who sent me here, but God; and Has made me a father to Pharaoh and lord of all his household and ruler over all the land of Egypt"* (Genesis 45:8).

Four hundred years later, Moses, a man groomed to be the leader of Egypt, had to flee the country, and he found himself sitting at a well in the desert like an outlaw in the badlands. Of course everyone remembers how Moses led the Jews out of Egypt and received the Ten Commandments from God. But we often forget that he spent 40 years in the outback herding sheep before he came back to confront Pharaoh.

Jesus endured the ultimate in suffering and He is our best role model.

And remember the apostle Paul. He probably was the most brilliant mind of his time, yet he suffered incredible hardships and spent much of his life in jail. Didn't he deserve better? Well, you and I might think so, but Paul had a different perspective. Listen to what he had to say about his situation. *"And we know that God causes all things to work together for good to those who love God, to those who are called according to His purpose"* (Romans 8:28).

Of course Jesus endured the ultimate in suffering and He is our best role model. He had a clear insight into the big picture and knew His suffering had a purpose. He experienced tremendous anguish in facing the sin of the world and its consequences; yet, He trusted the Father for results that ultimately would come.

You may find it difficult to relate to these biblical examples; a closer role model may be helpful. Look around your community and find others who have experienced discouragement and see how they have handled it. As you do, you'll understand that everyone encounters hardships and difficulties from time to time; suffering is a part of life.

During my time as a POW, I was about the youngest person in the camp so, naturally, I looked to some of the older officers for strength and inspiration. When I was scared and discouraged, their courage and faithfulness encouraged me to hang on and have hope for a brighter day.

Because I was a Christian, I also knew that God was in control and that He cared about me personally. I didn't know what His plan was for my life, but I knew it had to be better than anything I could orchestrate from my cell. In many ways my experience was a blessing, because I had no alternative but to trust in the Lord—my life was out of my control.

If you are suffering and feel your life is out of control, it could be the greatest opportunity you'll ever have to really learn to trust in Him rather than lean on your own understanding. It is sad but true that hardships often bring us back under the wing of the Father where we can find the protection and nurture we need.

A few years ago, when our Bible study group was working through the Sermon on the Mount, God gave me new insight: "Blessed are those who realize they are incapable of making it on their own and choose to totally depend on God." It is a great blessing to be able to trust in the Lord.

I hope these words have been encouraging, but I know you also will need some practical steps to help you work through difficult times. Let's look at a few.

1. Study God's Word regularly.

Jesus is both the Word and Bread of Life. *"In the beginning was the Word, and the Word was with God, and the Word was God"* (John 1:1). To be spiritually strong, you need daily nourishment from His Word.

2. Pray and meditate.

As we come to know the mind of God, we are able to pray in His will. Ask others to pray with you and for you. It's especially important to have a same-sex prayer partner who will meet with you and commit to praying regularly for you. *"Therefore, confess your sins to one another, and pray for one another, so that you may be healed. The effective prayer of a righteous man can accomplish much"* (James 5:16).

3. Seek godly counsel.

This can come from several sources: spouse, parent, friend, pastor, deacon, elder, prayer partner, or Christian counselor. *"Without consultation, plans are frustrated, but with many counselors they succeed"* (Proverbs 15:22).

4. Get involved with the body of Christ.

The responsibilities of the body of believers include bearing one another's burdens and sharing fellowship and love during difficult times. Whether your needs are emotional, financial, spiritual, or physical, you need to let others in your church know. If you are not in a church, find one, and become a part of it. *"Be on guard for yourselves and for all the flock, among which the Holy Spirit has made you overseers, to shepherd the church of God which He purchased with His own blood"* (Acts 20:28).

Once you've experienced suffering, God can use you to help someone else along the way.

---

5. Read encouraging books.

We have included a recommended reading list in the Appendix. Check with your church library and Christian bookstore for others.

6. Make a plan and start following it.

Your role is to do the process; God will take care of the results. Diligence and persistence are important principles and must be applied in every area of our lives. *"The mind of man plans his way, but the Lord directs his steps"* (Proverbs 16:9).

7. Avoid bitterness.

It only takes the slightest amount of bitterness to ruin your attitude and undercut your joy. Others will notice your attitude and begin to avoid you. Bitterness is a problem, so identify the root cause and deal with it. Don't point the finger at others; they don't control your attitude. *"Put on a heart of compassion, kindness, humility, gentleness and patience; bearing with one another, and forgiving each other . . . just as the Lord forgave you"* (Colossians 3:12–13).

8. Look for ways God can use your adversity to His glory.

Remember Joseph in Egypt; he realized it was for God's glory that he was sold into slavery. Once you've experienced suffering, God can use you to help someone else along the way. *"Blessed be the God and Father of our Lord Jesus Christ . . . who comforts us in all our affliction so that we may be able to comfort those who are in any affliction with the comfort with which we ourselves are comforted by God"* (2 Corinthians 1:3–4).

9. Wash someone's feet.

Look around your community and find people who need uplifting. Go to their aid; be a servant to them as Jesus was when He washed the feet of the disciples. In doing so you'll gain a new perspective of your situation and you'll begin to see God's grace in your life. *"[Jesus] said to them, 'If anyone wants to be first, he shall be last of all, and servant of all'"* (Mark 9:35.)

10. Acknowledge the love of God.

Stop and think of what it means to be a child of God—unconditionally loved by the Creator and Ruler of the universe. Even though our natural tendency is to reject Him, He has forgiven us, restored us, and made it possible for us to be with Him eternally. *"Having been justified by faith, we have peace with God through our Lord Jesus Christ, through whom also we have obtained our introduction by faith into this grace in which we stand; and we exult in hope of the glory of God"* (Romans 5:1–2).

11. Rejoice and praise the Lord.

When we are discouraged, we would do well to read again that short, four-paged letter written by Paul to the Philippians. It can be summed up in the following.

"Finally, my brothers, rejoice in the Lord. . . . I count all things to be loss in view of the surpassing value of knowing Christ Jesus my Lord. . . . that I may know Him, and the power of His resurrection and the fellowship of His sufferings, being conformed to His death; in order that I may attain to the resurrection from the dead" (Philippians 3:1, 8, 10–11).

Notes

Chapter 1—The Workplace Is Changing

1. As reported in *The Old Farmers Almanac*. Dublin, NH: Yankee Publishing Inc., p. 26.
2. William Neikirk, "New Industrial Revolution Hits U.S. Big Business," *Chicago Tribune*, © February 21, 1993, Chicago Tribune Company. All rights reserved. Used with permission.
3. Richard A. Swenson, *Margin*. Colorado Springs, CO: NavPress, 1992.
4. *Fortune* magazine, January 23, 1993, pp. 86–93; February 8, 1993, pp. 106–115.
5. Ibid., May 3, 1993, pp. 36–42.

Chapter 2—Adapting to Changes in the Workplace

1. Frank Grazian, *Communication Briefings*, December 1992.
2. Noel M. Tichy and Stratford Sherman, *Control Your Destiny Or Someone Else Will.* New York: Bantam Doubleday, 1993, p. 247.
3. *Wall Street Journal*, June 24, 1991.

Chapter 6—Good Career Decisions Are Based on Truth

1. Tony Campolo, *Everything You've Heard Is Wrong*. Dallas, TX: Word Publishing, 1992, p. 33. Used with permission.
2. Doug Sherman and William Hendricks, *Your Work Matters to God*. Colorado Springs, CO: NavPress, 1987.
3. Tony Campolo, *Everything You've Heard Is Wrong*. Dallas, TX: Word, Inc., 1992, p. 28. Used with permission.

Chapter 7—Factors That Affect Career Decisions

1. Donald O. Clifton and Paula Nelson, *Soar with Your Strengths*. New York: Delacorte Press (Dell Publishing), 1992.

Chapter 8—How Parents Influence Career Decisions

1. Ralph Mattson and Thom Black, *Discovering Your Child's Design*. Elgin, IL: Lifejourney Books/David C. Cook Publishing Co., 1989.

Chapter 9—Planning for Retirement Career Decisions

1. Elisabeth Elliot, *Shadow of the Almighty*. New York: Harper & Row, 1956.

Chapter 11—Identify Your Vocational Interests, Work Priorities, and Values

1. John L. Holland, *Making Vocational Choices*. Englewood, NJ: Prentice Hall, 1973.
2. Joseph M. Stowell, *The Dawn's Early Light*. Chicago, IL: Moody Press, 1990, p. 39. Used with permission.

Chapter 12—Understand Your Personality Strengths

1. Adapted from *The Leadership Series*, Ken Voges, © 1991, In His Grace Inc. Used with permission.
2. Edgar F. Puryear, Jr., *19 Stars, A Study in Military Character and Leadership*. Vanato, CA: Presidio Press, 1984.

Chapter 13—The Dominant Personality

1. Gary Smalley and John Trent, *The Two Sides of Love*. Colorado Springs, CO: Focus on the Family Publishing, 1990.
2. Tim LaHaye, *Spirit Controlled Temperament*. Wheaton, IL: Tyndale House, 1966.

Chapter 14—The Influencing Personality

1. Gary Smalley and John Trent, *The Two Sides of Love*. Colorado Springs, CO: Focus on the Family Publishing, 1990.

Chapter 15—The Steady Personality

1. Gary Smalley and John Trent, *The Two Sides of Love*. Colorado Springs, CO: Focus on the Family Publishing, 1990.

Chapter 16—The Conscientious Personality

1. Gary Smalley and John Trent, *The Two Sides of Love*. Colorado Springs, CO: Focus on the Family Publishing, 1990.

Chapter 17—Preparing Through Education and Training

1. Carol Klieman, *The 100 Best Jobs for the 1990s & Beyond*, Chicago, IL: Dearborn Financial Publishing Inc., 1992.
2. U.S. Department of Labor Report 838, February 1993, p. 3.
3. Noel M. Tichy and Stratford Sherman, *Control Your Destiny Or Someone Else Will*. New York: Bantam Doubleday, 1993, p. 244.

Chapter 18—Conducting a Job Search, Part I

1. Belous, Richard (economist with National Planning Association of Washington D.C.), as quoted in AP, February 3, 1993.
2. Dewey Sadka, president of Tempforce, quoted in *Atlanta Constitution*, September 8, 1991 in article by Sherry Jenkins.

Chapter 22—Dealing with Discouragement

1. Norhtwestern National Life Insurance Company, "Employee Burnout: America's Newest Epidemic," 1991. Used by permission.

Recommended Reading List

CODEPENDENCY AND DYSFUNCTIONAL FAMILY ISSUES

Codependency—A Christian Perspective. Pat Swingle, Dallas, TX: Word Publishing, 1991.

The Search for Significance. Robert S. McGee, Houston, TX: Rapha Publishing, 1990.

FAMILY RELATED ISSUES

The Blessing. Gary Smalley and John Trent, Nashville, TN: Thomas Nelson Publishers, 1986.

Your Family Voyage. P. Roger Hillerstrom, Grand Rapids, MI: Fleming H. Revell, 1993.

FINANCIAL MANAGEMENT

The Coming Economic Earthquake. Larry Burkett, Chicago, IL: Moody Press, 1991.

The Complete Financial Guide for Single Parents. Larry Burkett, Wheaton, IL: Victor Books, 1991.

Debt-Free Living. Larry Burkett, Chicago, IL: Moody Press, 1989.

Get a Grip on Your Money. Larry Burkett, Chicago, IL: Moody Press, 1989.

Surviving the Money Jungle. Larry Burkett, Colorado Springs, CO: Focus on the Family Publishing, 1990. (A workbook designed to teach teens about money management.)

Your Finances in Changing Times. Larry Burkett, Chicago, IL: Moody Press, 1982.

LIFE PRIORITIES

The Dawn's Early Light. Joseph M. Stowell, Chicago, IL: Moody Press, 1990.

Everything You've Heard Is Wrong. Tony Campolo, Dallas, TX: Word Publishing, 1992.

How to Balance Competing Time Demands. Doug Sherman and William Hendricks, Colorado Springs, CO: NavPress, 1989.

The Man in the Mirror: Solving the 24 Problems Men Face. Patrick Morley, Brentwood, TN: Wolgemuth & Hyatt, 1989.

Margin. Richard A. Swenson, M.D., Colorado Springs, CO: NavPress, 1992.

MAKING CAREER DECISIONS

The following books are from a general perspective and relate to career planning.

Career: *Take This Job and Love It.* Peter Menconi, Richard Peace, and Lyman Coleman, Colorado Springs, CO: NavPress, 1989.

Discovering Your Child's Design. Ralph Mattson and Thom Black, Elgin, IL: David C. Cook Publishing Co., 1989.

Finding A Job You Can Love. Ralph Mattson and Arthur Miller, Nashville, TN: Thomas Nelson, Inc., 1982.

The Great Niche Hunt. David J. Frahm with Paula Rinehart, Colorado Springs, CO: NavPress, 1991.

How to Succeed Where It Really Counts. Doug Sherman and William Hendricks, Colorado Springs, CO: NavPress, 1989.

Keeping Your Ethical Edge Sharp. Doug Sherman and William Hendricks, Colorado Springs, CO: NavPress, 1989.

Keeping Your Head Up When Your Job's Got You Down. Doug Sherman, Brentwood, TN: Wolgemuth & Hyatt Publishers, 1991.

Love Your Work. Daniel McKenna, Wheaton, IL: Victor Books, 1990.

The 100 Best Jobs for the 1990s and Beyond. Carol Kleiman, Chicago, IL: Dearborn Financial, 1992.

Soar with Your Strengths. Donald O. Clifton and Paula Nelson, New York, NY: Delacorte Press (Dell Publishing), 1992.

The Survivor's Guide to Unemployment. Tom Morton, Colorado Springs, CO: Pinon Press, 1992.

The Three Boxes of Life and How to Get Out of Them. Richard N. Bolles, Berkeley, CA: Ten Speed Press, 1981.

Unlocking Your Sixth Suitcase. John Bradley and Jay Carty, Colorado Springs, CO: NavPress, 1991.

Your Work Matters to God. Doug Sherman and William Hendricks, Colorado Springs, CO: NavPress, 1987.

What Color Is Your Parachute? Richard N. Bolles, Berkeley, CA: Ten Speed Press, 1978.

PERSONALITY (DISC OR SIMILAR SYSTEM)

All the books in this section use the DISC or an equivalent system to explain personality. All are written from a Christian perspective.

Connections, Using Personality Types to Draw Parents & Kids Closer. Jim Brauner with Duncan Jaenicke, Chicago, IL: Moody Press, 1991.

Kids in Sports, Shaping a Child's Character from the Sidelines. Bill Perking with Rod Cooper, Portland, OR: Multnomah Press, 1989.

Personality Plus. Florence Littauer, Tarrytown, NY: Fleming H. Revell, 1983.

Personality Puzzle. Florence Littauer and Morita Littauer, Grand Rapids, MI: Fleming H. Revell (Baker Book House), 1992.

Spirit-Controlled Temperament. Tim LaHaye, Wheaton, IL: Tyndale House, 1966.

The Two Sides of Love. Gary Smalley and John Trent, Colorado Springs, CO: Focus on the Family Publishing, 1990.

Understanding How Others Misunderstand You. Ken Voges and Ron Braund, Chicago, IL: Moody Press, 1991. (The workbook by the same name is excellent and contains two Biblical Personal Profile Instruments.)

Understanding Jesus, A Personality Profile. Ken Voges and Mike Kempainen, Chicago, IL: Moody Press, 1992.

The Winning Hand—Making the Most of Your Family's Personality Differences. Wayne Richerson, Colorado Springs, CO: NavPress, 1991.

STARTING A BUSINESS

Business by the Book. Larry Burkett, Nashville, TN: Thomas Nelson, 1990.

Home Business 101. Sharon Carr, Old Tappan, NJ: Fleming H. Revell, 1989.

Homemade Business. Donna Partow, Colorado Springs, CO: Focus on the Family Publishing, 1992.

Working at Home. Lindsey O'Connor, Eugene, OR: Harvest House, 1990. (Contains an excellent resource section for any new business.)

TEXTBOOKS

Career Choices. Mindy Bingham and Sandy Stryker, Santa Barbara, CA: Able Publishing, 1990.

Where Do I Go from Here with My Life? Richard N. Bolles, Berkeley, CA: Ten Speed Press, 1978.

Lee Ellis served as a career Air Force officer until his retirement in 1989. During the Vietnam war, his aircraft was shot down and he was a prisoner of war for over five years.

During Lee's military career, his assignments included duty as a pilot, flight instructor, staff officer, flying squadron commander, and supervisor in higher education. His last assignment prior to retirement was Chairman of Aerospace Studies at the University of Georgia.

In addition to earning a Bachelor of Arts degree in history from the University of Georgia and a Master of Science degree in counseling and human development from Troy State University, Lee is a graduate of the Armed Forces Staff College and the Air War College.

While in the Air Force Lee became a volunteer teacher and counselor for Christian Financial Concepts. During his seventeen years of supervising, educating, and training young people, he saw clearly how God has gifted people with different talents. Lee's gifts and experiences make him well suited for his present role as the director of Life Pathways.

Life Pathways is the career guidance outreach of Christian Financial Concepts (CFC) of Gainesville, Georgia. Since 1976, under the leadership of Larry Burkett, CFC has focused its ministry on teaching biblical principles of handling money. Life Pathways expands CFC's emphasis on stewardship to include stewardship of other talents, i.e., our unique gifts, abilities, and personal styles of work.

The Life Pathways program is based on the biblical teaching that God has a purpose for each individual. That purpose can be fulfilled to a great extent through our life work—occupation, career, or profession. Life Pathways seeks to help individuals discover their talents and career direction by providing education, assessment, feedback, encouragement, and resource materials.

For more information, write to Life Pathways, PO Box 1476, Gainesville, GA 30503-1476, or call 1-800-722-1976.